A PETRAKIS READER

Books by Harry Mark Petrakis

Novels
LION AT MY HEART
THE ODYSSEY OF KOSTAS VOLAKIS
A DREAM OF KINGS
IN THE LAND OF MORNING
THE HOUR OF THE BELL

Short Stories
PERICLES ON 31ST STREET
THE WAVES OF NIGHT
A PETRAKIS READER

Autobiography
STELMARK

A PETRAKIS READER

Harry Mark Petrakis

1978

DOUBLEDAY & COMPANY, INC.

GARDEN CITY, NEW YORK

P446p

The material in A PETRAKIS READER first appeared as follows:

"The Shearing of Samson," "The Victim," and "Zena Dawn" in *U.S. Catholic;* "Homecoming" in *U.S. Catholic and Jubilee,* Copyright © 1967 by Claretian Publications; "Pericles on 31st Street" (as "Pericles on 34th Street"), "Courtship of the Blue Widow," "The Passing of the Ice," "The Legacy of Leontis," and "Pa and the Sad Turkeys" in *The Atlantic Monthly;* "End of Winter" in *Cavalier,* Copyright © 1962 by Fawcett Publications, Inc.; "The Judgment" in *Chicago Guide,* Copyright © 1973 by WFMT, Inc.; "The Prison" in *Chicago Review;* "The Song of Rhodanthe" in *Country Beautiful;* "The Witness" and "Dark Eye" in *Playboy,* Copyright © 1967, 1968, respectively, by HMH Publishing Company, Inc.; "A Hand for Tomorrow" (as "The Little Store on Bleecker Street"), "The Ballad of Daphne and Apollo" (as "A Knowledge of Her Past"), and "The Wooing of Ariadne" in *The Saturday Evening Post;* "The Journal of a Wife-Beater" in *Harper's Bazaar;* "Matsoukas" and "The Bastards of Thanos" in *Chicago Magazine,* Copyright © 1965, 1969, respectively, by New Chicago Foundation; "The Return of Katerina" in *Greek Heritage,* Copyright © 1963 by Athenian Corp.; "The Sweet Life" in *Confrontation,* Copyright © 1968 by Long Island University; "The Eyes of Love" in *Cavalier;* "The Miracle" in *Playboy;* "Chrisoula" in *Chicago Tribune Magazine;* "Rosemary" in *Mademoiselle,* Copyright © 1968 by The Condé Nast Publications Inc.; "The Waves of Night" in the book THE WAVES OF NIGHT AND OTHER STORIES.

ISBN: 0-385-13421-5 Trade
       0-385-13508-4 Paperbound
Library of Congress Catalog Card Number 77-15180
Copyright © 1957, 1958, 1959, 1960, 1961, 1962, 1963, 1964, 1967, 1969, 1978 by Harry Mark Petrakis
All rights reserved
Printed in the United States of America
First Edition

For my beloved nephews,
LEO, FRANK, and STEVE MANTA,
and for their wives,
SOPHIE, DENISE, and DENA.

About The Author

Harry Mark Petrakis, born in St. Louis in 1923 the son of a Greek Orthodox priest, has spent most of his life in Chicago. His five published novels, two collections of short stories and a work of autobiography include the highly acclaimed *The Hour of the Bell*, and *A Dream of Kings*, which was nominated for a National Book Award, as was *Pericles on 31st Street*, a collection of short stories. He has won an Atlantic First Award and a Benjamin Franklin Citation for his stories, which have appeared in *Atlantic Monthly*, *Harper's Bazaar*, *Playboy*, and many other magazines here and overseas. He lectures extensively, and in the old bardic tradition reads his stories to college and club audiences. He is married and has three sons.

Contents

                              so we'll live,
And pray, and sing, and tell old tales. . . .

                              KING LEAR

A PETRAKIS READER

℄ Almost thirty years ago, when I owned a small, shabby lunchroom in a factory neighborhood near a railroad station, a young girl came in one night when I was about to close. She told me an unhappy story about having come from downstate Illinois to meet a young soldier so they could be married. She had waited all day in the station and he never appeared. Feeling sympathetic to her, I took her home to spend the night with my wife and myself in our small apartment. The next day, I bought her a bus ticket for her home and took her to the station. She promised to send me the money. I never heard from her again, and to this day I'm not sure whether she was telling me the truth.

Rosemary

"I must be nuts," Korshak, the white-haired railroad guard sitting at the counter, said. "Every meal I eat in here brings me a month closer to death."

"The complaint department is out the kitchen door and down the alley, third can from the right," Nick Manos, the lunchroom owner, said. He was a stocky, strong-bodied man in his late thirties, a soiled apron tied about his waist. He had dark unruly hair, a somber face, and even when cleanly shaven, his cheeks appeared shadowed.

"Ain't nothing wrong with this food," a tall, lean baggage handler named Noodles said, "long as your insurance premium is paid up."

Nick sighed. He scribbled on a pad and tore off a check that he put down in front of Korshak. "Eighty-six cents," he said.

The guard shook his head. "A shame I got to pay for a meal like that," he said sadly.

"You ate it," Nick said.

"I couldn't imagine it would taste as bad as it looked," Korshak winked.

"How much do I owe you, Nick?" Noodles slid off his stool.

"Sixty-three cents," Nick said. He shrugged wryly. "Sixty-three cents and eighty-six cents. If I ever get a customer with a check over a buck, I'll give him the place."

"He would want change," Korshak said sagely.

Noodles placed a few coins beside his check. "Guess I'll wash up later tonight after work," he said, and gave Nick a broad leer, "and drift around over to the Poinsetta Hotel."

"Better stay away from there, Noodles," Korshak warned. "That place full of tarts is due for a raid soon."

"Why don't you find a nice girl?" Nick said.

"Are there girls like that?" Noodles smirked.

"There are decent girls around," Nick said. "You meet one and get to know her and stop chasing whores."

Noodles laughed rejecting the advice and walked out to the dark street. Korshak brought his check to the register and put it down with a dollar bill. Nick rang up the amount and returned his change.

"About time to close up," Korshak said.

"Twenty more minutes," Nick said. "Just in time, too. By the end of the day this place becomes a prison."

He waved Korshak good night and walked along the counter to pick up the last dishes. He carried them to the kitchen and placed them on the shelf beside the battered metal sinks.

He stood for a moment over the sinks seeing the whole shabby and squalid lunchroom reflected in the rancid water. The place had been owned by his father for twenty years until his death six years earlier when Nick inherited it. He had made a few halfhearted efforts to scrub the floor and paint the walls. Then he gave up and consoled himself he could really do nothing with the aged stains of gravies and soups on the floor boards, the strong smells of wilted vegetables, the crusts of dried hard grease on the stove, the scarred and unmendable counter and stools. He planned to hold the place just long enough to build a small stake and then dump it for whatever he could get. But without his father's capacity to salvage and utilize scraps, he barely made enough on which to live and a little more to give his mother who lived with his married sister. In addition, as time went on he found himself forced to work longer hours every day in an effort to achieve even that meager return.

He dipped his hands savagely into the dishwater and saw his blurred image among the particles of food and whorls of grease floating on the surface. He considered draining the sink and running in fresh water but decided against the additional delay.

When he finished the last dishes, he drained the water and dried his hands. He carried a broom out to the front to sweep the floor. He was surprised to see a young woman sitting at the far end of the counter.

"I'm sorry, lady," Nick said. "I didn't hear you come in."

"I heard you working in the kitchen and didn't want to bother you," the girl said. "All I want is a cup of coffee."

He filled a cup of coffee from the urn and carried it to her. The only women who patronized his place in the shadow of the trucking depots and the railroad terminal were the assemblers and coilers from the factory across the street. They were beefy-armed, robust-breasted women with huge rumps that engulfed the stools. This girl was slim and no more than twenty-three or twenty-four. Her face was pale, her features even and small, her eyes large and dark. Her hair was dark brown and long and she wore a narrow band of black velvet across her crown, a band studded with tiny stars.

The band was strangely familiar and then as if the past were a crust that suddenly shattered he remembered a girl he had known when he was a young boy. He could not remember her name but they had skated together in the winter on the frozen ponds, whirling and laughing, their arms holding one another, their breath joining swift spirals of mist in the cold clear air. She had worn a short red skating skirt, white stockings, a fur-collared jacket, and in her hair a black velvet band studded with tiny stars.

Still unsettled by nostalgia, he finished sweeping the floor and then wiped the pie case. He closed at ten and when he looked at the clock again it was a few minutes past that time. The girl was smoking over her coffee, lost in reveries of her own. He walked to the door and flicked the switch that turned off the light above the sign outside and darkened the row of small lights in the window. When he turned back she had risen from the stool.

"Time to go," she said. With a nervous flutter of her fingers she crushed the tip of her cigarette into an ashtray. She wore a dark cloth coat and she tugged the collar higher about her throat and stared with foreboding out at the street. He felt sorry for her.

"I won't be leaving for a few minutes yet," Nick said. "Have another cup of coffee on the house before I empty the urn."

She looked at him gratefully and then nodded slowly and sat down. He brought her another cup of coffee and watched her begin to sip it. The coffee moistened her lips and they were full and well curved with a tiny cleft in one corner. She caught him staring and he turned brusquely to finish his work. He emptied the urn and put in a fresh bag for morning. She finished her coffee and brought him the cup and saucer. Then she fumbled in her purse for change. He waved her money aside.

"It's on the house."

"Thank you."

"You live close by?" he asked and was startled by the loudness of his voice. "I mean it's late and do you have a car?"

He sensed a sudden distress about her. She was silent for a long moment before she answered.

"I don't live in the city," she said. She stared through the plate-glass window at the railroad station looming above the roofs of the buildings across the street. "I was supposed to meet someone earlier today. A soldier who was coming from out of town, too. I was to have met him at two this afternoon." The illuminated clock in the tower of the station had black hands shining at twenty minutes past ten.

"He could have had his leave canceled," Nick said. "That happens, you know."

"I knew by late afternoon he wasn't coming," she said slowly. "I waited even though I knew he wasn't coming."

A truck rumbled past on the narrow darkened street and the old wooden floor quivered slightly under their feet. A gust of wind whipped a shred of newspaper against the window. It hung there a moment and then whirled off.

"You know anybody in the city you can phone?" Nick asked. "I mean do you have any family or friends here?"

She shook her head. A slight tremor swept her shoulders. He wondered uneasily if she were going to cry.

"I'll walk over to the station," she said, "and wait for a train back home. I think there is one in a couple of hours."

"Just wait a minute now," he frowned and stood thinking for a moment. "I'm just closing. I'll walk you back to the station. This isn't the neighborhood for a girl to walk around at night."

He walked quickly to the kitchen, pulling off his apron on the way. He made sure the back door was locked and got his coat from the locker. He snapped off the remaining lights, completely darkening the lunchroom except for a small bulb that threw an eerie beam over the desolate counters and stools.

She moved aside and he opened the door. A gust of cold air chilled their ankles. He locked the door and they started walking toward the railroad station.

"I'm glad to get out of that place," he said. "My father owned it, worked it eighteen hours a day for twenty years until he died."

"Do you work it that way, too?"

Another truck rumbled by sweeping their bodies with twin beams of light. From the railroad yards a bell tolled a sharp harsh sound. He shivered and pushed his hands deeper into the pockets of his coat.

"I made the old man a promise to stick it out and I've got my mother to support. But I have other plans. A good friend of mine has been writing me to come help him run a big fancy hotel in Denver with several hundred rooms. He wants me to manage the restaurant and bar. I'm planning to go soon."

At the corner he took her elbow and through her coat felt the firm young flesh of her arm. He was seized by a flutter of unrest in his stomach. They walked up the stairs to the station and he noticed her legs were long and slender in sheer nylons and high-heeled pumps.

They entered the large station waiting room, gray walls and concrete floors and worn benches, the air stale with old smoke and rancid steam from the radiators. The waiting room was almost deserted except for a few soldiers and sailors sleeping on some of the benches, duffel and sea bags cradling their heads. A porter swept a mop across a segment of the concrete floor with a weary flinging motion of his arms. Beyond the waiting room were the ticket windows, all closed but one, a bald man suspended within the lighted square.

"There might be a message for you with the agent," he said.

She nodded slowly and he watched her walking toward the ticket window on her slender legs, her back slim and straight. He wondered whether the soldier and the girl were lovers and jealousy bit his flesh. He moved toward a bench away from those occupied by the sleeping servicemen and after a few moments she joined him.

"There's no message," she said. "I didn't think there would be."

She spoke softly and calmly, sorrow apparent only in her voice, and he admired her restraint.

"When does your train leave?" he asked.

She opened her purse and drew out a small red ticket stamped for Champaign, Illinois. "In an hour and a half," she said.

"I'll wait with you, if it's O.K."

"You don't have to stay," she said. "You must be tired. I'll be all right now."

He shrugged. "I'm used to it."

She sat down at the end of the bench and he sat down beside her, making sure a few inches of the bench was visible between their bodies. They sat without speaking for a few moments. He stole several glances at her face, noting the strange weary and uneasy lines around her mouth. He felt a flare of indignation at the man who let her wait in the station alone.

"Do you like stations?" she asked.

"I don't know," he said. "I don't have any feeling about them one way or another."

"I love to come and just sit in them," she said. "I do it sometimes even when I don't have anyplace to go. I make believe I'm going on a trip, or that I have just returned, and that family and friends are going to meet me. You ever noticed how happy people who travel are?" He shook his head.

"It's usually true," she said. "They're going to visit friends or relatives or going on vacations. For a while there may be separations but then the reunions are joyful."

"I never thought of it that way," he said. "I guess you're right."

"It isn't always true," she said quietly. "Sometimes there is unhappiness, too. And then there are the soldiers and sailors like those asleep over there. They have to go where they are sent, from one camp to another, and then perhaps overseas, away from their families and sweethearts for a long time." She shook her head. "Some of them are just kids."

"You're not much more than a kid yourself," he smiled.

She answered with a brusque short laugh.

"I mean it," he said. "How old are you?"

"Twenty-three," she said. "And you?"

"Thirty-six," he said and felt foolish because he had cut a year and then regretted he had not severed several more. "I'm thirty-six and still unmarried," he shrugged wryly.

She studied him for a long moment and he grew uneasy under her gaze.

"Someday a fortunate girl is going to get you," she said.

He looked at her sharply, wondering if she were mocking him.

"It's true," she said gravely. "When you offered me the second cup of coffee so I could stay inside a little longer and when you walked me here to the station because you were concerned something might happen to me, I knew you were special."

"That was nothing," he said.

"You were kind," she said slowly. "Kindness is rare and when you have it you are someone special."

"That's enough about me," he said, and his voice came out strong and jubilant. "You know I don't even know your name?"

She smiled and he felt the two of them drawn closer.

"Rosemary," she said.

"That's a lovely name."

"Some people hate their names," she said, "and wish they had been called by another. But I have always thought Rosemary sounds like a flower."

He nodded and spoke softly under his breath. "Mine is Nick," he said. "Not much of a name but I'm stuck with it. Actually it's Nicholas."

"I like Nicholas better than Nick," she said. "But I suppose everybody calls you Nick?"

"Nick and a lot of other things," he laughed. "Most of my trade are railroad workers and baggage handlers and truck drivers. Rough, maybe, but good guys."

"They must like you," she said. "They must come to talk to you if they have troubles."

He remembered her grief and it sobered his pleasure. He looked at the young sleeping soldiers.

"Sometimes it helps to talk," he said. "But you don't have to talk about your friend if you don't want to."

"I don't mind talking about him," she said quietly. She

put her hands together in her lap and he saw how meagerly the flesh hinged across the wrists.

"I'm not bitter or angry with him, either," she said. "In the beginning after we first met, he wrote me almost every day. Beautiful letters that I will always treasure. In the last two months he wrote me only twice. I felt he had met another girl, loved her as he had once loved me, and I wrote asking for the truth. At first he denied it and then we agreed to meet in the station today, to talk over what we were going to do." She spoke softly, her voice barely more than a whisper, and he leaned slightly closer to hear. "He must have felt this way would be easier than having to tell me," she said. "I don't blame him, and I'm not bitter. Shall I tell you why?"

He nodded although he found it hard to understand why she should not have been angry.

"Even if I had known it would end like this," she said, "waiting for hours in a station and taking a train home alone, even if I had known, I wouldn't have given up a single hour of the time we had together, the letters, or the dreams." He saw her face with its spare flesh stretched tightly over small bones, a redness in the corners of her eyes. "True love is worth any sorrow and any grief and I will remember as long as I live that I had such love for a little while."

He heard the anguish in her voice and the loneliness and he was moved. He closed his eyes for a moment, locking himself in darkness.

"I understand," he said. "I had love like that once, too. A girl I was going to marry years ago. She became ill and died." He opened his eyes and looked at her. A quick and tender compassion for him swept her face.

"It happened years ago," he said. "I think I loved her in the way you speak of because I have never been able to feel the same about anyone else since. I think of her now at different times during the day but mostly at night, after a

long tired day in the lunchroom, at night when I can't sleep
and wonder what my life would be like if she had lived."

They were both silent for a moment and then she moved
her hand from her lap, slowly, bringing it to rest on his
wrist, her slim fingers touching his arm lightly in consolation. The moment passed and she drew her hand away. He
was embarrassed and grateful when the hoarse almost unin-
telligible voice of a man sounded over the loud-speaker announcing the arrival of a train. A soldier on one of the
benches raised his head like a startled bird and then lowered it slowly to the bag on the bench. A redcap emerged
from a baggage room and walked leisurely toward the gate.

"Maybe you're hungry," he said cheerfully. "The refresh-
ment counter is closed but they've got vending machines in
an alcove. I can get you a sandwich and a Coke if you like,
or maybe some candy."

"I'm not hungry, but thanks," she said and smiled. He
smiled at her and felt his weariness lifted like a rock from
his back.

"You know it's strange," he said. "Strange the way we've
met. Do you know what I mean? It's almost like fate, you
coming into the lunchroom just a few minutes before I
closed and coming back here together and talking like this."

"I believe in fate," she said, and smiled again. "Maybe
there's something here neither of us can understand." She
looked down at her fingers in her lap. "Both of us sharing a
grief and a memory of love," she said gravely.

They fell silent and he looked with concern at the clock.
There was so little time before her train. Yet Champaign
was only a few hours away and he imagined himself driving
down for a weekend. He felt a quick sharp excitement
through his body.

"Rosemary," he said. "This may sound crazy because we
just met tonight, and I know how you feel about this young
man, and I'm a good deal older than you . . . but I wonder
if I could write to you . . . just a letter or two in the beginning . . ."

He was interrupted by a noisy outburst of voices in shouts and laughter. A group of half a dozen men had entered through one of the gates, loudly roistering their way through the station.

"Some of the guys from the yards," he said resenting the distraction, "on their way for a beer." He turned back to her feeling a flurry of panic because he might have assumed too much, pressed too quickly against a still raw grief.

"You don't have to write me back if you don't feel like it," he said. "But I'd like to write you a few letters so you can get to know me better. When I go to Denver I can write you what my experiences are and whenever you feel like dropping me a short note you can let me know how you are, too."

The men drew closer and he recognized a casual patron or two and one nodded and the other waved his hand in a brief greeting. Then the lean wry face of Noodles emerged from the group, as he fell a step behind the others when he spotted Nick.

"Hi ya, Nick, boy," he cried loudly. "Skipping town to evade the Health Department?" He noticed the girl and fell silent. A surprised and twisted smirk crossed his cheeks. "Hello, Netta," he said. He winked and pursed his lips. "Take good care of Nick, will you?" He grinned and rolled his eyes. "He's a buddy of mine." He moved off after the men who had reached the door. They all left the station.

For a moment Nick did not move. There was a stunned fumbling in his head and a whirling of sound in his ears. Sweat erupted across his back and chest. He rose from the bench and he felt himself trembling. "Jesus Christ," he said, and the words came slurred from his lips. "Jesus Christ."

She looked up at him with her face shocked as his, her cheeks white as gravestones, her lips frozen.

"Are you crazy?" Nick said hoarsely. "Is this some kind of goddam joke?"

She shook her head numbly and a great shudder swept her body.

"I didn't mean any harm," she said, and the words stumbled in a frantic whisper from her lips. "I just came in for a cup of coffee and you were nice to me and I just started making things up. . . . I swear to God I didn't mean any harm."

He felt an outrage at her deceit, and even more anger at his own gullibility. She had tricked him, cheated him into exposing himself, duped him into pleading. He reached down and snatched the purse from her side. He snapped open the clasp and reached in and drew out the ticket.

"What the hell did you buy the ticket for?" he cried in a low harsh voice. "Ride there and ride all the way back so you could carry the trick right through to the end! Have me see you off, have me put you on the goddam train and wave goodbye so that you could laugh all the way to Champaign and back! You must be nuts!"

In a wild eruption of fury he tore the ticket into shreds and threw the pieces on the floor at her feet.

She stared down at the floor as if he had torn her up as well. She bent slowly and picked up one of the fragments. He saw the band of stars in her hair and felt a furious urge to tear it from her head. She looked back up at him with her face like a mask of death.

"You goddam lying whore!" he said. He twisted away from her and hurried from the station.

He wandered the dark cold streets around the depot for a long time. A wind carrying the chill of the frozen lake whipped his flushed cheeks. Anger died slowly in little spasms within him. He passed the lunchroom and looked with a sudden loathing at the shadowed interior, the dingy counters, the battered coffee urn. In less than five hours he would be back in that prison again.

He walked to the boulevard that ran parallel to the park. He passed under the gaunt trees, his shadow sweeping the deserted benches that glittered under the swaying street lights. The wind blew scraps of newspaper around the base of the stone monument erected to some heroic dead. He shivered and the station clock struck twelve, the resonant peals lingering in the desolate night.

He climbed the stairs to the bridge over the maze of tracks, rested his elbows on the ledge in the center, and listened to the banging of freight cars being shunted in the dark yards below. He looked up, trying to make out the clarity of a star against the darkness of the sky but suddenly the frail paleness of Rosemary's face intruded before his eyes.

He closed his eyes tightly for a moment and when he opened them he stared at the buildings gleaming in the distance, lighted tiny windows still resembling remote stars. Something closer caught his attention and over the bare frozen branches and boughs of trees a mile or so away he saw a clearing with a glistening pond of ice. He could just make out the small dark forms of a boy and girl skating together, the two of them alone on the pond. They moved as if locked by their arms, skimming in circles around the pond until the girl broke free and whirled gracefully.

He leaned forward on the bridge imagining he could hear the shrill whistling of her skates on the ice, almost see her face sparkling with the joy of her flight. He felt his heart straining to join her, to share her delight. He was seized suddenly with trembling.

He left the bridge, retraced his walk leaving the park, and hurried back to the station. He walked up the stairs and entered the doors, with his blood pulsing. When he saw she was gone, the bench where they had been, empty, he almost cried out.

Confused and uncertain what to do next, he thought of finding Noodles. Then he recalled the Poinsetta Hotel where she might have a room.

He walked quickly down to the street again, passed the lunchroom without a glance, crossed the boulevard entering the settlement of small dingy hotels, dim smoky taverns, and strip joints masquerading as clubs. When he saw the misted amber sign of the Poinsetta Hotel, he ran until he reached it. He entered the lobby short of breath. A night clerk with

cheeks like granite and eyes like chips of stone sat behind
the desk reading a newspaper.

"Is Netta here?" Nick asked.

The clerk raised his head for a moment. A slight stiff curl
of his lips denied the name. He looked back at his paper.

"I'm not a cop," Nick said. "I work right here in the
neighborhood. I know her."

The clerk kept his eyes on the paper.

"Listen," Nick said desperately. "Noodles is a friend of
mine. He told me to ask for her."

The clerk studied him for a long hard instant. He motioned finally toward a house phone around the side of the
desk. He left his chair and as Nick picked up the receiver,
he plugged in a line at the switchboard. There was a buzz-
ing in the receiver and Nick held his breath. When he heard
her voice, a small fire cut the darkness.

"This is Nick," he said. "Nick Manos."

She did not answer.

"I want to see you, please," he said. "I want to come up
for a minute."

There was another tight moment of silence and then he
heard her voice, quiet and without emotion.

"Room 314," she said.

He hung up the phone and walked toward the elevator.
The door was open and he entered, pushed the button for
three, and the doors closed. The elevator creaked and
whined up.

On the third floor he emerged into a faintly lit corridor. A
phonograph wailed a scratched tuneless melody carrying
from a nearby room. He peered closely at one of the numbers and then saw a feeble square of light at the end of the
corridor. He walked slowly toward it.

The door was open and Netta stood inside a narrow room
lit only by the gloomy light from a tiny lamp on a bedstand
behind her. He could make out the bed, a dresser, and an
armchair. Her face was shrouded in shadow and she wore a
quilted robe that hung to her ankles. Her feet were bare,

slim and white on the darker carpet, the toes like small shining shells.

He hesitated a moment and then stepped into the room. He closed the door behind him. Almost at once he breathed the scent of some strange perfume, an odor of withered flowers or musty leaves.

"There is something I want to tell you," he said, and his words whispered like an echo. "I've been walking around for a long time and I had to come and tell you I'm sorry. I'm sorry for what I said."

She stood concealed in shadow and silence and he tried to see within the shrouded hollows and circles of her face.

"There is something else, too," he said. "I'm not stuck in the lunchroom because it was my father's dying wish. I'm stuck in it because I'm lazy and worthless and don't know what else I want to do. I don't have any ambition and I don't have any hope."

The silence tightened and drew thin between them. She did not move or make a sound. The spread on the bed reflected tiny metallic points of light.

"I don't have any friend in Denver who owns a fancy hotel," he said, "and who wants me to handle the restaurant and bar. The only job I been offered in the past five years was to take bets for a bookie who hangs out in the men's room of the railroad station."

He had a sense of the wretched months and years moving past his lips, falling with an ache from his flesh. He looked down at the scuffed worn tips of his shoes.

"The girl I might have married years ago," he said. "She didn't get sick and die. She became pregnant and I would have married her but I was afraid that the kid wasn't mine. She had an abortion and couldn't stand the sight of me afterward. I don't know where she is now."

His voice fell away and he finished in a futile silence.

For an instant it seemed something stirred under the shadowed flesh of her cheeks. Then she moved around and walked a few steps to the other side of the bed. She turned back to him.

He saw her face in the gleam of the lamp and she appeared a stranger. The flesh puffed slightly about the eyes, the skin of her cheeks gray and sallow, the hair dull and lank. But it was her eyes that were altered the most, hard cold buds suspended between the womb and the grave.

"I'm a whore not a priest," she said, and the words came frozen and quiet from her lips. "If you want to stick around, it's ten bucks a jump."

He looked at her and tried to answer. The words stuck in his throat. He heard a moan beginning somewhere deep in his body and as it sought to burst from his heart, he turned for the door and fled.

⊄ I have read this story before a hundred college and club audiences across the United States. The girls in the audience will clap for Nitsa and hiss Vasili, and the boys will cheer Vasili and boo Nitsa. The result is like an old movie, where one cheers or hisses, depending upon one's sympathies. No other story I have written has provided me as much fun.

In the question periods that follow the reading, someone invariably asks if the story is autobiographical. I explain solemnly that my wife and I have a nonaggression pact. If I do not beat her, she will not beat me.

The Journal
of a Wife Beater

OCTOBER 2: Today I beat my wife, Nitsa, for the first time! I preserve this momentous event for future generations by beginning this Journal and recording this first entry with some pride.

I did not beat her hard, really not hard at all. I gave her several clouts across her head with my open palm, enough to make her stagger and daze her a little. Then I led her courteously to a chair to show her I was not punishing her in anger.

"Why?" she asked, and there were small tears glistening in the corners of her eyes.

"Nothing of great significance," I said amiably. "The coffee you served me was not hot enough this morning and after the last few washings my shirts have not had enough starch. Yesterday and the day before you were late in arriving at the restaurant. All of these are small imprudences that display a growing laxity on your part. I felt it was time to suggest improvement."

She watched me with her lips trembling. How artfully women suffer!

"You have never struck me before," she said thoughtfully.

"In the year since we married, Vasili, you have never struck me before."

"One does not wish to begin correction too soon," I said. "It would be unjust to expect a new bride to attain perfection overnight. A period of flexibility is required."

Her big black eyes brooded, but she said nothing.

"You understand," I said consolingly. "This does not mean I do not love you." I shook my head firmly to emphasize my words. "It is exactly because I do care for you that I desire to improve you. On a number of occasions in my father's house I can remember him beating my mother. Not hard you understand. A clout across the head, and a box upon the ear. Once when she left the barn door open and the cows strayed out, he kicked her, but that was an exception. My mother was a happy and contented woman all her life."

The conversation ended there, but Nitsa was silent and meditative as we prepared for bed. She did not speak again until we were under the covers in the darkness.

"Vasili," she asked quietly, "will you strike me again?"

"Only when I feel you need it," I said. "It should not be required too often. You are a sensible girl and I am sure are most anxious to please me by being a good wife and a competent homemaker."

She turned away on her pillow and did not say another word.

OCTOBER 3: I slept splendidly last night!

OCTOBER 5: Since I have a few moments of leisure this evening, I will fill in certain background information about Nitsa and myself so that future generations may better understand this record of an ideal marriage relationship.

First I must record my immense satisfaction in the results of the beating. Nitsa has improved tremendously the past two days. She has taken the whole affair as sensibly as any man could have wished.

Her good sense was what first impressed me about Nitsa. I met her about a year ago at a dance in the church hall, sponsored by the Daughters of Athens. I drank a little beer and danced once with each of a number of young ladies whose zealous mothers beamed at me from chairs along the wall. I might add here that before my marriage a year ago I was a very desirable catch for some fortunate girl. I was just a year past forty, an inch above average height, with all of my own hair and most of my own teeth, a number of which have been capped with gold. I had, and of course still have, a prosperous restaurant on Dart Street and a substantial sum in United States Savings Bonds. Finally, I myself was interested in marriage to a well-bred young lady. My first inclination was to return to Greece and select some daughter born to respect the traditions of the family; but as our parish priest, Father Antoniou, pointed out with his usual keen discernment, this would have been grossly unfair to the countless girls in our community who hoped for me as a bridegroom. Although marriage to any one of them would dismay the others, it would be better than if I scorned them all for a wife from overseas.

Nitsa impressed me because she was not as young as most of the other girls, perhaps in her late twenties, a tall athletic-looking girl who appeared capable of bearing my sturdy sons. She was not as beautiful a girl as I felt I deserved, but she made a neat and pleasant appearance. Most attractive young girls are too flighty and arrogant. They are not sensible enough to be grateful when a successful man pays them attention. Bringing one of them into a man's home is much the same as bringing in a puppy that has not yet been housebroken. Too much time is spent on fundamentals!

Imagine my delight when, in inquiry regarding Nitsa's family that night, I learned she was the niece of our revered priest, Father Antoniou, visiting him from Cleveland.

I danced several American dances with her to demonstrate I was not old-fashioned and spoke to her at some length of my assets and my prospects. She listened with un-

concealed interest. We sat and drank coffee afterward until
a group of my friends called to me to lead one of the old
country dances. Conscious of her watching me, I danced
with even more than my usual grace and flourish, and
leaped higher off the floor than I had in some time.

A day or two later I spoke seriously to Father Antoniou.
He was frankly delighted. He phoned his sister, Nitsa's
mother in Cleveland, and in no time at all the arrangements
were made. As I had accurately surmised, the whole family,
including Nitsa, were more than willing.

Several weeks later we were married. It was a festive
affair and the reception cost a little over a thousand dollars
which I insisted her father pay. He was a housepainter who
worked irregularly, but in view of the fact that Nitsa
brought me no dowry I felt he should demonstrate the good
faith of the family by paying for the reception.

Nitsa and I spent a weekend at the Mortimer Hotel for
our honeymoon, so I could return to count the cash when
the restaurant closed each evening. As it was, God only
knows what the waitresses stole from me those two days.
During our absence I had the bedroom of my apartment
painted, and after considerable deliberation bought a new
stove. I write this as proof of my thoughtfulness. The stove I
had was only twelve years old, but I am worldly enough to
understand how all women love new stoves. If permitted by
weak and easily swayed husbands they would trade them in
on newer models every year.

In recalling our first year together, while it was not quite
what I expected, I was not completely disillusioned. There
was a certain boldness and immodesty about Nitsa which I
found displeasing, but one must bear with this in a healthy
young woman.

As time went on she spent a good part of the day with me
in the restaurant taking cash. She became familiar enough
with my business so that when the wholesale produce and
meat salesman called she could be trusted to order some of
the staple items. But I noticed a certain laxity developing, a

carelessness in her approach to her responsibilities, and remembering my father's success with my mother, it was then I beat her for the first time.

I am pleased that it seems to have prompted unreserved improvement. Bravo, Vasili!

OCTOBER 7: It is after midnight and I am alone in the restaurant which is closed until morning. I am sitting at the small table in the kitchen and can hardly bear to write the shameful and disgraceful episode which follows.

Last night after returning from the restaurant I went to bed because I was tired. Nitsa came into the room as I was slipping under the covers. I had noticed a rather somber quietness about her all that day, but I attributed it to that time of the female month. When she had donned her night clothes and gotten into bed beside me, I raised my cheek for her to kiss me goodnight. She turned her back on me and for a moment I was peeved, but remembering her indisposition I turned off the lamp and said nothing.

I fell asleep shortly and had a stirring dream. I fought beside Achilles on the plains before Troy. I carried a mighty shield and a long sword. Suddenly a massive Trojan appeared before me and we engaged each other in combat. After I brilliantly parried a number of his blows he seemed to recognize he was doomed. He retreated and I pressed him hard. While we slashed back and forth, another Trojan rose beside me as if he had sprung from the earth, and swung his weapon at my head. I raised my shield swiftly but not quite in time and the flat of his sword landed across my head. The pain was so terrible I shrieked out loud, and suddenly the plains of Troy and the helmeted warriors were all swept away and my eyes exploded open to the sight of Nitsa bent over me, calmly preparing to strike again!

I bellowed and clawed to sit up, and tried desperately to flee from the bed. The stick she swung bounced again across my head and the pain was ferocious. I fell off the bed in a tangle of sheets at her feet; then I jumped up frantically and

ran to the other side of the bed, looking back in desperation
to see if she followed. She stood dreadfully calm with the
stick still in her hand.

"Are you mad!" I shouted. My nose seemed to be swelling
and my head stung and I tasted blood from my cut lip. "You
must be mad or in the employ of the devil! You have split
me open!"

"I owed you one," she said quietly. "A debt that had to
be paid."

I looked at her in astonishment and rubbed my aching
head. I could not comprehend the desecration of a wife
striking her husband. "Your senses have come apart," I bellowed. "You might have broken my head!"

"I don't think so," she said. "You have an unusually dense
head."

I was horrified. On top of my injuries her insolence could
not be tolerated. I ran around the bed and pulled the stick
from her hands. I swung it up and down. When it landed
across her shoulders she winced and gave a shrill squeal.
Then I went to bathe my swollen head. A harrowing and
terrible experience indeed!

OCTOBER 11: Plague and damnation! Blood and unspeak-
able horror! She has done it again.

That wench of evil design waited just long enough for the
swelling of my nose to recede and my lip to heal. All week
she had been quiet and reserved. She came to work promptly
and performed her duties efficiently. While I could never
forget that night in bed when she struck me, I was willing
to forgive. Women are by nature as emotionally unstable as
dogs under the mad light of a full moon. But I am a generous man and in this foul manner was my generosity re-
warded.

It happened shortly after the rush at lunch was over. The
restaurant was deserted except for Nitsa at the register and
the waitresses chattering beside the urns of coffee. I was sitting at the small table in the kitchen, smoking a cigar, and

pondering whether to order short ribs or pork loins for lunch on Thursday. Suddenly I was conscious of an uneasy chill in the center of my back. A strange quick dread possessed me and I turned swiftly around and Nitsa was there. Almost at the same instant the pot she was swinging landed with a horrible clatter on my head. I let out a roar of outrage and pain, and jumped up holding my thundering head. I found it impossible to focus my eyes, and for a frenzied moment I imagined I was surrounded by a dozen Nitsas. I roared again in fear and anger, and ran to seek sanctuary behind the big stove. She made no move to follow me but stood quietly by the table with the pot in her hand.

"You must be mad!" I shrieked. "I will call the doctor and have him exchange your bloody head!"

The dishwasher, who had come from the back room where he had been eating, watched us with his great idiot eyes, and the waitresses, cousins of imbeciles, peered through the porthole of the swinging door.

"I owed you one," Nitsa said quietly. She put down the pot and walked from the kitchen past the awed and silent waitresses.

As I write this now, words are inadequate to describe my distress. Fiercer by far than the abominable lump on my head is the vision of chaos and disorder. In the name of all that is sacred, where is the moral and ordered world of my father?

OCTOBER 15: Disturbed and agitated as I have been for the past few days, tonight I decided something had to be done. I went to speak to Father Antoniou.

Nitsa, that shrew, has been at the restaurant for several days now acting as if nothing had happened. She joked with the customers and took cash calmly. Heartless wench without the decency to show some shred of remorse!

Last night I slept locked in the bathroom. Even then I was apprehensive and kept one eye open on the door. While it was true that by her immoral standards we were even, she could not be trusted. I feared she would take it into her stony soul to surge into a shameful lead. Finally tonight, because I knew the situation had become intolerable, I visited the priest.

He greeted me courteously and took me into his study. He brought out a bottle of good sherry. We sat silent for a moment, sipping the fine vintage.

"You may speak now, my dear friend," he said gently. "You are troubled."

"How can you tell, Father?" I asked.

He smiled sagely. He was indeed a fountain of wisdom.

"Well, Father," I struggled for the mortifying words. "It is Nitsa. To put it plainly, she has struck me not once, but twice, with a stout stick and a heavy pot."

He sat upright in his chair.

"May God watch over us!" he said. "Surely, Vasili, you are jesting!"

I made my cross and bent my head to show him the hard lump that still dwelt there. He rose from his chair and came to examine it. When he touched the lump, I jumped.

He paced the floor in agitation, his black cassock swirling about his ankles.

"She must be demented," he said slowly. "The poor girl must be losing her mind."

"That is what I thought at first," I said seriously. "But she seems so calm. Each time she strikes she merely says, 'I owed you one.'"

"Aaaaah!" the priest said eagerly. "Now we approach the core of truth." His voice lowered. "What did you do to her for which she seeks revenge?" He winked slyly. "I know you hot-blooded Spartans. Perhaps a little too passionate for a shy young girl?"

"Nothing, Father!" I said in indignation, although I could not help being pleased at his suggestion. "Absolutely nothing."

"Nothing?" he repeated.

"I have clouted her several times across her head," I said.

"My prerogative as a husband to discipline my wife. Certainly nothing to warrant the violence of her blows."

"Incredible," the priest said. He sat silent and thoughtful, then shook his head. "A woman raising her hand to her husband in my parish, and that woman my niece. Incredible!" He wrung his hands fretfully. "A stain upon the sacred vows of marriage." He paused as if struck by a sudden thought. "Tell me, Vasili, has she been watching much television? Sometimes it tends to confuse a woman."

"Our picture tube is burned out now several months, Father," I said.

"Incredible," the priest said.

"Perhaps if you talk to her, Father," I said. "Explain what it is to be a dutiful wife. Define the rights of a husband."

The priest shook his head sadly. "When I first entered the priesthood," he said somberly, "I learned never to attempt to reason with a woman. The two words should never be used in the same sentence. The emancipation of these crafty scheming descendants of Eve has hurled man into a second Dark Ages."

I was impressed by the gravity of his words and had to agree I had spoken hastily.

"My son," the priest said finally, a thin edge of desperation in his voice. "I confess I am helpless to know what to advise. If you came to seek counsel because she drank to excess or because she had succumbed to the wiles of another man . . . but for this! I will have to contact the Bishop."

I sipped my sherry and felt anger coming to a head on my flesh as if it were a festered boil pressing to break. I, Vasili Makris, subjected to these indignities! Humiliated before my own dishwasher! Driving my parish priest to consult with the Bishop!

"There is only one answer, Father," I said, and my voice rang out boldly, a call to battle. "I have clouted her too lightly. There is nothing further to be done but for me to give her a beating she will not forget!" I waved my hand. "Rest assured I will remember my own strength. I will not break any bones, but I will teach her respect." I became more pleased with that solution by the moment. "That is the answer, Father," I said. "A beating that will once and for all end this insufferable mutiny!"

We watched each other for a long wordless moment. I could sense that good man struggling between a moral objection to violence and an awareness there was no other way.

"They who live by the sword," he said dolefully, and he paused to permit me to finish the quotation in my mind. "This cancer must be cut out," he said, "before it spreads infection through the parish."

Father Antoniou raised his glass and toasted me gravely. "Consider yourself embarked on a holy crusade," he said in a voice trembling with emotion. "Recapture the sanctity of your manhood. Go, Vasili Makris, with God."

I kissed his revered hand and left.

OCTOBER 17: The promised retribution has been delayed because a waitress has been sick and I cannot afford to incapacitate Nitsa at the same time. But I vow her reprieve will be brief!

OCTOBER 19: Tonight is the night! The restaurant is closed and we are alone. I am sitting in the kitchen making this entry while she finishes cleaning out the urns of coffee. When the work is all done I will call her into the kitchen for judgment.

Nitsa! Misguided and arrogant woman, your hour of punishment is here!

OCTOBER 23: In the life of every noble man there are moments of decisive discovery and events of inspired revelation. I hasten with fire and zeal to record such an experience in this Journal!

That epic night when Nitsa came to the kitchen of the restaurant after finishing her work, without a word of explanation I struck her. Quick as a flash she struck me back. I was prepared for that and hit her harder. She replied with a thump on my head that staggered me. I threw all hesitation to the winds and landed a fierce blow upon her. Instead of submitting, she became a flame of baleful fury. She twisted violently in search of some weapon to implement her rage, and scooped up a meat cleaver off the block! I let out a hoarse shout of panic and turned desperately and fled! I heard her pounding like a maddened mare after me, and I made the door leading to the alley and bounded out with a wild cry! I forgot completely the accursed stairs and spun like a top in the air and landed on my head. I woke in the hospital where I am at present and X-rays have indicated no damage beyond a possible concussion that still causes me some dizziness.

At the first opportunity I examined myself secretly for additional reassurance that some vital part of me had not been dismembered by that frightful cleaver. Then I sat and recollected each detail of that experience with somber horror. A blow now and then, delivered in good faith, is one of the prerogatives of marriage. Malevolent assault and savage butchery are quite another matter!

However, as my first sense of appalled outrage and angry resentment passed, I found the entire situation developing conclusive compensations. I had fancied myself married to a mortal woman and instead was united to a Goddess, a fierce Diana, a cyclonic Juno! I realized with a shock of recognition that one eagle had found another, perched on Olympian peaks, high above the obscure valley of pigeons and sheep.

O fortunate woman! You have gained my mercy and forbearance and have proven to my satisfaction that you deserve my virile love and are worthy of my intrepid manhood!

Nitsa, rejoice! You need no longer tremble or fear that I will ever strike you again!

¶ I had been working several days on a review of a book of poems by the Greek poet from Alexandria, Constantine Cavafy. When I finished the review I was steeped in the aura of sadness surrounding the gentle, sybaritic old poet who revealed so precisely how age and death are always in the shadow of the delight of love. I began writing this story, but the poet who emerged, Thanos, was a totally different person, sharing with Cavafy only his love of the poem.

The Bastards of Thanos

The island hospital stood on a small hill overlooking the city, a battered stuccoed two-story building that had endured rain and wind and storm. At the foot of the hill the narrow winding streets teemed with the trade of bazaars, stalls and shops vending spices and silks, cheeses and wines, shrimp and squid. Greek and Jewish and Egyptian merchants haggled and bartered in a babble of harsh and reedy dialects and tongues.

From where Thanos lay in the corner bed of the second floor pauper's ward, he could see the harbor beyond the city, the piers and docks with a few freighters at anchor. He watched the ships make port and sail with the tides and on sharp clear days he marked the flight of gulls that skimmed and soared above the water. At other times he stared at the ceiling above his bed, the surface upon which particles of sun and cloud and the reflections of water shimmered like the billows of the sea itself. During these hours he fashioned his verses, appending each word slowly and arduously, composing another fragment of the long unfinished poem he had begun ten years before. In this way the day would pass until twilight curtained his window. He waited for the lights of the city and the harbor to flicker on proclaiming the beginning of another roisterous night of drinking, gambling and love.

Though there were twenty other occupied beds in his

ward, a screen beside his bed and another at the foot shielded him from the remainder of the patients. He heard the clatter of utensils, the skirmishing murmur of voices, the curses and the groans. He inhaled the fetid stench of pus and decay mingled with the antiseptic scents of alcohol, iodine and carbolic acid. But the smells and the sounds of the ward came to him as if from a distance, while in his bed he breathed and endured the cesspool of his own body.

He knew he was dying. The scent of death rose like swamp mist from his pores. His flesh withering on his bones. Even his once strong hands now skewered between fatal illness and age, his fingers brittle twigs needing only a slight jerk to snap them from the frail stem of his wrists.

When he had first been brought to the hospital several months before, the diagnosis had been unanimous and clear. Accepting the coming of his death he fought all efforts to soften his abrasive will, to medicate and console him. He rejected the banal ministrations of the nurses and doctors, scorned their aseptic routine visits that merely served to chart his decline. He vehemently refused the drugs they sought to give him for his pain, unwilling to narcotize the wellsprings from which his poem flowed. He would suffer the pain until he could bear it no longer rather than dull his senses. And even if pain made him howl like a dog to the end he would seek to contour and define even the assembling spectres of darkness and death.

For a little while each morning he had his only visitor, the island Greek priest who came dutifully to attend him on his rounds of the sick. He was a meek and resigned man with a pale, sepulchral face. Fasts and prayer, celibacy and ingratitude, these had drained his spirit and he lived and moved like a shadow drawing what small warmth he could from the candles of his faith.

"How are you today, Thanos?" the priest asked in a frail voice that he tried to make sound vigorous. Thanos knew he regarded the few moments of his visit as a penance.

"Absurdity is still king," Thanos said. "And the poem is the only canon still worthy of faith."

The priest sat down awkwardly in the chair at the screen. He drew his bony legs cloaked in shabby black trousers together and stared at the worn tips of his scuffed shoes. He forced himself to look back at Thanos and managed a wan smile.

"You are looking better today," he said.

"You are a dreadful liar," Thanos said. "Each day all my selfish desires and my absurd vanities decline further into impotence and ugliness. In a short while I will be hollowed out, old as the ages, bare bone and dry brush. And you look about the same."

The priest fumbled his fingers together.

"How is the poem going?" he asked.

"It resembles the old man of the sea," Thanos said. "The Proteus who constantly eludes the grasp, forever changes his shape. But here and there in a word, in a line, it captures pleasure and folly, misfortune and love, vice and elegance, perfidy, betrayal, ineptitude, cunning."

"Is there a place in all of this for God?" the priest said.

"He is there too," Thanos said, "holding aloft the lance and the cup and the Holy Grail. Where He is the water does not flow, love is sterile, crops fail, and animals do not reproduce."

"You build a statue without a pedestal," the priest said patiently. "We are saved by hope and not by memory."

"Spare me your vesicular oblations," Thanos said. "I would not trade a single folly or vice of my life for an eternity of redemption. Your paradise is duller than the landscape of your dismal and surrendered face."

"I have had no reason to laugh in twenty years," the priest sighed. "Even a smile threatens to crack my jaw. Yet although I cannot help my sad face, God may still help you. Believe in Him and you may find your burdens lightened."

"I have always believed in the essentials," Thanos said. "Dancing and laughter, yeast and flour, grapes and wine, desire and love, noon and night, words and poems. Why should I forsake them now?"

"There are mysteries we can enter only through faith," the priest said.

"The mystery lies not in the end but in the beginning," Thanos said.

For a moment longer the priest wavered and then he slowly rose. He bent and raised his small black communion bag.

"I will see you again in the morning," he said. He hesitated and for an instant closed his eyes. When he opened them the lids were heavy with despair. "I pray for a sign," he said slowly. "A sign to prove the power and glory of God. A small miracle to enable you to accept communion."

Thanos uttered a low growl of laughter. "I have swallowed wine by the barrel," he said, "and savored bread by the ovenful. Your chalice of crumbs and droplets is an abomination."

The priest turned forlornly to leave.

Thanos called after him. The priest turned back.

"Show me a sign of His power and His glory," Thanos said, "and I pledge to take your communion." He grinned a crooked tearing back of flesh from about his hardened and discolored gums. "But if you cannot provide me a sign then you must admit your life has been useless deprivation and waste. We may still be able to provide you a few meager vices with which to adorn your last years."

The priest coughed a final futile sigh and left.

Thanos did not mind the visits of the priest. He looked forward to them, secretly yearned for them to last longer. They offered him a momentary release from the sputtering and spasms of his organs as they expired.

After the priest had gone, he returned to his poem, forming the words deep in his throat, feeling them hiss and sing through the crumbling canyons of his body. He cherished the words born of sight, smell, touch, taste, hearing and spirit. The fertile element was life, the sterile element was

death, and the purifying element was the poem. In the
throes of his creation he could still feel the wild strong cries
of his soul.

When he needed a respite from the words and lines, he
assaulted his memories. He used the myriad events of his
life as herbs and potions, sharpening the treasured reveries
for battle against the great savage pain he knew would
come just before the end. He carefully reviewed the succulent meals he had eaten, the juicy rare meats, the redolent
oil and garlic salads, the candled midnight tables of walnuts,
cheese and fruit. Upon the parched desert of his palate he
trickled once more in fantasy the wines of Bordeaux and
Burgundy, Porto and Marsala, still wines and sparkling
wines, pale amber champagne and glowing ruby clarets.

He retraced his multifarious journeys across the world. An
orphan at six, a seaman at fifteen, fifty years as a poet. He
remembered the hundreds of women he had possessed, the
countless courtships and consummations. The cycles of desire, the sadness after love, but also, reborn like the phoenix
from the ashes, the love after sadness. He tried to extricate
the hundreds of shimmering bodies, the lovely faces, knowing that many of them were dead now or grown cold and
old with skin like ship's canvas and bodies gnarled and
twisted like the trunks and branches of old island trees. But
in the fertile valleys of his assignations they would always
be young. Brown handsome Polynesians who walked with
the pride of Queens. Black wenches in Africa with gleaming
flanks and armored breasts. Coal-eyed Jewesses, descended
of Bathsheba, like smoke in a man's arms. Moslem girl children with breasts like plums. Delicate yellow women with
the shyness of virgins in their eyes and a whore's skill in the
arts of love. He heard them whimpering and shrieking and
cursing and giggling and pouting and teasing in the rocking
beds of a hundred ports. He fought to hold the vicarious
heat of the visions, until finally, shaking and exhausted, he
watched them fading into the twilight that engulfed his

bed. He cried out then, a bitter lament deep in his body, for the joys he had once savored and would garner no more.

Early one morning in that week he had another visitor. During the night his pains had goaded him almost to the threshold of screams and he had found himself thinking with frenzy of the numbing drugs. The dawn came bleak and pale, the sky a gray shroud against his window. He was staring at the window when a young man entered between the screens around his bed, pausing for a moment as if he were expecting to find someone else.

Thanos turned his head on the pillow and for a time they stared at one another in silence. The youth was tall, with dark eyes and dark hair, dressed in a seaman's jacket, a seaman's knit cap in his hands. Against the sunweathered skin of his cheek the slit of a scar gleamed white.

"Are you Thanos, the poet?" he asked finally. He spoke in a low and earnest voice.

The pain had made Thanos angry and uneasy. "What do you want?" he asked harshly.

"My name is Petros," the young man said. "Petros Potamis. My mother was Magdalina."

"My mother was the Blessed Virgin," Thanos said. "What do you want?"

"Magdalina Potamis of Athens," Petros said tensely. "You were in Athens for a while years ago, weren't you?"

"I have been in fifty countries and in five hundred cities," Thanos said impatiently.

Petros raised his hand, fumbling with his fingers at the scar on his cheek.

"I am your son," he said.

For a startled moment Thanos was silent. Then he began to laugh, a mirthless sniggering from between his lips. Petros stood stolidly until his fit had subsided, until he could hoarsely regain his breath.

"I have no sons or daughters," Thanos said and snorted again. "I have never been chained in marriage and my unions have been unsanctified. You have made a mistake."

"I am your bastard son," the young man said quietly. "My mother was Magdalina Potamis and you knew her in Athens more than twenty years ago. She has married twice, has other children by those husbands, but you are my father. She told me when I was fifteen."

"We all dream of the father," Thanos said. "The comedy begins when we think we have found him."

"My mother told me you had been a sailor," Petros said. "When I was sixteen I went to sea. I asked about you in a score of ports. A few men remembered your drinking and your fighting. Some remembered you shouting out your poems." He gestured with his hands in awkward apology. "I even talked to a few of the women who remembered you."

"You heard about me in some brothel," Thanos cried, "and have come to mock me or to discover if I have an inheritance of treasure to leave. I have nothing but a thousand lines of an unfinished poem that will die soon with me."

Petros fumbled in the pocket of his jacket and brought out a small, worn and faded, paper-covered booklet.

"These are your poems," he said. "I have read them many times. On nights in the Islands of the Indies and on watch in the Galapagos. I have heard them echo in the cries of birds on the shores of Greenland."

"Where did you get the scar?" Thanos asked.

Petros shrugged a slight drawing together of his shoulder, his lips parting in a spare wry admission.

"A fight over a girl in Vera Cruz," he said.

"That could be evidence of my paternity," Thanos said with a snigger.

"My mother gave me the poems," Petros said. "There is one of them, a poem she told me you had written of her. Do you remember?"

"Read it to me," Thanos said.

The young man opened the booklet and began to read in a clear and strong voice.

> A single candle was not needed
> To light our hours close together.

In the distance, the sea,
The harbor white under the moon.

On the flanks of the mountains,
Wildflowers and the evening star.

Secret places of our heart's love,
Wind and night our bower.

Old and ill I will still remember,
In darkness savor once more the light.

From a yard below the hospital window, a rooster screamed raucously. A dog answered with a short harsh bark. Thanos struggled vainly to separate flowers sundered in the wind of years, petals scattered in the wake of endless tides. With the poem in his hands Petros waited in a silence like the drifting of a ship in a dead still sea, heart and soul ardent for the first quiver of wind.

"I remember," Thanos said. "I remember your mother now." He felt a sliver of pain moving in his blood.

A flame leaped into the youth's dark eyes.

"I have searched for you for six years," he said and his voice trembled. "Searching six years to find a father I had never seen. In Alexandria, two months ago, an old salt you had sailed with told me he had heard you were here. When we anchored yesterday I swept the city for you, wandered all night through the bars that had not seen you in months. Now I have found you and my ship sails in an hour on the tide."

"You found me in time," Thanos said. "A few more days might have been too late."

"I can stay if you want me to stay," Petros said. "I can jump ship and hide until after she sails. I can stay with you until you are well."

"There is no need of that," Thanos said. "I cannot escape the shipwreck of my body and the end of my voyage is very near."

"I knew I would find you," Petros said. "I swore to my mother I would find you."

"When you see her again, give her a message for me,"
Thanos said. "Tell her I loved her most of all."

"I will tell her," Petros cried softly. "As God is my judge,
I will tell her in just those words."

"I have no possessions to leave you," Thanos said. "Remember these words, my only legacy to you. I was what you
are. You will become what I am. Think of those words and
you will unravel the way to live."

"I will," Petros said. "I will."

"Hurry now to your ship," Thanos said.

Petros came closer to the bed and knelt quickly. Before
Thanos could draw his hand away the son had clasped his
palm and gently kissed his stiff dry fingers. The touch of the
youth's mouth upon his cold wasted flesh filled him with a
strange quivering warmth.

Petros rose and moved toward the opening between the
screens. He paused as if to make another plea or effort to
remain.

"Don't miss your ship and your mates!" Thanos cried. "A
hundred gilded ports are waiting for you, a hundred scented
lovely girls. Hurry!"

The young man turned and fled.

Later that morning the priest came on his daily rounds.
He stood for a moment uncertainly at the foot of the bed.

"How are you today, Thanos?" he asked.

"Rejoicing," Thanos said, and the words came with a slur-
ring burden from his lips. "Because I am purified by every
devilment, sanctified by every depravity, beyond sentiment
and fatigue, nearing the realm of pure spirit."

The priest sat wearily down drawing the small black bag
close to his feet.

"You are looking better today, Thanos," he said with a
frail smile.

Thanos groaned. "Day by day you parrot your miasmic
clichés," he said. "A worthy spiritual leader for this parish of
drunks, thieves, and syphilitics."

The priest looked submissively at his pale-fingered hands in his lap.

"I had a visitor this morning," Thanos said. "I have been waiting to tell you about him. A bastard son from a far-off port that I did not know I had whelped. He has been searching for me for six years and finds me on the eve of my death. What does St. John say to that?"

The priest rose trembling to his feet and made his cross. "God has heard my prayers," he said in a shaken voice. "To send you a son so close to the end. It is a sign of His power and His glory."

"It was a sign," Thanos said. "A moment of deliverance, an event of revelation."

"God be praised!" the priest cried softly and closed his eyes.

"If there is one son," Thanos said, "how many others might there be, bastard spawn of my wild beds, born of virgins and whores . . ."

"No!" the priest gasped. "That is not the sign I meant!"

"Think of it!" Thanos cried hoarsely. "Perhaps as many as fifty or more androgynous mongrels of my rampaging journeys, devoted to life and drink and love as I have been, a virile host to carry on after I am gone, hurling my unrepentant seed into myriad races and through endless generations!"

The priest shook his head, a moan of despair falling from his lips. "No," he pleaded. "That is not the meaning."

"That is my meaning," Thanos said.

The priest stood in silence for another moment. His breathing grew calmer slowly, his agitation quieted. The weariness and the resignation settled once more in his pale cheeks. He bent heavily for his small bag and turned slowly to leave.

"I will see you in the morning, Thanos," he said.

"Before you go," Thanos said, "I would like communion."

The priest stared at him numbly.

"Communion, you know, the last rites," Thanos said. "A sign is a sign and I honor my pledges."

For a labored moment longer the priest stared benumbed at Thanos. Then he placed his small bag on the chair. He opened the worn clasp and drew out the golden chalice, the tiny bottle of wine, the container of meager bread. He worked with slow stiff fumblings, praying under his breath as he blended the wine and the bread.

He brought the chalice to the bed. He dipped the small golden spoon into the wine and bent toward Thanos.

"My God, my God," he whispered, and there were tears in his eyes. "Thy mysterious ways are beyond thy servant's understanding."

Thanos parted his lips and received the tiny spoon of sweet wine and the sodden pellet of bread.

After the priest had gone, he lay staring at the ceiling. The arc of day gave way to the shades of dusk. In the twilight the wild rooster screamed again and he heard a savage burst of pain answer in his body.

He fought his fear and panic and slowly, carefully, he cast and forged the words and lines of his poem.

¶ I have read this story to audiences almost as many times as I have read "The Journal of a Wife Beater," but the response is quite different. The origins of the story must go back to my youth, when I admired the lovely, black-haired and dark-eyed Greek girls in church, who were encircled by zealous brothers and grim fathers. Sometimes, staring at one of those girls, I would catch a brother bristling and quickly avert my glance. I remember thinking then how only the most reckless and fool-hardy of suitors would dare to pass the inspection of that fierce and prickly Greek garrison.

The Song of Rhodanthe

I was twenty-seven years old that spring. Papa had still not given up hope that a man would be found to marry me. My brothers, Kostas and Marko and Niko, were married and had numerous children of their own. They were all concerned about me.

It was true that I wanted to be married. Papa had presented a number of men to me for my approval. I was not beautiful but neither was I so homely that I had to accept one of them. They were either too old or too loud or red-faced from drinking too much beer and wine. I think Papa grieved most about me when wine made him tearful. His only daughter, twenty-seven, and still unmarried. Friends who were bachelors drank and grieved with him. In the end they offered themselves as suitors to ease Papa's despair.

After an evening with one of them Papa waited for my decision. I told him I refused to accept such a man.

"You are twenty-seven years old!" he cried. "A daughter still unmarried at twenty-seven is a plague on a man's spirit. I cannot sleep for worrying about you. My health is breaking down. At the market everyone asks me, Panfelio, is your daughter married yet? Is she even engaged? I cannot bear much more."

"Yes, Papa."

"What was the matter with Gerontis?" he asked.

"He is too old," I said, "and his false teeth whistle when he speaks."

"You are too choosy!" Papa shouted. "Remember you are twenty-seven years old."

"Yes, Papa."

"What was the matter with Makris?" he asked. "He is a younger man than Gerontis."

"He is younger," I said. "But he greases his hair until it drips oil down his cheeks and he spent all evening telling me how he can crack open a crate with his bare hands."

"I can still crack open a crate with my bare hands," Papa shouted. "Your poor Mama was never the worse for it. You forget, my girl, you are twenty-seven years old."

"Yes, Papa."

One evening a week, my brothers brought their wives and children to our house to eat supper. The wives were red-cheeked with great bosoms and ate like contented mares. The house became a bedlam with children hanging from the lamps and chairs collapsing with a sound of thunder. We assembled at the table and bowed our heads and Papa said grace.

"We are grateful, O Lord, that we are well and together and for the food upon this table. Bring us together again next week and let there be a man for Rhodanthe among us. Amen."

When dinner was over and it was time to leave, each of the wives of my brothers kissed me benevolently on the cheek. One after the other my big brothers embraced me sadly and kissed me somberly. Every parting was a festival of grief. Poor Rhodanthe.

I told Papa goodnight and kissed him tenderly because I loved him very much. He was foolish sometimes and shouted a great deal but I knew how much he loved me too.

I went to my room and prepared for bed. I sat before the

mirror and brushed my long hair. In those moments I fiercely felt a wish to be married and raise children of my own. Sometimes I thought I wanted that as much for Papa and Kostas and Marko and Niko as for myself.

The last cold months of winter passed. The winds grew gentle. The rain fell during the night and in the daylight the earth smelled fresh as if it were awakened from a long sleep. One morning I saw a robin sitting on a branch of the cherry tree in our yard and I knew the spring had really come.

Each morning Kostas and Marko and Niko drove up in their trucks to have a cup of coffee while Papa ate breakfast. I knew they did that for me so that I would not feel too lonely during the day.

They sat around the kitchen table, big strong men that made the kitchen seem smaller than it really was. The cups looked tiny and fragile in their massive hands. They smoked cigars and spoke in loud gruff voices to each other. But they were soft and gentle when they spoke to me.

When they had left with Papa for the market, I washed the dishes and cleaned the house. I worked quickly and felt a glow in my cheeks.

Because that day was so beautiful I decided to take the bedding outside to air. I carried the sheets and blankets to the back yard and draped them across a line. When I finished hanging them up I was a little out of breath.

There was the sound of whistling in the alley in back of the yard and a young man appeared. He was striding along with his hands in his pockets and his head flung back and a wild jubilant whistling ringing from his lips. I had heard whistling before, even the strong bass whistling of my brothers, but never a sound like he made. It was as if the spring had burst into song. As if the first slim green buds and the blades of new grass and the soft fresh wind had suddenly found a voice.

When he saw me standing there he paused. For a quick tight moment the whistling ceased. His hair was thick and dark and an untamed and errant curl glittered across his forehead. He smiled then and his smile was as reckless and daring as his whistle. Then he walked on quickly and the wild whistling rang out again. As the sound faded a terrible loneliness overcame me. I went quickly into the house.

That night at supper I broke a cup and spilled soup from the pot while pouring it into a bowl.

"What is the matter with you?" Papa said. "You are nervous as a cat tonight."

"Nothing is the matter, Papa," I said and felt a quick flame in my cheeks.

He cleared his throat and sighed heavily.

"It is not normal," he said somberly. "Twenty-seven years old and still unmarried. You will become sick."

"I will not become sick, Papa," I said. "Do not worry about me."

"How can I help worrying?" he said. "What kind of father would I be if I did not worry about my daughter, still unmarried at twenty-seven?" His lips quivered and he wiped a stray tear from his eye.

"Yes, Papa."

"You are too choosy!" he shouted. "You have not that right at your age. Gastis passed the market today. He asked how you were. He was taken with you. What in God's name was the matter with Gastis?"

"I have told you before, Papa," I said.

"Tell me again!"

"His face is like one of his grapefruit," I said. "He never smiles. Whatever time of day you are with him always appears to be night."

Papa threw up his hands in despair.

"One is too young," he said. "And one is too old. One laughs like an idiot and one does not laugh enough. One is a banana and one is a grapefruit. I am telling you, my girl, I am losing patience!"

"Yes, Papa."

"What kind of man do you want?" he shouted again. "Tell me what kind of man you want?"

I paused for a moment in the doorway of the kitchen. A reckless excitement swept my tongue.

"I want a young man with dark hair," I said boldly. "And a wild dark curl across his forehead. A man who whistles and makes the earth burst into song."

Papa made his cross.

"What I have feared has come to pass," he said sadly. "You have become unbalanced."

"Yes, Papa," I said, and I ran back to him and kissed him gently. "Good night, Papa."

In the morning I could not wait for all of them to leave. They sat over their coffee for what seemed to be an eternity. Yet each time I looked at the clock I saw they were no later than they usually were.

When they had gone I ran to my room and carefully brushed my hair and tied it with my brightest ribbon. I touched my lips with a light red stain and pinched my cheeks. I went quickly downstairs and out the back door. A moment of panic seized me when I realized I could not just stand there waiting. I hurried back into the house and pulled the blankets from my bed and ran with them down the stairs. I had just finished hanging them across the line when I heard the sound of the whistling again.

He came down the alley just as he had the morning before. His head flung back and his legs walking with great strong strides and that wonderful wild whistle singing on his lips.

When he saw me he stopped. He smiled again, a perfect and riotous smile. I could not help myself and smiled back. He walked slowly to the fence and carelessly and with a supple grace leaned his elbows upon it and put his face in his hands.

"You live here?" he asked. And he had a deep man's voice but not nearly as harsh a voice as Papa had, and with revelry in it, unlike the voices of Marko and Kostas and Niko.

"Yes," I said.

"With your husband?" he asked slyly.

"With my father," I said quickly. "I am not married."

"Good," he said, and he smiled again and threw back his head and laughed a festival of tuneful laughter from his throat. "Good," he said again and then he waved goodby and started striding down the alley.

There were a dozen questions I wanted to call after him, a dozen things I wanted to say. I was ashamed because I had answered and yet I felt strange and alive for the first time in my life. I looked at the budding leaves and at the first blades of grass and at the early tulips and felt a fervent kinship with them.

The next morning it rained and I was in despair. I could not stand in the rain waiting for him to pass, or hang blankets on a line in the downpour. After a while I gave up hoping it would stop in time and consoled myself that the following morning the sun might shine again.

I finished the kitchen and wiped the last breakfast cups without spirit. I hung the dish towel upon the rack, and heard a light tapping at the window.

My heart leaped because he was there. He waved to me through the rain-smeared glass. I ran to the door and flung it open. He came in dripping from the rain and the dark curly hair matted upon his head.

"You are soaked!" I said. "You'll catch cold! I'll get a towel."

He took the clean towel from my hands and began briskly to dry his hair. He rubbed his cheeks with vigor and smiled and shook his head.

"You weren't in the yard," he said.

I looked at him helplessly.

"It was raining so hard," I said. "I wasn't sure you would come."

When I realized what I had said I put my hand quickly to my mouth. But he only laughed softly.

"The rain is nothing," he said. "I missed you."

We looked at each other and there was taunting merriment in his dark eyes. I tried to think of something to say but all my senses seemed to have fled.

"I've got to go in a minute," he said. "I'll be late for work."

"A cup of coffee," I said. "It's still hot. It will warm you."

He came to the table and he was not as tall as any of my brothers and not as broad in the shoulders as my father, but there was grace and strength in the way he moved.

I brought the pot of coffee to the table and filled his cup. I could sense him watching me and I spilled some into the saucer.

"Weren't you afraid to let me in?" he said.

I turned away and shook my head.

"What's your name?" he said.

"Rhodanthe," I said. I put the pot back on the stove and then turned to face him.

"A pretty name," he said. "A name for a flower."

I looked down at the floor because I was sure the frantic beating of my heart would show in my cheeks.

"I know a great deal about you," he said and when I looked up he winked slyly. "I know more about you than you realize."

"You do?" I said.

"I know you are sometimes sad," he said, "because you do not smile. I know you are sometimes lonely because you do not laugh."

We were both silent for a moment and I marveled at how well he understood. And how natural it seemed that he should be sitting at my table drinking coffee.

He pushed back his cup and rose from the table and walked to the door. I followed him there and he turned and paused with his hand on the knob. He bent a little and kissed me. A quick impulsive kiss that brushed my lips with the grace of the spring wind.

I stepped back shocked.

"You had no right!" I said. "You should not have done that."

"I wanted to kiss you," he said and smiled wickedly. "I do what I want."

Then he was walking swiftly with long strong strides through the rain.

That night the family gathered again. All the rosy-cheeked wives and the multitude of children. I worked with a jubilation I found hard to conceal. I even sang a little to myself and several times noticed one of my brothers watching me strangely.

At the end of the meal the children scrambled from the table to resume playing in another room. The wives picked up the plates and carried them to the kitchen. Niko, the youngest of my brothers, caught my arm.

"What makes you sparkle tonight?" he said. "I have never seen you like this before." He gestured at Papa. "What has happened to this girl?"

I tried to shake off his hand but he laughed and held me tight. All of them watched me and I felt my cheeks flaming.

"She is blushing," Marko cried. "Blushing like a school-girl."

"Let me go," I said to Niko, "or I will bring this plate of bones across your head."

"She is in love!" Kostas roared. "The girl's in love!"

A reverent quiet descended upon the room. The wives came from the kitchen to stand in the doorway with their eyes open to great bursting cups. Niko let me go slowly. All of them watched me in some kind of awe.

"Rhodanthe," Papa said and there was a great joy stirring in his voice. "Is this true?"

My heart went out to him. He was growing old and loved me so much. I looked at each of my brothers and felt a great wave of affection for them. I could even forgive their smug wives, secure in marriage to good men, who listened in the doorway.

"Yes," I said. "Yes."

"Thunder and lightning!" Kostas roared. He beat with his big fist upon the table. The dishes rattled and jumped.

"Hurrah!" Niko cried.

"I'll be damned!" Marko shouted.

Everybody looked at Papa. He silently made his cross and looked as if he were about to cry.

"God be praised," he said and his voice trembled. "I knew you must come to your senses. I have brought you some good men. Which one of them have you reconsidered?"

"Five bucks to a buck it's Makris!" Niko shouted.

"That grease pot?" Kostas cried. "She wouldn't touch him with a yardstick."

"It must be Gastis!" Marko said. "It has to be Gastis!"

"Silence!" Papa roared. "Silence!"

The room went quiet. No sound except for the shrieking children in the parlor.

"Silence those little monsters!" Papa roared again. One of the wives went quickly to the parlor and a moment later silence fell in every part of the house. She came back and softly closed the door.

"Which one is it?" Papa spoke to me gently.

I stood at the foot of the table and folded my hands. I took a deep breath and for one brief moment closed my eyes and then opened them again.

"It is none of the men you have brought home," I said.

They all looked shocked. A rumbling began around the table. Papa waved his hand fiercely for silence.

"I do not understand," he said slowly. "It is not Gastis or Makris or Sarantis or Gerontis or any of those other good men?"

"No, Papa," I said.

"Who the devil is it then?" Marko said angrily.

A flare of panic seized me but I had gone too far to turn back.

"A young man who passes on his way to work in the

morning," I said. "He has dark and curly hair and he whistles in a way I have never heard anyone whistle before."

For a long startled moment no one spoke.

"She has gone nuts!" Kostas cried. He looked around for confirmation.

"Who is this guy?" Marko shouted. "I'll teach him to whistle at my sister!"

"Dirty hoodlum!" Niko spit between his teeth.

Papa beat with his fist upon the table. Everyone became quiet again.

"You are joking?" Papa said and he made an effort to laugh and one of the wives began to laugh with him. Papa stopped laughing and glared at her and she almost choked closing her mouth.

"I am not joking," I said. "He is a young man that I have spoken to a number of times. This morning we had coffee together."

"He had coffee with you this morning?" Marko shouted angrily. "In this house alone with you?"

"We'll have his teeth hot from his mouth!" Kostas cried.

"Dirty hoodlum!" Niko shouted. "Sneaking behind our backs."

"Who is he?" Papa cried. "Who is he?"

"I don't know his name," I said. I knew how that sounded but I was becoming angry too.

Papa exploded for all of them. Shock and anger ripping his face. The wives cowered in the doorway.

"You don't know his name!" Papa thundered. "You don't know his name!"

They all began roaring at once. I bit my lips hard trying to stop the tears that burned to break from my eyes.

"I don't know his name!" I cried angrily. "I don't know his name! I know I love him! I heard him whistling and saw him and everything changed. This morning it rained and I could have cried because I would not see him and then he knocked on the window." They all sat staring at me and I struggled furiously to find words to overwhelm them.

"There were other men I might have loved years ago," I said. "Men who were frightened off by your shouts and your fists. But you will not take this man from me. He told me he knew I was sad because I did not smile and that I was lonely because I did not laugh and then he kissed me!" I felt a tremor shake my body and my voice rose fiercely. "I don't know his name! I only know I love him!"

They were sorry afterwards. Papa came to my room and kissed me and cried a little. Then Marko and Niko and Kostas came and touched my hair gently with their big hands and tried to speak with their eyes. I forgave them because I knew how much they cared for me. And I consented to let Niko wait with me in the morning to see the young man.

But he did not come the next morning. I thought perhaps he knew about Niko and the following day I waited alone. I waited in the yard with the spring wild and tangled about my head and the blossoms breaking on the branches of the trees and the earth flowing and alive.

He did not come. And the spring passed into summer and the leaves grew long and green on the trees and the sunflowers bloomed among the stones and the birds were everywhere. The speckled robins and the gray starlings and the brownish redwings.

After a while I knew Papa and the others thought I had made it all up. That I had grown weary of the procession of sad suitors and made the story up to keep others away.

They do not understand that someday he will come back. On a morning when the green hearts of the lilac bushes tremble awake in the wind. When the first slim green buds break upon the branches of the maples and the catalpas.

He will come striding along with his hands in his pockets and his reckless head flung back and the wild jubilant whistle ringing from his lips. And I will feel once again that the early green buds and the first fragile flowers and the soft new winds have suddenly burst into song.

¶ This story is one of my favorites and stems from a year when I worked as a night dispatcher in an ice depot. The theme encompasses decline and age as well as those resonances of the past I often draw upon in my stories. If these men are not Homeric Greeks but Polish icemen, I saw them as heroic figures suffering the same fate.

The fine film director Sam Peckinpah once made me promise to grant him first reading on any novel I wrote about the icemen. I hope I can write it before one or the other of us passes.

The Passing of the Ice

That morning, standing before Toby's desk in the dispatch office, Mike felt the moment of his discharge had come. The straw boss sat overflowing his chair with the great rolls of fat around his waist and loins, his heavy fingers leafing through the papers on the desk.

"How you feel today, Mike?" Toby asked.

"I feel fine," Mike said. "I feel like an iceman. How do you feel?"

"You look tired, Mike," Toby said. "A man should not look as tired as you so early in the morning."

"We are all tired," Mike said. "But a heavy man covers his weariness and a skinny man shows it to the bone."

The straw boss sat stiffly at the desk staring intently at the papers, as if he had forgotten anyone was there. His way was to loosen his grip just enough to allow a man to think he might escape, and then clamp his big hand on him tighter. Mike had seen others squirm and sweat before the desk. He showed no fear, because his dread was not of the fat man but of being forced to accept the measure of his days.

"Somebody left ice out." Toby spit the words between his thin lips. "An old hand like you should watch there is no goddam ice left on the trucks overnight."

"I'll watch," Mike said.

Outside the office the loaded trucks stood idling with the

blocks wedged beneath the wheels. The voices of the drivers and helpers carried in a chorus of curses and laughter. J. C. would have his truck gassed and loaded with the cakes of four-hundred-pounders stacked to the tailgate.

"Why don't you give up?" Toby said, and his voice was a harsh and ugly whisper. "You can't move around on the cars like you used to. It won't be long anyway."

Mike felt a violence deep in his belly, the fury of a temper that had plagued his younger days. He waited until the hard knot eased, and tried to speak quietly.

"I get around," he said. "I work twice as hard because I know you don't want to lose me."

"Get out." Toby's eyes were bright in anger. "Get out, old man, and do your work."

Mike left the office. Outside he stood for a moment in the spring morning with the smell of the earth fresh and cool, and found himself trembling. He walked across the roadway to where J. C. waited in the cab of the truck, feeling that Toby had risen from his desk and was watching at the window.

"Roll your truck, Mike," Sargent cried from behind the wheel. "We late now."

On the running board of the next truck, tall and lean-flanked Noodles swung an arm toward the sky.

"O sun," Noodles sang. "You have displayed your backside long enough. Winter has been fierce and the icemen are weary. O sun, grow strong and warm poor old Noodles."

From the tailgate of Noodles' truck, his helper Gomez waved a greeting to Mike.

"This is the season," Gomez said, turning his face to the sky, "the time I would like to own a small farm and work in the fields."

"You, a farmer?" Noodles said. "Gomez, you couldn't grow foam on a glass of beer."

"You making noise with your mouth," Gomez said. "My father was a farmer. I would have been a good farmer."

"Sure you would have," Mike said. "Lay off quail hunting

every night with Noodles, and save your money. Get back to the farm."

When Mike reached his truck, J. C. kicked out the blocks that wedged the wheels and swung into the cab beside him.

"Let 'em roll!" Mike shouted savagely. "C'mon, you dead-rumped coal hikers that call yourselves icemen. Roll them loads!"

Noodles waved and hollered something that was lost in the roar of the motors.

A few moments later, driving with the windows open and the air cool against his cheeks, Mike's trembling had eased. J. C. rode in silent fury beside him.

"The bastard was on you again," J. C. said. "The bastard was riding your back again." His black cheeks corded, and a curse came bitten from his mouth.

"What you talking about?" Mike said. "He poured me a cup of coffee and shared his chocolate doughnut with me. You got that big and friendly man all wrong."

They looked at each other and smiled. J. C. laughed. Mike felt the old pleasure returning, the rocking feel of the wheel in his hands, the pull of the loaded trailer, and a good friend beside him.

"You can smell the spring," Mike said. "In a few more weeks the summer, and then another year almost gone."

"To hell with the season," J. C. said. "Icemen freeze in winter and roast in summer. You know the ice don't care what time of year."

"Amen," Mike said.

Mike knew the ice. He had worked with the pick and tongs for almost forty years. Sometimes in the summer, with the dry railroad cars waiting to be iced, and in his rushing back to the hill to reload, he forgot for a little while that the icing was not the way it had been. Bungo was dead, and the great Orchowski no longer roared his wild songs from the top of the cars. Each year brought more icing machines, and the old icemen were gone. Now in the beginning of summer the young wandering Blacks and the Irish gandy dancers came to work on the trucks. They were strong without skill and lifted to show off their strength. Foolish young men who tried to lift the three- and four-hundred-pound blocks with their backs or with their arms. Mike tried to teach them how to lift by using their legs and how to hook the tongs just the right distance from the score marks. But he worked beside them uneasily, aware how a man could be maimed or crushed by the carelessness of others.

There were a few good men among them. J. C., the young Black on his truck, had some of the strength and spirit of the old icemen. Noodles knew how to handle his Hilift. The dark and bitter Sargent could cut and throw the way Chino once had. But they were just a few among the sportive young men who came for the summer pay and took no pride in their work and left wearily in the autumn.

Mike had been the smallest of the giants, and now he was alone. But time and the ice had not left him untouched. Each year the burden of his back and legs began earlier in the day, until by the middle of the afternoon his muscles were knotted and each movement of icing was scored with pain. More and more often he was seized with a strange despair.

He could not do much of anything else. He could eat and drink and sleep and in season go to see a ball game. He could lie in the darkness next to Zeba and sometimes still feel the wild and sudden tenderness that briefly let his weariness drop aside. Afterward he could not help but laugh, remembering himself as a bantam rooster and the women as the hens. Of all the women he had known and loved, only Zeba remained. She had never been very pretty, and she was no longer young. Little pouches of flesh had gathered beneath her chin, and in the morning he noticed how the strap of her slip was held by a pin, or how the seam of her stocking might run all around her leg. But in the evening there was hot food on the table. When he brought J. C. home, she baked them spareribs and went down to the corner and

brought them back cold beer. She was kind to his friend,
and for this he was grateful. When it was time to go to
bed, Zeba rubbed Mike's back and legs with ointment, her
big warm hands bringing a temporary comfort to his body.
Afterward they lay side by side, and she spoke of the years
they had spent together. She talked low and soft in the dark
room, and knowing his weariness, she did not ask a question
or expect him to say a word. Sometimes she laughed at
something she remembered, secretively, yet always including him. He would feel himself easing into the darkness and
her voice fading and the last low stirrings of her laughter.

"How come I let you be my driver?" J. C. bared his teeth
in a broad grin. "You too skinny to be a good driver for a
big boy like me."

"Fat ass don't make a good iceman," Mike said.

J. C. laughed and struck his big fist against his chest.

"Never been an ice crew like us," he said. "Someday we
going to ice together in hell. Damn devil going to say, 'J. C.,
where that skinny driver you come down with? Oh, there he
is hiding in the cab. All right, now you both here, let the
number-one ice crew start to work and cool off hell.'"

"You crazy." Mike smiled. "I taught you all I know, and
now you wear your pants too high. Between tall pockets and
big feet you got a head like a sponge."

"I'm an iceman," J. C. said. "All icemen got a sponge for a
head. It goes with the job."

"Amen," Mike said.

When they reached their first stop, at the Harley Depot,
the yardmaster located their cars on the spur. Mike pulled
the truck alongside the first car to be iced, and carrying
picks and tongs, he and J. C. swung up on the back of the
truck.

The elevator rose slowly to the height of the car. They
began to work, cutting the blocks into chunks to fit the
bunkers. Swiftly they fell into the rhythm, and the ice flew.
To save their wind they did not speak, but J. C. hummed a

broken snatch of melody. Their picks rose and fell, and the ice split into chunks for the tongs to grab and throw. They moved quickly and surely on the narrow runway. They closed the lids and lifted the plugs with a steady pull. As fast as they finished a car they moved on to the next.

A little past noon they stopped for lunch at Chino's small bar on Laramie Street. They ordered beef sandwiches garnished with pickle and onion, and steins of lager beer. Sitting in a rear booth of the darkened room, Mike was grateful for the chance to rest among the warm shadows.

Chino, bent with arthritis but still taller than most men, came to sit in the booth with them. He had been one of the icemen with Mike in the days of Bungo and Orchowski. When his joints became inflamed and his body twisted, he bought an interest in the small bar. He kept it shadowed, as if ashamed to be seen by the men who still worked the trucks.

"How's business, Chino?" Mike asked.

"Ain't doing nothing," the old iceman said gloomily. "We get a little movement at lunch, and the rest of the day is like a graveyard. See." He motioned with his stiff and swollen fingers around the room.

"Sure," J. C. said. "You stop watering your beer and stop making sandwiches so skinny, you get some more business."

"You just a punk," Chino said. "You don't know like Mike and me know. The ice is passing. There ain't no more trade from the locations. In a few more years the machines will do all the icing and the last icemen will be working in the goddam coalyards."

Mike shut his eyes, and for a moment the years fell away and he worked with Bungo and Orchowski, and Chino was a tall young giant, wilder than all the rest.

"You remember?" Chino said. "Mike, you remember how it used to be?"

"I remember," Mike said.

Chino twisted his head around like a frightened bird suddenly trying to take flight. He raised his hand from the table and held it for a moment poised in the air and then slowly lowered it again to the scarred surface of the wood.

"It ain't no use thinking about how it used to be," Chino said. "I think and think but it ain't no use. Things are just the way they are and nothing can change them. The old ice days are gone, and they ain't never going to come back."

J. C. finished the last of the beer in the stein and wiped his mouth with the back of his hand. "You make it sound like we all dead now," he said.

"You just a punk," Chino said. "You don't remember the ice trucks lined up for blocks. Tarpans and Shaws and the crews from Proviso. A few years back, even after I was off the Hilifts, they would fill this place for lunch. But not one of them a damn iceman like we was in the old days. Ain't that right, Mike?"

Mike stood up to leave, suddenly not wanting to listen to Chino any longer.

"You still talk just as much," Mike said. "By God, Chino, you talk as much now as before."

"I got a right," Chino said. "Business is bad and my back hurts and all I got to do is sit and remember."

"Stuff it," J. C. said. "Trouble with you is you see the whole world hung up. You ain't the only man pushing to see daylight."

"Listen, Chino," Mike said. "Tomorrow make the beef a little leaner. Today was too much fat." He put his hand briefly on the old man's shoulder and felt the block of strength beneath the swollen joints.

Outside, the sunlight hurt their eyes, and for a moment they stood squinting while the shavings of ice melting on the truck dripped into puddles in the gutter.

"He's right about one thing," J. C. said. "You the only ice-man left. Rest of us don't count for crap."

"Chino and me make noise with our mouths"—Mike shook his head and spoke gruffly—"because we can't shake our rumps the way we used to."

He climbed into the cab of the truck. J. C. walked to the other side and swung in beside him.

"He's right anyway," J. C. said. "I know the old man is right because you the only hump at the hill don't scare when Toby talks. Rest of us call him bastard but inside we sweat. Maybe it's how you think about the ice. Not like the rest of us, just a job. I see you close and I know."

Mike turned the key, and the motor kicked over with a roar. Then he reached over and brought his bunched fist down hard on J. C.'s leg above the knee. The helper bellowed with a cry of pain that almost drowned the noise of the motor.

"You're right," Mike said. "No one any damn good but me."

J. C. rubbed his leg and began to laugh.

"Daddy," he said. "When I grow up, daddy, can I be an iceman like you?"

They laughed together, and Mike pulled the truck from the curb and started back to the hill to reload.

By the time they got to the big ice storage house at the top of the hill, the rest at lunch had worn off and Mike was aware again of the burden of his body. He backed the truck to the edge of the platform. He waited with his tongs at the ramp while J. C. opened the heavy door and entered the icehouse. In a moment the helper backed out swiftly dragging the first four-hundred-pound block, his powerful back and big-muscled arms handling the ice easily.

Mike watched him and marveled at his strength and realized that even in his prime years he had perhaps not been as strong as J. C. Yet he still could have beaten him at work, because cutting and throwing the ice were like something he had been born to do, the main reason he had been put on earth. Now, like Chino said, it was too late. No good to hide in a dark bar and remember the way it used to be in sunlight. No good to hang with the ice and fall under weariness and age.

"Sometimes," Mike said, and there was a fierce edge to his voice, "I want to drag out that ice and cut it down and throw it as far as I can, throw it to hell and gone. I want to empty the big house once of every last block and scatter every last damn chunk over the hill. Make the fat man sit up. Make everyone understand that after forty years an iceman don't just lay down his pick and tongs with a goddam whimper."

J. C. paused and watched him silently for a long moment and then finally flashed his big white teeth.

"You too little to empty the big house," he said. "A little chewed-up runt like you can't do it alone. You need J. C. help to cut down the big house."

"Shove it," Mike hooted. "The only edge you got is a fat head and feet six sizes bigger than you need."

Together they put on the last blocks to make a full load. They climbed back into the cab, and Mike started the truck down the hill. Another truck passed them going up the hill to reload, and Noodles and Gomez waved from the cab.

In front of the dispatch office, Toby stood by the gas pumps waiting for them.

"Hot dog," J. C. said. "Run over the bastard!"

Mike stopped and braked beside the pumps and kept the motor idling. Toby looked up at him unsmiling, and as he stood there without the partial cover of his desk, the great rolls of fat hung upon his frame and made him appear rooted, like some shapeless and heavy-footed animal, to the earth. In that moment Mike was aware how unlike the icemen the fat man was. Where they were lean and quick, he was leaden and slow. Where they tried to sing in their work, he was angry with envy and reminded them it was a burden.

"You took a long time loading," Toby said.

J. C. shifted restlessly beside him, and Mike did not say a word but marveled suddenly how clearly he saw the place of the fat man in the passing of the ice.

"When you come back in," Toby said, "put any ice left

into the big house. Don't let any ice sit overnight on the damn truck."

"OK," Mike said, and for a moment he pitied the fat man and his load.

That night in the darkness of their rooms Zeba moved closer to him in the bed, and her body soothed the pain that rioted through his bones. He felt the pressure of her full breasts against his arm, and he twisted in the bed, curling closer to her warmth.

"Sleep," she said, and her voice was soft and husky in the darkness. "Sleep, my old rooster, sleep."

He touched her, but there was no desire in his hands and no wish for her to respond. He wanted only to rest, to banish weariness and pain.

When he fell asleep, in a restless dream the first days of the ice returned. He saw again the great heaving horses pulling the dray, hauling the ice with block and tackle. He worked swiftly beside the wild young men and cut and threw, and then he stood alone. There was only the mournful face of Chino and in a mist the lost faces of the giants and over them all the cloud of Toby, soft and angry, waiting for him to fall and for the mountains of ice to crumble.

He moaned in his sleep and felt Zeba's fingers and dimly heard her comforting voice. He moved gratefully against her body and slipped again into fitful sleep.

In the beginning of September, the pain which had cramped his body through the summer eased up. He was not sure whether he felt less weary because of the shorter hours on the truck or the first clear, cool days. In the early twilight, driving back from icing at one of the depots, he sang loudly, and J. C. joined in, and the two of them bellowed over the roaring of the old motor. Later, as they unloaded the few remaining blocks into the big house, a great round and orange moon hung in the sky above the hill.

September was the time of year the drivers and helpers lingered in the locker room after punching out. A few more

weeks would see most of them gone, so they talked of the
journeys they would make, following the sun. They would
recall the rumble of the freights and the small dark towns
that swept by in the night and, finally, the great sweet or-
chards with the ripe fruit like little pieces of sunlight. They
talked confidently of returning in the spring, and at those
times Mike tried to convince himself that perhaps he and
Chino were wrong. The winter would be quiet as it had always been, but in the spring the Hilifts would rock down
the hill again. The dry cars with empty bunkers would stand
in long trains. The young Blacks would come up from the
South, and the husky gandy dancers would tumble in off the
freights, and among them would be another Bungo or another Chino, and they would bring the mighty ice days
back. Even as he told himself that story, he did not really
believe it might be true.

There was a day near the end of September. His pain returned fiercely late in the afternoon as they iced dry potato
cars at Dart Street. He stood for a moment uneasy and surprised. It had been weeks since he had felt it quite so
sharply.

A little later, uncomfortable in his chest and stomach, he
had to catch his breath, and on a car runway he let go his
tongs and straightened up quickly, feeling a cramp knotting
in his chest. The ice seemed to become heavier through the
afternoon, and by the time they finished their last car and
were on their way in, empty, his arms and back felt stiff and
raw. When he pulled up the hill and parked, Noodles and
Gomez had just unloaded the few blocks of ice left on their
truck into the big house, and the four of them walked together down the hill.

The locker room was thick with smoke and laughter and
the jubilation of men leaving to eat and meet their women.
Mike sat on a bench in the corner beside a paned window
and rested his head against the wall. He wanted to wash
and change to the clean shirt hanging in his locker, but sud-

denly he was far too tired for the effort that required. J. C. came over and shook his shoulder gently.

"C'mon, daddy," J. C. said. "Your lady is baking spareribs and I'm invited. You feel better after some of them ribs."

Noodles turned from his locker and laughed.

"Couple of pigeons picking for ribs," he said. "Old Noodles going picking for something else with more meat on it than them ribs." He winked broadly and flexed his muscles. "I seen a gal today," he said. "She come out of no place while we was icing and just stand and watch. Pretty gal with big eyes and hair like golden corn."

"Sheik," Gomez said. "Oh, sheik."

"I told her, honey," Noodles said, "honey, you need an iceman?"

"She was shaken with your hot charm," J. C. said. "I bet she took one look at you and fell right down under the wheels of your truck." He laughed down at Mike, who tried to smile against the stiffness in his cheeks and around his mouth.

"She told me—" Noodles said slowly. "She told me she got an electric icebox."

"Sheik," Gomez said, "tell them what you told her then."

"I told her"—Noodles grinned and slapped his leg—"I told that gal wasn't nothing better than hand icing by an iceman who knew his stuff."

"That's what he told her." Gomez shook his head and chuckled.

The room seemed unreal to Mike, the stiffness spreading to his arms and a slow pounding beginning in his head. Through the grimy glass of the window he could see the shadowed rows of frame houses further down the hill with their kitchens lit for supper. And far over the edge of the city the sun had left a strange red glint in the twilight.

"I could tell that gal was crazy about me," Noodles said. "She probably still there waiting for me."

"I had a gal crazy about me once," Sargent said. "Waited for me every night when I got off work. I borrowed two dollars, and we chased down a preacher. Now we got six kids waiting for me every night when I get off work."

Mike wanted to sleep. He felt suddenly that it would be comforting to be able to lay his head down on the bench and close his eyes and have J. C. and the young icemen close by.

"You all right?" J. C. said. "Daddy, you with me?"

The faces of the men around the room blurred, and in quick panic Mike struggled and recalled them and then lost them again. In sweeping darkness and without moving he seemed to be stretching for something just out of reach. A terrible heat suddenly blazed in his chest, and he wanted to cry out, but the wonder of what was happening kept him silent. He was torn by fear and a strange joy. In the moment of deciding which was stronger, the heat burst within him.

The voices of the men fell away and there was silence in the room. J. C. stood beside the bench, and Noodles came to his side.

"He's sleeping," Noodles said. "He just fell down asleep."

The others moved and gathered uncertainly around the bench.

"He's dead," Sargent said quietly. "I seen them in the army. I know the look. He's a dead man."

"You talk crazy!" Noodles snapped at him. "Old Mike just sleeping!"

"Goddam!" Sargent said savagely. "I know a dead man when I see one. Was you in the army and seen the dead piled up like me, you know too."

"Someone call a doctor," Gomez said in a shocked voice. "Someone better go for a doctor."

"He's dead." Sargent shook his head. "Doctor don't do no good for a dead man."

"Jesus Christ," Noodles said, and made a quick sign of the cross. "Jesus Christ."

For the first time J. C. moved and bent slightly to peer closely at Mike and straightened up and looked around at the circle of men with a stunned and terrible grief on his face.

"He was tired and just died," J. C. said. "He been an iceman a long time, and he got tired and he died."

The silence spread again, and no one moved. One of the men cleared his throat, and another shifted restlessly from one foot to the other.

"Phone the fat man," Sargent said. "Tell him to turn off that TV. Tell him an iceman died."

J. C. reached down and put his arms under Mike's back and legs and lifted his body. He held him easily against his chest. He left the locker room, and no one made a move to follow.

He carried the body to the top of the hill. Once or twice he stopped and for a moment stood unmoving beneath the dark sky pinned with a crescent moon. He started walking again toward the row of parked trucks, and bracing the body against his knees, he opened the cab of Mike's truck and slid him in upon the seat. He fumbled on the floor and found Mike's pick and tongs.

He crossed the hill and climbed the ladder to the big house's platform. He opened the heavy door and in the pale light of the moon saw the blocks of ice in glistening rows waiting to be loaded on the trucks in the morning.

He hooked his tongs on a block in the nearest row and dragged it swiftly through the door to the edge of the platform. He swung his pick and split the scored block. The chunks fell apart, and he switched back to tongs and caught up the chunks one after the other, and swinging them between his legs, flung the ice out into the darkness. When he had finished one block he went in and dragged out another and cut it down and again scattered the ice across the earth. He worked faster and faster, and shattered shavings of ice stung his cheeks. He kept dragging out the blocks and cutting them down and heaving the ice into the darkness. His breathing became hoarse and tight in his chest, and he cut desperately and threw more savagely. He dragged out block

after block, throwing farther and farther, the chunks cracking against other chunks that littered the ground.

When the big house was empty, he stood for a moment on
the platform, his lungs heaving for air, and then with a great
and final fling he hurled the pick and tongs far out into the
night.

He climbed down the ladder and walked through the field
of broken ice back to the truck. In the cab he moved Mike's
head gently to rest against his shoulder. He turned the key,
and the motor roared like an animal coming awake. He
wheeled the truck out of line and started down the hill to
take Mike home.

¶ An editor once at *Chicago Review* asked me to contribute a story for an issue they were doing on writing in Chicago. Since literary magazines pay off in subscriptions, I leafed through some rejected stories, thinking they would be grateful to accept even less than vintage Petrakis. They promptly returned the story I sent them with thanks.

Slightly nettled, I pulled out another rejected story but, feeling uneasy about the possibility of a second peremptory rejection, rewrote it. They published "The Prison" happily. And the story was later included in the O. Henry Awards Prize Stories collection for that year.

There may well be a moral here. . . .

The Prison

Harry Kladis met Alexandra when he was forty-five and she was forty. For twelve years he had worked with his father in their small candy store. She was a librarian at the neighborhood branch. He admitted to himself that she was not very pretty and a little older than he would have wished but he was drawn to her by the soft abundance of dark hair that she wore to her shoulders and by an air of shyness he suspected concealed loneliness as distressing as his own. One night after she had been coming into the candy store for almost three months, he mustered the courage and asked to take her out. He was so pleased when she accepted that he insisted she take three pounds of her favorite chocolate mints as a gift.

On their first date they walked for hours and talked endlessly. In the beginning they tried shyly to suggest they were accustomed to dating many others. After a while this posturing seemed foolish to both of them. He told her about a girl, handsome and raven-haired, that he had lost to a bolder man years before. She told him of a salesman, tall with sensitive eyes, who held her devotion until, transferred to another territory, he ceased to answer her letters. These melancholy recitals drew them together. They were de-

lighted to find they both enjoyed concerts and chop suey
with black pekoe tea and almond cookies. After a month of
seeing each other several evenings a week they accepted
with grateful happiness that they were in love.

Two weeks before the day scheduled for their wedding,
Harry's father died. Returning from an evening with Alexandra, Harry found the old man in the back room of the
store where he had suffered a stroke while mixing a batch of
fresh milk chocolate.

They recognized it would have been unseemly to marry
so close upon death and they delayed their wedding for a
few months. Harry wished to sell the store as soon as possible. He had studied accounting some years before and considered taking additional courses to qualify himself for that
profession. But his mother insisted he keep the thin security
of the store that was all her husband had left to provide for
her old age. The first weeks after the funeral seemed merely
to sharpen the blades of her sorrow.

"My father and I were all she ever cared for," Harry said
to Alexandra. "He is gone now but she wonders what will
happen to me if I sell the store and cannot make a go of accounting."

"You will be a good accountant," Alexandra said. "I have
my job to help out. It will be better for your mother in the
long run."

"I should have made the decision years ago," Harry said
and he was ashamed. "I never really cared for the store but
I have let the years slide by." He turned away to conceal his
distress. "Just a while longer," he said. "I don't want to
press Mama in her grief now. Just a little longer."

But he could not make chocolates as well as his father and
business fell off. The price he might have received for selling the store declined as well. He worried and worked for
longer hours. At the end of six months from his father's
death they postponed their wedding once more.

His mother's continued despair confused him and made
him unhappy. They tried to include the old lady in the

things they did but she did not care for music and could not stand the sight or smell of chop suey. In desperation to appease her relentless grief they spent most of their evenings at home with her. She talked ceaselessly of the past and of joining her husband in death to remove herself as a burden on Harry. He spent the evening assuring her of his love and devotion. The only moments he managed alone with Alexandra were during the brief period when he walked her home. Then bedeviled by the evening of his mother's lament, he had little to say. When he returned home, he had to listen to his mother stitch the final ornament on the hours before he could flee to bed.

"Sitting in with me instead of being out with her," his mother said and a long sigh came wracked from her flesh. "She must resent me and blame me."

"She does not blame you for anything, Mama," Harry said. "She has never spoken a single word against you."

"I want you to marry," his mother said. "I want you to be happy." She looked in dismay at her son. "You were our only child. You are my life now. I would swear to die tonight if you thought I did not want your happiness."

"Stop it now," Harry said. "When Alexandra and I are married, you will live with us and we will look after you."

The old lady shook her head somberly. "You were two years old when your father's sister Sophoula died," she said. "The last ten years of her life she lived with us. I bathed her and fed her and cleaned up her slop. I would say my prayers at night and ask God to forgive me because I hated her on my back and wished her dead." She paused and with her dark dried fingers made her trembling cross. "There were nights I would hear her calling to me," she said. "I would hold my ears and make off I was asleep. And she would call in a voice like a bird for a long time." She bared her teeth in a harsh and cold smile. "My sins have come home to roost. I am the old woman now."

"What more can I say, Mama?" Harry asked. "As long as

I live I will love you and look after you. And Alexandra will
love you as I do."

The old lady looked at him silently for a long time. He
felt himself reduced to the condition of a child unaware of
reality and the grim shades of life. She rose slowly and heavily to her feet.

Harry kissed her goodnight with tenderness. For a moment she clung to him fiercely. He felt her fear of death and
loneliness riot through his own flesh.

Winter passed into spring. The hours of daylight grew
longer. From blossoming gardens in the park came the
aroma of new flowers. Within the foliage of trees sounded
the shrill-throated songs of birds. In the twilight the moths
writhed their wings about the street lamps. The young
lovers whispered and laughed in the sheltered groves beyond the walk.

With the coming of spring, Harry and Alexandra felt their
spirits rising. Sunday afternoons they spent looking for an
apartment with an extra bedroom. They talked confidently
of the future. The season filled them with new strength.

On the last Sunday in April they found a bright apartment not far from the park and only a few blocks from the
library and candy store. Alexandra was enchanted with it
but Harry could not subdue his apprehension. He could already feel the dark attendance of his mother. And closing
their bedroom door at night would not shut out her brooding
presence.

Afterwards they walked silently in the park. They passed
old men with bony faces who sat on benches like withered
roosters soaking up the sun, old men who bore the marks of
neglect and impending death.

"We will take the apartment!" Harry spoke in a furious
effort to break free. "We will go back and take it."

"You did not want it," Alexandra said quietly. "We have
been searching for a place like that for weeks and when we
found it you did not want it."

He fumbled helplessly for her hand and felt her slim-boned fingers against his palm. "In every room I could feel my mother," he said. "Like all the curtains were drawn and the shades pulled down."

"She cannot live alone," Alexandra said. "We have to work it out."

"She is sure we will come to hate her," he said. "Maybe she is right. I love her and feel a terrible pity for her. I love you too and I don't know what to do."

They paused before a deserted bench and sat down. He put his arm around her slim shoulders and drew her close.

"When I found you I had given up hope of love," she said quietly. "I had put that dream away like a flower pressed between the pages of a book." She moved her head slightly and he felt her breath against his throat. "Now I brush my hair as I did when I was a girl. Every mirror makes me realize I am no longer young. I want you to love me and find me beautiful. I want you to love me before I grow old."

"We will work things out," Harry said and for a moment tightly closed his eyes. "We won't lose each other. We will work things out."

Summer passed. The hours of daylight grew shorter. Dusk and dark advanced as the autumn nights closed in. The earth stirred and waited for the winter.

His mother grew more feeble. She could not bear to be alone and in the afternoon had a neighbor woman help her to the store. She sat in a corner and watched Harry as he worked. In the evening the neighbor returned and took her home so that she could prepare Harry's supper. She sat watching him silently as he ate.

Afterwards he helped put her to bed. She was driven with fear that death would claim her while she slept so she delayed sleeping as long as possible, holding Harry's hand, and talking aimlessly of the past. There were moments when she looked at her son with a strange burning pity. "There is no answer for us on this earth," she said and made her cross. "God save you by taking me soon."

After she slept Harry went to his bed on the couch in the next room and lay awake for a long time. Finally weary and tormented by his thoughts, he fell asleep.

In December of that year Harry and Alexandra parted. They had been seeing each other less frequently as the weeks passed, each meeting marked by a silent grievance and rebuke. They were lonely away from one another and yet miserable when they were together. He made the suggestion, trying to hold back his tears, and she mutely agreed.

That night Harry did not go home. He knew his mother would be in terror at being alone but he remained all night in the store and mixed more chocolate than he would be able to use in months. He kept all the lights burning and tried furiously to keep busy. In the dawn when weariness finally overcame him, he sank down on a chair and laid his head on the table smelling of sweet chocolate. In that moment he envied his father who was dead.

For almost three years Harry did not see Alexandra. From an acquaintance he knew she still worked at the library. He was often tempted to walk by the library in the hope of catching a glimpse of her. He was afraid she might see him and this kept him away.

He saw her often in his dreams. Her thin mournful face and the long hair about her pale cheeks and her slim fingers quiet in her lap. In the morning he woke unrested and faced the day with a burden on his heart.

His mother grew a little stronger. Now that she had him to herself she made fewer demands upon him and let him alone. They never spoke of Alexandra.

He had always been careful about his diet but as time went on he ate as much as he wished and gained weight. When he shaved in the morning he was repelled at how suddenly he seemed to have aged. He was not yet fifty but he felt much older.

More and more the pattern of his life assumed the dimensions that had governed the last years of his father. He rose early and went to the store. He worked through the day and in the evening went home to eat the supper his mother prepared. Afterwards he sat and read the paper while she rocked silently in her chair. When she was in bed he smoked a cigar as furtively as his father had done because she had always complained about the rank odor. He had trouble sleeping and after a while began using sleeping pills that a doctor prescribed.

In the beginning of the fourth year after he and Alexandra separated, his mother died. A cold had plagued her for several weeks. She ran a high fever and had to be moved to the hospital. The fever blazed up and down in spurts while she struggled fiercely to live. A priest came and dispensed the last rites. She died late one night in her sleep.

After the funeral Harry returned to the flat alone. He walked slowly about her bedroom. Every possession of hers, every article of clothing or spool of thread seemed to belong to someone he could hardly remember. He felt suddenly as if she had been dead for a long time.

He went for a walk. Without awareness of direction he found himself across the street from the library. In a panic that Alexandra might see him for the first time in three years on the day of his mother's funeral, he fled back home.

In the next few days he kept thinking about Alexandra. He yearned to go to her and yet shame kept him away. He studied himself in the mirror and mourned how seedy he had become. He determined desperately to diet again and brushed his hair in a way that concealed the growing patch of baldness.

After closing the store in the evening he detoured on his way home to pass the library. He stood hidden in the darkness of the small park across the street. When she came out and started to walk home he knew that he still loved her.

One night that he stood beneath the shadow of the trees a

longing to talk to her overcame his shame and fear. When she emerged from the library he crossed the street and called out her name.

It was a strange moment. She did not seem surprised to find him there. He was stunned at the sight of her and the changes that three years had made. She looked much older than he remembered, the last traces of youth gone. He trembled knowing that he too had changed and that she might see her own ravages reflected in him.

They walked home together as they had done so many times in the past. He was careful not to walk too close beside her. For a block they were silent and then they spoke a little. She had become head librarian. He mentioned a concert he had attended a few months before.

They paused before her building. He was about to say goodnight and try and muster the courage to ask to see her again.

"Would you like some tea?" she asked quietly.

For a moment, choked by gratefulness, he could not speak. They walked slowly up the stairs. He sat in her small parlor while she heated water in the kitchen. Everything appeared the same. The rows of books and records in the corner, the photograph of her dead parents, the small plaster bust of Beethoven on the mantel. The room even retained the delicate scent of her powder and he leaned back slightly and closed his eyes. He felt for an overwhelming moment that he was back where he had always belonged.

She brought in the pot of tea and set the cups upon the small table. She poured carefully and filled a plate with a few almond cookies. He had not eaten them in years.

"Do you still like chop suey?" he asked gently.

She shook her head. "Not any more," she said. Her hands, pale and slim-fingered, moved restlessly about the cups of fragrant tea.

"I don't care for it any more either," he said. He was silent a moment, wondering if he had suggested too much.

When he finished his tea he rose slowly to his feet. He wanted to stay longer and yet was afraid to ask.

She brought him his coat. "You have gained weight," she said.

He fumbled hurriedly into the concealment of the coat. "I have started to diet again," he said.

"Your cheeks have no color," she said. "And you are growing bald."

He made a mute and helpless gesture with his hands.

"Do you find me changed?" she asked and a certain tightness had entered her voice.

"Hardly at all," he said quickly. He was sorry the moment he uttered that naked lie.

"Three years have passed," she said and the words came cold from her lips. "I was not young when you first met me. I am much older now."

"Alexandra," he felt a furious need to console her. "Alexandra," he drew a deep breath and then could not control the wild tumble of words. "Can you care a little for me again? Can you let me love you once more?"

She made a stiff and violent motion of her arm to silence him. He was shocked at the fury blazing suddenly in her eyes.

"Three years are two words," she said. "Two words easy to say. But three years are a thousand lonely nights and a thousand bitter cups of tea and a thousand withered flowers."

She raised her hand and struck him hard across the cheek. "For the thousand lonely nights!" she said and the words came in flame. "For the thousand bitter cups of tea! For the thousand withered flowers!" She struck him again more savagely than before.

He turned then and fled. He went quickly out the door, down the stairs to the sidewalk, across the street into the darkened doorway of a closed store. He stood there seeing the dark reflection of his face in the glass and felt his heart

as if it were about to burst. He began to cry, the tears running down his stinging cheeks. And he did not know in that
terrible moment of despair whether he was crying for Alexandra or for himself.

¶ This was my first published story, accepted by *The Atlantic* in December 1956 and published in their April 1957 issue. I had been writing and submitting stories unsuccessfully for ten years. That December, I was working in real estate sales and the prospects were bleak for my family's Christmas. I wired the great *Atlantic* editor Edward Weeks, who had been encouraging and supportive of my efforts for years, that they had been holding the story more than three months. They could take as much time as they needed, but if there was any good news, I would be grateful to hear from them before Christmas. Since it is not good practice to wire editors about one's stories, I never really expected an answer. But, a day later, Ted Weeks wired me back that they were taking the story as an Atlantic First. He added his congratulations and best wishes for a Merry Christmas.

The ten years I had been writing without publishing, from the age of twenty-two until thirty-two, were in some way redeemed for me in that moment when I received the wire. I felt like Lazarus. . . .

Pericles on 31st Street

Louie Debella's bar was located on the corner of 31st Street and Dart Avenue, the last store in a group of five stores owned by Leonard Barsevick, who besides being a landlord operated the Lark Wholesale Clothing Company across the street.

My name is George. My last name is not important. I'm Louie Debella's night bartender and I count myself a good bartender. I might mention a few of the quality places I have tended bar, but that has nothing to do with this story.

If I have learned anything from fifteen years of tending bar it is that a bartender cannot take sides with anything that goes on across the bar. He has got to be strictly nonpartisan. A cousin of mine in South Bend, also in the business, once tried to mediate an argument about Calvin Coolidge. Somebody hit him in the back of the head with a bottle of beer that was not yet empty, and besides needing stitches he got wet. Now when I am on the job I never take sides. That is, I never did until the episode of Pericles.

As I understand it this fellow Pericles was a Greek general and statesman who lived back in those Greek golden years you read about in the school history books. From all reports he was a pretty complete sort of guy who laid down a set of rules and was tough on everybody who did not read them right.

If you are wondering what a Greek who lived a couple of thousand years ago has got to do with this story, I guess it all started because the storekeepers in our row of stores gathered in the bar in the evening after they locked their doors for a glass of beer.

The first man in was usually Dan Ryan, who had the butcher shop. Ryan was a heavy beer man and needed the head start on the others. A little later Olaf Johnson, who ran the Sunlight lunchroom, came in with Sol Reidman the tailor. Olaf had a huge belly that was impossible to keep under a coat. Sol liked nothing better than to tease Olaf about when the triplets were expected.

The last man in was Bernard Klioris, who had a little grocery next to Sol's tailor shop. Bernard usually got lost in the arguments, and swung back and forth like a kitchen door in a restaurant. He had a sad thin face and was not so bright, but among our patrons you could hardly tell.

Last Tuesday night after I had served Ryan his fourth beer, Olaf and Sol and Bernard came in together, with Olaf and Sol arguing as usual.

"She told me she was a Republican," Olaf said. "They want some lunk for Congress. I told her to come by you and get her petition signed."

Sol waggled his bald head indignantly. "Who gave you leave to advertise my business?" he said. "A man's politics is a sacred trust that belongs to him alone."

"She only had a petition, not a gun," Olaf said. "I knew you was a Republican so I sent her."

"How can anyone," Ryan said from the bar, "be in his right mind and still be a Republican?"

Sol waved a warning finger. "Be careful," he said. "You are stepping on the Constitution when you ridicule a man's politics."

"I read about the Constitution," Bernard said.

They lined up at the bar. I poured them beer. All they ever drank was beer.

The door opened and Nick Simonakis came in. He was the vendor who took his stand at night on the corner of 31st and Dart. He had a glassed-in wagon that he pushed into place under the street lamp, and from the wagon he sold hot dogs and tamales and peanuts. Several times during the evening he locked up the wagon and came into the bar for a glass of wine. He would sit alone at a table to the side of the room, his dark eyes in his hollow-cheeked face glaring at the room from above the white handlebar mustache. Every now and then he would sip his wine and shake his head, making his thick white hair hang more disordered over his forehead.

Other men might have thought he was a little crazy because sometimes he sat there alone talking to himself, but like I said, I do not take sides. At other times he gave up muttering and loudly berated the drinkers of beer. "Only Turks would drink beer," he said, "when they could drink wine. One for the belly and the other for wisdom." He would sip his wine slowly, mocking their guzzling of beer, and the storekeepers would try to ignore him.

"The sun-ripened grapes," Simonakis said, "hanging until they become sweet. Then the trampling by the young maidens to extract the lovely juices. A ceremony of the earth."

"Beer don't just grow in barrels," Olaf said. "Good beer takes a lot of making."

The old man laughed softly as if he was amused. "You are a Turk," he said. "I excuse you because you think and talk like a Turk."

"Say, old man," Sol said. "Someone wants a bag of peanuts. You are losing business."

Simonakis looked at Sol with bright piercing eyes. "I will lose business," he said. "I am drinking my wine."

"He must be rich," Ryan said, "and pushing business away. I wish I had gone into peddling peanuts myself."

"It is not a case of wealth," Simonakis said. "There is a time for labor and a time for leisure. A man must have time to sit and think. This made Greece great."

"Made who what?" Olaf asked with sarcasm.

The old man swept him with contempt. "In ancient Greece," he said coldly, "an elephant like you would have been packed on a mountaintop as bait for buzzards."

"Watch the language," Olaf said. "I don't have to take that stuff from an old goat like you."

"A land of ruined temples," Sol said, and he moved from the bar and carried his beer to a nearby table. "A land of philosophers without shoes."

"A land of men!" Simonakis spit out. "We gave the world learning and courage. We taught men how to live and how to die."

Ryan and Bernard and Olaf had followed Sol to the table, drawing their chairs.

"Would you mind, old man," Ryan said as he sat down, "leaving a little bit of credit to the Irish?"

"I give them credit," Simonakis said, "for inventing the wheelbarrow, and giving the world men to push it."

"Did you hear that!" Ryan said indignantly and looked fiercely at the old man.

The old man went on as if he had not heard. "A model of courage for the world," he said. "Leonidas with three hundred men holding the pass at Thermopylae against the Persian hordes. Themistocles destroying the great fleet of Xerxes at Salamis."

"That's history," Olaf said. "What have they done lately?"

Simonakis ignored him. He motioned to me and I took him the bottle of port. He raised the full glass and held it up and spoke in Greek to the wine as if performing some kind of ceremony. The men watched him and somebody laughed.

Simonakis glared at them. "Laugh, barbarians," he said. "Laugh and forget your debt to Greece. Forget the golden age and the men like lions. Hide in your smoking cities and drown in your stinking beer."

"What a goat," Olaf said.

Sol shook his head sadly. "It is a pity to see a man ruined by drink," he said. "That wine he waves has soaked his head."

"Wheelbarrow indeed," Ryan said, and he glared back at the old man.

2

At that moment the front door opened and Leonard Barsevick, the landlord, walked in. He carried an air of elegance into the bar. Maybe because of his Homburg and the black chesterfield coat he wore.

The storekeepers greeted him in a respectful chorus. He waved his hand around like a politician at a beer rally and smiled broadly. "Evening, boys," he said. "Only got a minute but I couldn't pass by without stopping to buy a few of my tenants a beer. George, set up the drinks and mark it on my tab."

"Thank you, Mr. Barsevick," Olaf said. "You sure look like a million bucks tonight."

Barsevick laughed and looked pleased. "Got to keep up a front, Olaf," he said. "If a man in my position gets a spot on his suit he might as well give up."

"That's right, Mr. Barsevick," Ryan said. "A man in your position has got to keep up with the best and you sure do."

"Say, Mr. Barsevick," Bernard said. "You know the leak in the roof at my store I spoke to you about last month. It hasn't been fixed yet and that rain the other night . . ."

"Wait a minute, Bernie," Barsevick laughed. "Not tonight. If I promised to fix it, I'm going to have it fixed. Leonard Barsevick is a man of his word. Ain't that right, boys?"

They all nodded and Olaf said, "Yes, sir," emphatically.

"But not tonight," Barsevick said. "Tonight I'm out for a little relaxation with a baby doll that looks like Jayne Mansfield." He made a suggestive noise with his mouth.

"You're sure a lucky man, Mr. Barsevick," Olaf said admiringly.

"Not luck at all, Olaf," Barsevick said, and his voice took on a tone of serious confidence. "It's perseverance and the ability to get along with people. I always say if I didn't know how to get along with people I wouldn't be where I am today."

"That's sure right, Mr. Barsevick," Ryan said. The others nodded agreement.

"Fine," Barsevick beamed. "All right, boys, drink up, and pass your best wishes to Leonard Barsevick for a successful evening." He winked broadly.

The storekeepers laughed and raised their glasses. Everybody toasted Barsevick but Simonakis. He sat scowling at the landlord from beneath his shaggy brows. Barsevick noticed him.

"You didn't give this gentleman a drink, George," he said. "What are you drinking, sir?"

"He ain't no gentleman," Olaf said. "He is a peanut peddler."

"An authority on wheelbarrows," Ryan said.

Simonakis cocked a thumb at Barsevick. "Hurry, landlord," he said, "your Mansfield is waiting."

Barsevick gave him a cool glance, but the old man just looked bored. Finally the landlord gave up and turned away, pulling on his suede gloves. He strode to the door cutting a fancy figure and waved grandly. "Good night, boys," he said.

The boys wished him good night. Simonakis belched.

3

On the following Thursday the notices came from Barsevick's bookkeeper announcing a fifteen per cent rent increase all along the block. All the storekeepers got a notice of the raise becoming effective with the expiration of their leases about a month away. Louie was so disturbed he called me down in the middle of the afternoon and took off early.

That night the storekeepers were a sad bunch. They sat around the table over their beer, looking like their visas had expired.

"I don't understand it," Ryan said. "Mr. Barsevick knows that business has not been good. Fifteen per cent at this time makes for an awful load."

"With license fees and the rest," Olaf said, "a lunchroom ain't hardly worth while. I was not making nothing before. With this increase it ain't going to get no better."

"Two hands to sew pants will not be enough," Sol said. "I must sew with four hands, all my own."

Bernard looked distressed. "Mr. Barsevick must have a good reason," he said.

"He's got expenses," Olaf said.

"He should have mine," Ryan said. "Beef is up six cents a pound again."

Simonakis came into the bar pulling off his gloves. He ignored the men as he walked by them to his table against the wall and signaled to me for his bottle of wine.

"I am going to buy a wagon," Olaf said loudly, "and sell peanuts and hot dogs on the street."

"You must first," Simonakis said, "have the wisdom to tell them apart."

Olaf flushed and started to get up. Sol shook him down. "No time for games with crazy men tonight," Sol said. "This matter is serious. We must organize a delegation to speak to Mr. Barsevick. It must be explained that this increase imposes a terrible burden on us at this time. Perhaps a little later."

"Shoot him," Simonakis said. He waved the glass I had just filled with dark wine.

"You mind your own business, peddler," Ryan said. "Nobody is talking to you."

"A Greek would shoot him," Simonakis said. "But you are toads."

"I get my rent raised," Olaf said, "and now I got to sit here and be insulted by a peanut peddler."

The front door opened and the room went quiet.

Barsevick closed the door softly behind him and walked over to the storekeepers' table. He pulled up a chair and sat down like a sympathetic friend coming to share their grief.

I guess they were all as surprised as I was and for a long moment no one spoke and Barsevick looked solemnly from one to the other. "I hope you do not mind my butting in, boys," he said and he motioned to me. "George, bring the boys a round on me."

"Mr. Barsevick," Ryan said, "the boys and me were just discussing . . ."

Barsevick raised his hand gravely. "I know, Danny," he said. "I know what you are going to say. I want to go on record first as saying there is nobody any sorrier than Leonard Barsevick about this. That is why I am here. My bookkeeper said I did not have to come over tonight and talk to you. I told him I would not stand for that, that you boys were not just tenants, you were friends of mine."

"It is a lot of money, Mr. Barsevick," Olaf said. "I mean if we were making more, things might be different."

"I know that, Olaf," Barsevick said. "Believe me, if there was any other way I would jump at the chance. I said to Jack, my bookkeeper, 'Isn't there any other way?' I swear to you boys he said, 'Mr. Barsevick, if that rent is not increased it will be charity.'" I brought the tray of fresh beer and set the glasses around the table. "Not that I mind a little help to my friends," Barsevick said, "but it is not good business. I would be shamed before my competitors. 'There's Barsevick,' they would laugh, 'too soft to raise his tenants' rent.' They would put the screws on me and in no time at all I might be out of business."

Everybody was silent for a moment, probably examining

the prospect of Leonard Barsevick put out of business because of his soft heart.

"We know you got expenses," Ryan said.

Barsevick shook his head mournfully. "You got no idea,"
he said. "I mean you boys got no idea. I am afraid sometimes for the whole economy. Costs cannot keep rising and
still keep the country sound. Everything is going up. Believe
me, boys, being a landlord and a businessman is hell."

"Shoot him," Simonakis said loudly.

Barsevick stopped talking and looked across the tables at
the old man.

"He is a crazy man," Sol said. "That wine he drinks
makes him talk to himself."

Barsevick turned back to the men but he was disturbed.
He looked over at the old man once more like he was trying
to understand and then started to get up. "I got to go now,
boys," he said. "I'm working late tonight with my bookkeeper. If we see any other way to cut costs I will be glad to
reconsider the matter of the increase. That is my promise to
you boys as friends."

"We sure appreciate you stopping by, Mr. Barsevick,"
Ryan said. "We know there is many a landlord would not
have bothered."

Barsevick shook his head vigorously. "Not Leonard Barsevick," he said. "Not even his worst enemy will say that
Barsevick does not cut a straight corner when it comes to
friends."

"We know that, Mr. Barsevick," Olaf said.

"We sure do," Bernard said.

"Shoot him," Simonakis said. "Shoot him before he gets
away."

4

Barsevick whirled around and stared in some kind of
shock at the old man. I guess he was trying very fast to
figure out if the old man was serious.

"Don't pay him no mind, Mr. Barsevick," Olaf said. "He has been out in the rain too long."

"You are a demagogue." Simonakis spoke loudly to the landlord. "You wave your greedy fingers and tell them you are a friend. Aaaaaaaaa!" The old man smiled craftily. "I know your kind. In Athens they would tie you under a bull."

Barsevick stood there like rocks were being bounced off his head, his face turning a bright shade of red.

Sol motioned angrily at the old man. "Somebody wants a hot dog," he said. "You are losing business."

Simonakis looked at Sol for a moment with his mustache bristling, then looked at the others. "I have lost business," he said slowly. "You have lost courage."

A sound of hissing came from Barsevick, his red cheeks shaking off heat like a capped kettle trying to let off steam. "You goddam pig," he said huskily. "You unwashed old bum. You damn peddler of peanuts."

The old man would not give an inch. "You are a hypocrite," he said. "A hypocrite and a libertine. You live on the sweat of better men."

Barsevick's jaw was working furiously like he was trying to chew up the right words.

"Let me tell you," Simonakis said, and his voice took on a more moderate tone as if he were pleased to be able to pass information on to the landlord, "let me tell you how the hypocrite goes in the end. One day the people wake up. They know he is a liar and a thief. They pick up stones. They aim for his head." He pointed a big long finger at Barsevick and made a rattling sound rise from his throat. "What a mess a big head like yours would make."

Barsevick gasped and whirled to the men at the table. "He's threatening me," he shouted. "Did you hear him? Throw the old bastard out."

No one moved. I kept wiping glasses. A good bartender learns to keep working.

"Did you hear me!" Barsevick yelled. "Somebody throw him out."

"He is a crazy old man," Sol said. "He talks without meaning."

"Shut up!" Barsevick said. "You stick with him because you are no damn good either."

"I do not stick with him," Sol said, and he drew himself up hurt. "I am trying to be fair."

Barsevick turned to me. "George, throw him out!"

I kept wiping the glasses. "I am underpaid, Mr. Barsevick," I said. "My salary barely covers my work. Any extra service would be charity."

The old man took after him again. "Who likes you, landlord?" he said. "Be honest and speak truth before your tenants. Who likes you?"

"You shut up!" Barsevick shouted.

"I mean really likes you," Simonakis said. "I do not mean the poor girls you buy with your tainted money."

"I'll shut the old bastard up!" Barsevick hollered and started for the table against the wall.

Simonakis stood up and Barsevick stopped. The old man looked tall and menacing with his big hands and bright eyes and his white mustache standing out like a joyous challenge to battle. "You cannot shut up truth," Simonakis said. "And the truth is that you are a leech feeding on the labor of better men. You wish to become rich by making them poorer."

Barsevick stood a couple of tables away from the old man with his back bent a little waiting for a word to be raised in his defense. No one spoke and the old man stared at him with eyes like knives.

"You old bastard . . ." Barsevick said weakly.

Ryan made a sound clearing his throat. He wore a stern and studied look on his face. "Fifteen per cent is a steep raise," he said. "Right at this time when it is tough to make ends meet."

Barsevick whirled on him. "You keep out of this," he said. "You just mind your own business."

"I would say," Ryan said slowly, "fifteen per cent more rent to pay each month is my business."

"I'll make it twenty-five per cent," Barsevick shouted. "If you don't like it you can get out!"

"I have a lease," Ryan said quietly. He was looking at the landlord like he was seeing him for the first time.

"I will break it," Barsevick said. He looked angrily around at the other storekeepers. "I will break all your leases."

"I did not say nothing!" Bernard protested.

"The way of tyrants and thieves," Simonakis said. "All who oppose them suffer." He raised his head and fixed his eyes upon the ceiling. "O Pericles, lend us a stick so we may drive the tyrant from the market place."

"Stop calling me a tyrant," Barsevick fumed.

Simonakis kept his head raised praying to that guy Pericles.

"I'm going to put every one of you into the street," Barsevick said. "I'm going to teach you all not to be so damn smart."

Sol shook his head with measured contempt for the landlord on his face. "You will not put us out," he said. "First, you are too greedy for the rent. Second, you would not rent those leaking barns again without major repairs, and third . . ." He paused. "Third, I do not admire your personality."

"Amen," Bernard said. "My roof keeps leaking."

"O Pericles!" Simonakis suddenly cried out and everybody looked at him. "They are barbarians and not of Athens but they are honest men and need your help. Give them strength to destroy the common enemy. Lend them your courage to sweep out the tyrant."

"You are all crazy," Barsevick said and he looked driven and disordered. His tie was outside his coat and the Homburg perched lopsided over one ear.

"You are a tiger," Sol said. "Tell me what circus you live in and I will rent a cage to take you home."

"Do not be insulting," Ryan said to Sol. "You will hurt the landlord's feelings. He cannot help he has got a head like a loin of pork."

"You ignorant bastards!" Barsevick shouted.

Ryan got up and came over to the bar. He stepped behind and pulled out the little sawed-off bat Louie kept under the counter. He winked at me. "I am just borrowing it," he said. "I want to put a new crease in the landlord's hat."

Simonakis came back from calling on Pericles. "Do not strike him," he said. "Stone him. Stone him as they stoned tyrants in Athens." He looked at the floor and around the room excitedly searching for stones.

Barsevick in full retreat began to edge toward the door. He opened his mouth to try and speak some final word of defiance but one look at the bat in Ryan's hands must have choked off his wind.

"Tyrant!" Simonakis shouted.

"Vulture!" Olaf said. "Stop and eat on me, and I'll grind some glass for your salad!"

"Greedy pig!" Ryan said, and he waved the bat. "You try and collect that rent and we all move out!"

"Judas!" Sol said. "Come to me only to sew your shroud!"

"Fix my leaking roof!" Bernard said.

With one last helpless wail, Barsevick stumbled out through the door.

For a long moment after the door closed nobody moved. Then Ryan handed me back the bat. I put it under the counter. Olaf started to the bar with his glass. Bernard came after him. Soon all were lined up at the bar. All except Simonakis, who had gone back to sit down at his table staring moodily into his glass of wine.

Ryan turned his back to the bar and looked across the tables at Simonakis. He looked at him for a long time and no one spoke. The old man kept staring at his wine. Ryan looked back helplessly at Olaf and Sol and they watched him struggling. Bernard looked dazed. I held a wet towel in my hands and forgot to wipe the bar. When Ryan finally turned back to Simonakis, you could see he had made up his mind. He spoke slowly and carefully.

"Mr. Simonakis," he said.

The old man raised his head scowling.

"Mr. Simonakis," Ryan said. "Will you be kind enough to join my friends and me in a drink?"

The old man stopped scowling. He nodded gravely and stood up tall and straight, his mustache curved in dignity, and came to the bar. Ryan moved aside to make a place for him.

I began to pour the beer.

"No, George," Ryan said. "We will have wine this trip."

"Yes, sir," I said.

I took down the bottle of port and filled a row of small glasses.

Ryan raised his glass and looked belligerently at the others. "To the glory of Greece," he said.

The rest of them raised their glasses.

"To Athens," Sol said.

"To Mr. Simonakis," Olaf said.

"Ditto," Bernard said.

I took down another wineglass. I poured myself some wine. They all looked at me. I did not care I was abandoning a professional tradition of neutrality.

"To Pericles," I said.

Simonakis stroked his mustache and sipped his wine. The rest of us sipped right with him.

¶ When I was very young I thought that love, the bond shared by Heathcliff and Cathy in *Wuthering Heights*, endured even after death. As I grew older I understood that love contains only the façade of eternity. When we lose someone we love to death, after a time of mourning, driven by physical and emotional needs, we move again to the virginal experience of another love.

That isn't unfaithfulness, simply the rhythm of life. Still, we must allow a place for those haunted men and women who might indeed be able to love only once.

Chrisoula

She could not live the remainder of her life in mourning. For a while she would wear her widow's black raiment and grieve for her man murdered in the summer of his life. When she could no longer bear her cold and solitary bed, she would find another man to love her, a man, perhaps, she too might love. That was the way of the flesh and of life. But for as long as she lived, Petros would always remain, for her, the first of men and the best.

Yes, he was a man who could not tell a tale without dazzling lies. He held before him the vision of fair-seeming but false glories. He scorned that which was seemly and good, and blindly pursued that which was graceless and evil.

But he was also tall, raven-haired, with black eyes that gleamed like those of a gypsy. His lips glistened as if he had just bitten into a ripe, sweet plum. She had only to look at his lips and be filled with desire. His arms and shoulders were as powerful as a gymnast's and yet his waist was lean as that of a boy. To watch him enter or leave a room was a delight. He walked in a lithe, strong stride as if he were on his way to or returning from a festival.

He was a man of swift movement and strong beat, untamed and reckless and unafraid of anything on earth. He courted Chrisoula as a princess might be courted with a radiant grace. He brought her flowers, sang to her at night under her window while her sisters giggled and peeked from behind the blinds. He would eat dinner with her family on Sunday evenings and to her father's distress would jump up several times during the meal to regale them with a story that he acted out with fervence and skill. There were times he seemed a marvelous child adrift in a world of adults and at other moments, when they were alone, a mature man. He was twenty-five when they married in the autumn of that year and Chrisoula was twenty-two.

On the night before the wedding, her father took Chrisoula into the basement of their house, away from the ears of her mother and sisters.

"You love this man, I know," her father said. "You love deep in your blood in the way of our people. I am resigned to this love and understand nothing I say or do can spare you the grief you will endure. Go then and marry with my blessing. But when you take this man as your husband, forsake all thought of serenity, a peaceful house, a consoling old age."

"I love him, papa," Chrisoula said. "I will endure what must be endured."

"You will endure," her father said sadly, "but you cannot imagine how much. This man lives out of his time and his place. Centuries have passed him by. The stars and the rivers and the mountains call him back."

"I will help him, papa," she said. "My love will protect him from harm."

"It is not enough," he shook his head wearily. "One can more easily destroy than save with love."

He reached out to her then and with his fingers touched her cheek in a mute and consoling caress.

For a little while that autumn, Petros and Chrisoula lived as God must have wished men and women to live. They made a refuge and a haven of their three small rooms that looked out upon the street of shabby tenements and dingy stores. When they ventured out to shop for food and wine or to walk in the last fragrant twilights of October, people moved like shadows about them and sounds seemed to come from a distant world.

At night they lay naked together, watching from their bedroom window the sky like a moon-splashed sea and the stars glittering rings and circles of light.

"Do you know why I love you?" Petros asked.

"Because I am a peach and a pomegranate," she said. "Comely as the bride of Solomon with breasts that ravish your eyes."

"You are an insufferable woman!" he laughed. "You take a man's songs from his mouth before they are spoken!"

"I only tell you what you have told me before," she said and kissed him.

"That was before," he said. "Each day and night I love you differently. I savor your face when you laugh, cry out, or in your moments of melancholy."

"My darling," she whispered.

"Listen to me," he said, and his voice trembled. "I have seen many marvelous sights on this earth, a storm in the mountains, a ship under sail on an azure sea, a bride dancing at her wedding. But the naked loveliness of my beloved is the supreme sight of all."

She reveled in his endearments, delighted to feel him asleep beside her, their legs side by side, her toes touching his ankle. Above all she loved the moments of their passion, his fingers pressing her shoulders, his lips curling upon her breath. She felt then the shudders which began as ripples and rolled into great waves across her body. It was as if they rode the crest of a wild sea, their bed a tossing ship, the ceiling of their room a boundless sky.

Sometimes, afterwards, she would cry, the tears rolling slowly down her cheeks. He would hold her tightly and kiss her eyes.

"You foolish little girl," he said. "When you should be the happiest after we love, you cry."

"You are the foolish one if you do not understand why I

cry," she said. "After a moment so exquisite I cannot help but think of us as old, someday emptied of youth and passion, withered leaves falling to the earth to die."

"We mustn't waste time brooding about death," he said. "There is too much life to be lived." He leaped from the bed to stand like a naked young god above her.

"But if by some quirk or mischance I should die," he said gravely. "Ornament my body with basil and mint in the way my mother adorned the corpse of my father, and scatter the petals of flowers across my eyes . . ."

"Petros!" she cried, and her blood ran cold. "Petros, stop!"

"Make the house rock with your widow's grief for a while," he laughed, "and then find a hardy man for your lonely bed."

"Damn you, stop! Damn you, damn you, stop!"

He came quickly to kneel beside her on the bed.

"I am sorry," he said, and he was shaken with remorse. "I was only teasing. I am sorry, my beloved, forgive me." He kissed her temples and kissed her eyes. "Love is stronger than death," he whispered, "and our love will live forever, setting eternity ablaze with its burning song."

She took him then into her arms, holding him as a mother holds a child unaware of the grim shades of life. She held him until he had fallen asleep, her naked breasts a plumed pillow for his fine dark hair.

When they married, Petros was working as a bread truck driver, one of many jobs he had worked at through the last few years. He had been a bartender, counterman, had driven a produce truck, and loaded bags of potatoes at the market. After their marriage none of these jobs seemed to satisfy him. He was conscious suddenly of the responsibility of marriage. Chrisoula's father reluctantly offered him a junior partnership in his grocery business, but Petros scorned the offer as a gratuity. He grew vexed and sullen.

"There are many women on this street whose bodies have aged through too much work and too many children," he said. "They might have been lovely once but the years have hollowed them out. They can no longer laugh or sing. I will turn the saints out of heaven before I let that happen to you."

"I am young and strong," she said. "Don't worry about me."

"On my route in the stores where I deliver bread," he said, "I see the wives of other men in fine clothing, driving fine cars. Why should my wife have less than these women? Am I less a man than their men?"

"I have you," she tried to comfort him. "Those wealthy women would trade all their possessions and their sad husbands for someone like you."

He shook his head impatiently. "I am your husband now," he said. "I must look after you, provide you the things which people respect."

"People will respect us if we are true and live well in the eyes of God," she said.

"Chrisoula, will you listen!" he cried. "It is not what you are willing to settle for, but what I feel you should have."

"Petros, be patient," she pleaded. "We have our love, the days and nights we share together. The rest will come. Be patient, my darling."

"To hell with patience," he said, and closed his heart like a stone against her.

For several weeks afterwards, Petros brooded. He was late coming home from work and told her he had been looking for other employment. She knew by his breath and the sodden glint in his eye that he had spent the time in the taverns.

There was an evening in November, a sharp cold night, when she heard him shouting from the street below. She opened the window, shivering slightly in the cold air, and saw him standing on the sidewalk below with a man she recognized as Antonio Gallos.

"We are coming up!" he cried. "I am bringing Mr. Gallos up! Take out the glasses and the wine!"

He tugged Gallos by the arm and they entered the doorway. Chrisoula closed the window, confused and suddenly frightened.

Antonio Gallos was well known in their neighborhood. As a child she had heard her father curse after Gallos had driven past them in his great glittering car. He was a fat, heavy-jowled man who wore diamonds on his fingers, and expensive tailored clothes wasted on his obese frame. He owned a candle company and a bakery. He owned, as well, three gambling parlors packed all day with men wagering on the horses, dice and cards. The candle company and bakery he maintained as a facade of respectability which fooled no one since they all knew the gambling parlors provided him his wealth.

She took off her apron, started nervously to smooth back her hair and then angrily stopped. She walked to the door just as it burst open and Petros entered.

"Come in, come in, Mr. Gallos!" Petros motioned him over the threshold. Gallos entered wearing a fine black cashmere coat and a white silk scarf, in sharp contrast to Petros' jacket and cap.

"This is my wife, Soula," Petros said. "I told you she was a beauty, didn't I? Soula, this is Mr. Gallos."

Gallos stood staring at her, blinking slightly in approval. The skin of his face was sallow, his nose long and thin, his lips meager and colorless.

"Please come in," Soula said and avoided asking for his coat.

"Give me your coat, Mr. Gallos," Petros said and glared at her.

Gallos drew off his gloves slowly, and his hands were small, his fingers blunt and unsightly. On two fingers of each hand he wore sparkling diamonds.

Petros helped him off with his coat and Gallos walked into the small parlor and sat down heavily on the faded cushions of the couch. He drew his shiny pointed shoes back carefully from a threadbare section of carpet.

"I have brought Mr. Gallos home to meet you and to have a glass of wine," Petros said, a sullen anger beginning to stir in his voice. "Mr. Gallos has honored us by offering me a fine position."

"I'm sorry, there is no wine left," Chrisoula said. "We finished the bottle last night at dinner."

"No wine!" Petros cried in dismay. He made a gesture of apology to Gallos. "A house without wine is a body without blood. I will go downstairs and buy some."

"Never mind, Petros," Gallos made a small delicate shrug of his shoulders. "We can have a glass of wine together some other time."

"I beg your pardon, Mr. Gallos," Petros said, his voice rigid with pride. "In your house and in your business, you command and I will obey. In my house, as my guest, I will command. You will please wait just a few moments. Soula will keep you company. I will go just a few doors down the street and return instantly."

Then he was gone, rocking the door closed behind him, his feet beating a flurried descent.

For a long, stiff interval the room was silent.

"The weather seems to be turning colder," Gallos said finally, and looked down at his shoes.

"Yes," Chrisoula said.

He nodded. "To be expected, of course, this time of year."

"Mr. Gallos," Chrisoula said. "What work will Petros be doing for you?"

He brushed a speck of lint from his trousers and frowned as he looked toward the window. "A number of duties relating to my business," he said.

"Which business, Mr. Gallos?" she asked quietly.

He looked at her startled and blinked. A slight, uneasy smile trembled the thin flap of his upper lip.

"You are a handsome woman, Mrs. Zervas," he said, "and a blunt one too. I admire that quality in a woman. My blessed mother was like that, God rest her departed soul. Kept my poor father off balance all his life." He stared down at the rings on his fingers. "It is well known that I operate several gambling rooms in this neighborhood. But I maintain them as honestly as I can. I provide people a place for the excitement they find in gambling. This Christmas I will have been in business here forty years." He sighed. "Frankly, I am tired. After all, I am not as young as I used to be. And I find fewer and fewer men I can trust. Would you believe, Mrs. Zervas, that everyone steals from me? My managers and dealers and ticket writers and runners." He fumbled his fingers nervously together in his lap. "There are those who say that I operate outside the law. That is completely false! I am in perfect harmony with the law. I have one captain, three lieutenants, six sergeants on my payroll. Every Christmas more than a hundred policemen receive baskets from me with turkey, ham, cheese and fruit, and bottles of good wine. Their families enjoy a pleasanter Christmas because of my generosity."

"Forgive me, Mr. Gallos," Chrisoula said. "What role will Petros play in all of this activity?"

He did not answer for a moment. He stared anxiously at the door, as if eager for Petros to return. He looked back to Chrisoula.

"I have been watching Petros for quite a while," he said earnestly. "I admire his energy and his courage. He is bright and quick and people are drawn to him. I believe he is honest. What I wish him to do for me is to keep a close check on all phases of my business. Collect the monies from my managers, keep an eye on my dealers and runners. Satisfy my customers that they are being treated honestly. You need not worry about Petros if he works with me. I will look after him and he can go far with me."

"We may not wish to go your way," she said.

He nodded slowly and then sighed. "Long ago when I was young," he said, "I tried to be fair and good and make a living for myself in some conventional occupation. But I was ugly, sin enough, and worse than that, innocent. Yes, I admit my ugliness and my innocence. You see I can speak as bluntly as you. But I quickly learned that society is composed of thieves. Whether in mahogany-paneled offices on La Salle Street or in my gambling rooms, all steal in one way or another from others. He who steals the most achieves the greatest wealth and success."

"That is not true, Mr. Gallos."

"Please, Mrs. Zervas," he cut her off with a quick nervous flutter of his fingers. "Allow me to finish, I beg you. Petros will be back in a moment and I may not have another chance to explain this to you." He rubbed his palm gently in a caress across the rings on his other hand. "I want Petros to prevent others from stealing what is mine. It is as simple as that. In return, I will pay him well, and, who knows. I am childless and not well. After I am gone the business must belong to someone."

"No," she said, and felt a sliver of fear pierce her heart. "No."

"Yes!" he said, and for the first time a force and conviction entered his voice. "Yes! In this life there are only victims and masters. Petros will always remain a victim driving a bread truck."

At the bottom of the stairs the street door closed with a bang. Gallos jumped as if the noise had startled him.

"Remember what I say," he spoke in a hurried whisper. "Don't make your husband a wound to fit another man's arrows . . . help him fashion arrows of his own."

The door opened and Petros entered carrying a full case of wine on his shoulder. With ease he swung the case to the table. He reached in and pulled out two bottles of wine and held them high over his head. "Wine for my darling and for my new employer!" he cried. "Soula, the glasses!" His voice trembled with excitement. "The glasses so we can drink to the future!"

Chrisoula rose and started to the kitchen for the glasses,

fighting the despair that curled like a black snake in her body.

For the next few months, through the coldest part of winter, Petros supervised the handbooks for Gallos. He made sure they functioned in accord with Gallos' wishes. In return for this protection, Gallos was generous. Petros brought home more money each week than he ordinarily had earned in a month of work. After a few futile efforts to convince him that what he was doing was wrong, Chrisoula gave up and kept silent. And each week the money increased. Petros bought new suits for himself and new dresses for Chrisoula which she secretly returned.

When she refused to move from their small apartment to larger, more lavish quarters, Petros had all the old furniture carted away and replaced it with new chairs, bureaus, a table and a large, gaudy and expensive couch. One afternoon he drove home in a new car and she rode with him in it while he chattered as excitedly as a child.

Sometimes lying beside him at night, watching the pale winter moonlight sweep the ceiling of their room, feeling his body warm and quiet against her flesh, she rested within the serenity and love they had in the early months of their marriage. But in the morning she woke to another day filled with foreboding.

For all her despair, Petros was happier than he had been in years. Each triumph fed his vanity and his pride. Because of his energy and effort, Gallos prospered, and opened two additional handbooks, the first such expansion in more than twenty years. Petros tasted the respect and envy of other men and found it a savory wine. They called him the young crown prince and it was rumored that Gallos was as fond of him as if Petros were his son.

The marauders came from across the city, lean, hard men with the souls of maggots. They had heard of Gallos expanding his gambling and came for his spoils. They bombed one of his handbooks, and, in terror, Gallos wanted to give up. In his old age he feared for his useless life. But Petros scorned their threats. When two of them came to Gallos to present their ultimatum, they found Petros waiting for them instead. He took on the two of them, laughing with excitement as his powerful arms beat them into a bruised and bloody retreat. He regarded the fight as part of a jubilant game, a game in which the contestants were honorable men.

That night flushed with the heat of his triumph, he celebrated in a circle of admiring, shouting men while Gallos ordered case after case of wine for the hordes to toast the young prince of his realm.

Chrisoula waited for him to come home. She walked through the rooms, her shadow rising and falling in frantic sweepings along the walls. She marked each passing minute as if it were an hour. When she could endure waiting no longer, she went down to the street.

The night was bleak and cold, a smell of snow riding the air. She followed his triumphant trail from one tavern to another. In the last one, they told her he had left a few moments before to go home. He had convinced the neighborhood florist who had been drinking in the tavern to unlock his shop a few doors away so he could assemble a cluster of bright flowers to carry home to his wife.

She hurried the blocks back home and at the corner of their street, she saw him almost before the entrance to their door. She cried out his name, her voice shrill and clear across the frosted and silent street. He turned and waved the massive bouquet of flowers. Her heart flew out to him and she started to run to his arms.

She saw the lights of a parked car suddenly flash on, veiling Petros in a strange luminous mist. As he turned around, the car surged forward. A fearful cry from Chrisoula's throat was lost in the stuttering thunder of the shots.

For a moment Petros seemed to leap off the street, a great spring to carry him over the roofs of the buildings, a stunning and impossible effort to escape. Then, as if his heart had burst, he fell back to the earth and the flowers scattered in the wild wind of his wake.

When she reached his body and saw the blood, she screamed a great tearing apart of her flesh. She fell across his chest and kissed his mute limp mouth. Shouts and lights broke the night around her. Two men sought to pull her away and with her fingers curled like claws she went like a hawk for their eyes.

They let her alone. She knelt beside him and stared at his face, startled and shattered in death. A few flakes of snow fell and glistened on his temples and in his hair. She picked up petals of the strewn flowers and put them gently on his lips and over his eyes. The snow fell on the flowers and gave his face a misted and serene beauty.

Only when her father came would she allow Petros to be taken from her, to be washed and anointed and dressed. And in the old ways of their people to be decked with basil and mint.

In the sunless and damp room of the dead, the old women mourning and whispering like black crows, she knew he was gone. At the cemetery with the people standing like faceless statues around his grave and the cry of a bird falling shrilly from the sky, she knew he was gone. And for weeks afterwards in her solitary bed, her breasts and loins chilled as if death had become her lover, she knew Petros was gone and would never return.

The weeks passed into months and then the winter was over. The first traces of new green grass appeared in the vacant lots. A single tree, stunted in the shadow of bricks and mortar, sprouted a few fragile buds. In the twilight the air was shaken with fragrant wind from warmer land.

Each day the sun grew stronger. From the dismal buildings the old men emerged like moles to sit on their stone steps blinking in the glaring light. Children cast off the garments of winter and shrieked joyously in play.

With the renewal of spring, Chrisoula felt the resurgence

of her body. She walked the sunlit streets conscious of the bold staring eyes of men. At night she lay restlessly in her solitary bed, watching the haunting waves of the moon, hearing the husky laughter of couples passing in the darkness of the street below her window. Spires and towers moved through her fantasies. When she slept fitfully and wakened, the pillow which had been beneath her head was clasped tightly against her breasts and loins.

She came to understand in the lonely passage of those long spring nights that the time of love was brief and that vows of eternal fidelity faltered before the yearnings of her body. There was nothing the dead could offer the living but lament.

So she cried softly for Petros. Then she slept and dreamed of the wild laughing lover she would someday bring to her cold and dormant bed.

℄ Sometimes when men defer marrying until their fifties and sixties, they tend to select a much younger girl. The general reaction to them is that they are reprobates and lechers. I find myself sometimes sympathetic to them, particularly as I grow older. The old King David took the young Abishag to his bed so she might warm his cold bones.

In this story I made Leontis a sympathetic and unselfish man. That isn't impossible in someone over sixty.

The Legacy of Leontis

Leontis Marnas married Angeliki when he was fifty-eight years old. She was twenty-four. She had been in the United States only a little over two years. All that time she spent working from dawn to dark in the house of an older brother who had paid her passage from Greece. Her days were endured scrubbing floors and caring for his children. In addition, the unhappy girl did not get along with her brother's wife, who was a sullen and unfriendly woman.

Leontis was not aware at that time of how desperately Angeliki wished for liberation from her bondage. When he visited the house in the evening to play cards with her brother, she released upon him all the smoldering embers of her despair. He would have been ashamed to admit that he mistook her attention for affection and her desperation for passion. He was bewildered and yet wished ardently to believe that a young and comely woman could find him attractive. He could not help being flattered and soon imagined that he was madly in love.

In the twenty-eight years since Leontis emigrated from Greece to the United States, he had made a number of attempts to marry. Several times he almost reached the altar, but in the end these efforts were always unsuccessful. Even when he was a young man the bold girls had frightened him, and the shy sweet girls to whom he was attracted lacked the aggressiveness to encourage him. He was without sufficient confidence to make the first move, and as a result always lost his chance.

Sometimes despair and restlessness drove him to women that he paid for affection. As he grew older, however, these visits became much more infrequent, and when he realized they burdened rather than satisfied him, he gave them up.

A year came when he was forced to concede to himself that he would never marry. This caused him a good deal of remorse and self-reproach, but secretly he was also relieved to be spared additional disappointment. His mother, of whom he often said, God rest her departed soul, had affirmed that keeping busy prevented melancholia. He became active in a Hellenic lodge and sponsored the education of several war orphans overseas. He rearranged all the stock in his grocery at least twice in each six months. On Sundays, the hardest day of the week for him to sustain, he rode the trolley from one end of the city to the other. He visited museums and spent many hours at the zoo. He was strangely drawn to the monkey house and quietly marveled at his apparent resemblance to one somber old male in a corner of a cage who seemed untouched by the climate of social amiability that prevailed all around him.

During the week, after closing the store in the evening, he sometimes played cards with fellow members of his lodge. In the beginning, this was his reason for visiting the house of Angeliki's brother. Afterwards, although it took a while to admit it to himself, he went only to see her.

Later, in remembering that time, Leontis often considered how ridiculous his conviction that Angeliki loved him must have appeared to her brother. Perhaps he saw their union as an answer to his concern for the future of his sister. But whatever his reasons, her brother gave his approval and completed the alchemy created by the loneliness of Leontis and Angeliki's wish for freedom.

In the early spring of that year, with the first buds breaking in slim green shoots upon the trees, Angeliki and Leontis were married. But it did not take long for the poor girl to re-

alize she had merely substituted one form of despair for another. He could offer her every advantage but the one of
youth to match her own. Leontis knew she must have considered him ancient and unattractive, but his presence in
the rooms in which she bathed and slept must have created
in her an awareness of her body, and perhaps excited her as
well. She could see that he admired and adored her, and at
the same time he could not blame her impatience with his
fumblings.

She could not comprehend how difficult it was for him to
value himself as participant in the act of love. He had too
long lived vicariously on the perimeter of life. Yet he desired
her fervently and made a valiant effort to play the role of
lover. On a number of occasions he did manage to fulfill the
functions expected of him. But Angeliki grew petulant and
bitter at his inadequacies and began to ridicule his age and
appearance. A day came when his own long-suffering patience wore thin, and they exchanged hot and furious words.

"You married me for my money!" he said, and he knew
that was not true, but anger selects its own truth.

"No," she laughed bitterly. "I married you because you
were young and handsome."

He felt the black bile of despair through his body, and he
was tempted to strike her but understood helplessly that she
could not deny herself the release of some of her frustration.

"I married you because you were handsome!" she
shrieked. "A Greek god with a golden body!"

"Enough," he said, and suddenly his anger was gone and
he was only weary. He saw in that moment the absurdity of
his delusion and how much more he was to blame than she.

He fled down the stairs. In the store, Thomas Sarris, the
young man who worked for him, was stacking cans of coffee.
Leontis was ashamed and wondered if Thomas had heard
them quarreling.

Upstairs, Angeliki slammed a door, a loud and angry slam.
Thomas Sarris pretended he did not hear.

The following spring, a son was born to them. Through the months of Angeliki's pregnancy, observing her body curving incredibly into the shape of a pear, Leontis felt sure the doctor had made a mistake. For a long time he had accepted that he would never have a wife. The prospect of becoming a father had been additionally remote. Not until the moment in the hospital shortly after Angeliki returned from the delivery room was he able to accept the conception as real. He was shocked at the sight of her pale cheeks and her dark moist hair, combed stiffly, in the way of hair on a corpse. Fifty-nine years on earth without awareness of the struggle of birth had not prepared him for the emotion. He could not speak. A great tenderness for his young wife possessed him. He touched her cheeks softly and struggled vainly to find words to explain that he understood the ordeal she had endured alone.

When they brought the baby to Angeliki to be nursed, he was rooted with reverence and wonder. He had seen babies before, not quite as small and wrinkled, but that this baby should be a part of his flesh, a blossom of his passion, filled him with a wild strength. As if in some strange and secretive way he had cultivated a garden beyond the reaches of his own death.

Back at home, Angeliki was a devoted mother and cared diligently for the baby. She was dismayed and fretful at the disorderly abundance of affection Leontis showered upon the child. But he could not help himself. He worked in the store, and whether or not he was alone, a moment came when he was filled with an overwhelming longing to see his son. He would run up the stairs and burst through the kitchen into the room where the baby played. Angeliki would follow him, nagging fiercely, but he paid her no attention. He would bend over the baby and marvel at how beautiful he was. He would kiss the top of his soft head and kiss each of his tiny warm feet. The bell in the store rang endlessly.

Angeliki drove him finally from the room.

"You are mad! I will have you put away. You think of

nothing but that baby. Your store, your wife—nothing matters. We will end up in the street!"

He kept a few feet ahead of her, and puffing heavily he
hurried down the stairs.

A few weeks before the baby's first birthday they baptized him in the Greek Orthodox Church on Laramie Street.
Leontis planned a gigantic party. He had several whole
lambs roasted, and fifty gallons of wine, and forty trays of
honey-nut sweets. He rented the large Masonic hall and invited almost all of the congregation of the church to attend.
It was a wild and festive night, and everyone appeared to
marvel at the way Leontis danced. Angeliki at last caught
him in a corner.

"What an old fool! You will drop dead in the air. Everyone is laughing at you. They think you are crazy."

But full of wine and lamb and gratitude, Leontis just
smiled. He danced and sang for love of his son, and he did
not care what others thought.

Now, in that month of his son's baptism, sleeplessness,
which had troubled Leontis for years, grew worse. He lay
wakeful and still beside Angeliki and stared into the dark,
and sweats came, and chills, and strange forebodings rode
his restless dreams. He went secretly to his friend Doctor
Spiliotis. The old physician examined him silently and spoke
without sugar off his square tongue.

"Have you made out a will? If not, go home and attend to
it."

"I have a will made," Leontis said. "Thank you, old
friend, for the advice."

"No thanks to me," the doctor said brusquely. "Thank
that heart of yours, which has endured all the abuse you
could heap upon it. Many men have weak hearts. They live
long lives by taking care. You seem determined to leave as
quickly as possible."

"I have lived a long time," Leontis said. "Looking back, it
seems to me there is nothing but time."

The doctor looked down and stabbed fiercely with his hand through the air.

"I only treat physical ailments," he said. "They have specialists now for sickness of the mind. For aberrations of old men who marry strong young girls."

"You should have been a diplomat, old friend," Leontis said.

"Understand me, Leontis," the doctor said. "The time is past for jokes. Unless you go to bed at once and rest for a month to six weeks, I do not think you have long to live."

In that moment, Leontis understood the tangled emotion a man feels who hears sentence of his death. At the same time, it seemed his decision was clear.

"Who will attend the store?" Leontis asked. "Who will walk my son in the park in the afternoons? Who will sit with my family in church on Sunday mornings?" He paused for breath. "And if I go to bed, can this insure I will live a long time?"

"We can be sure of nothing on this earth," the doctor said.

"Then I will wait in the way I wish," Leontis said.

"Get out," the doctor said, but the affection of their long friendship softened his words. "I will send you a wreath, a big one, fit for a horse. It will be inscribed 'Athenian Fool.' "

"Save your wreath for someone less fortunate," Leontis said. "I have lived long enough, and I have a son who will carry on my name."

With the knowledge of his impending death, a strange calm descended upon Leontis. Recalling his sixty-odd years as dispassionately as he could did not permit him any reason for garish grief. He knew that except for his son there was nothing in his life worthy of exultation or outrage.

He was certain of Angeliki as a devoted mother who would love and attend the child. To provide them with economic security in addition to the store, he had been purchasing bonds in considerable quantity for years. Therefore, only the possibility of Angeliki's remarriage to a man who might mistreat the child caused him anxiety.

He began carefully studying the clerk in his store, Thomas Sarris. A young man of strong build and pleasant manner. On a number of occasions, Leontis had noticed him discreetly admiring Angeliki when she entered the store. For an instant, the thought of Thomas Sarris or any man replacing him as father to his son brought a terrible pang to his body, but reason calmed him. Thomas was not wild, as were many of the young men. He did not wish to be more than a good grocer, but he worked hard and would care for his own. He would know how to sweeten a girl like Angeliki and remove the memory of her bitterness in marriage to an old man.

He spoke cautiously to Thomas one afternoon.

"How old are you, Thomas?"

"Twenty-eight," Thomas said.

"Twenty-eight," Leontis repeated, and kept busy bagging loaves of fresh bread so that Thomas would not notice his agitation. "How is it you are not married yet? Many young men are in a great hurry to marry these days."

Thomas easily swung a heavy sack of potatoes from the floor to the counter.

"I have not found the right girl."

"Are you looking?" Leontis asked.

"I will be ready when I find her," Thomas said. "But I am intent on getting myself established first. Get a store of my own."

Leontis felt his pulse beat more quickly.

"Do you like this store?" he asked in what he felt was a casual voice.

Thomas shook his head enthusiastically.

"A wonderful store," he said. "A fine business. I would give anything to have one like it someday."

Leontis turned away so that Thomas would not see the sly and pleased smile that he was sure showed on his face.

From that day he brought the baby and Angeliki and

Thomas together. He invited the young man to dinner and afterwards encouraged him to play with the baby. He was gratified when Thomas was gentle and tolerant with the child. And the presence of the young man seemed to act as a balm upon Angeliki. She spoke more softly and laughed easily, and there was a strange sparkle in her eyes. Sometimes, in the course of those evenings, it seemed to Leontis that Angeliki and Thomas and the baby were the family and he the intruder. Awareness of this jolted him, and forgetting for an instant that this was his design, he would flee with the child to another room. He would sit in the dark, holding the child tightly in his arms, and with the bitter knowledge of their separation roweling his flesh, he sometimes cried, softly, so that Angeliki and Thomas would not hear.

Summer passed and autumn swept brown crisp leaves along the streets beside the torn scraps of newspaper. In the morning, opening the store, Leontis felt the strange turning of the earth and endured the vision of the sun growing paler each day.

He knew that it was too late, but he suddenly took great care not to exert himself and called to Thomas to move even the smallest box. More and more often, he left the younger man alone in the store and spent most of the day upstairs with Angeliki and the baby. In the beginning she reproached him for neglecting the store, but after a while she seemed to sense his weariness and left him alone. He sat and watched her work about the rooms and listened to the baby make soft squealing sounds at play. Sometimes Angeliki brought him the baby to hold, and they would sit together by the window, looking out upon the winter street.

One afternoon when it rained and the dark heavy sky filled him with unrest, he spoke to her for the first time of what was in his mind.

"Angeliki," he said. "If I died, what would you do?"

She looked up and paused in sewing a button on the sweater of the baby.

"What is the matter with you?" she answered sharply. "What makes you talk of dying?"

"I am getting older," he said. "It should be considered."

"I will not listen to nonsense," she said.

"Would you marry again?" he asked. "I would want you to marry again."

She did not answer, but bent again over her sewing.

"Thomas is a fine young man," he said. "He works hard in the store. He is gentle with the baby. He would make a fine father and husband."

Angeliki snapped down her sewing.

"What nonsense is this?" she said impatiently. "I have better things to do than sit here and listen to you talk nonsense." She rose to leave the room, but a slight flush had entered her cheeks at mention of the young man.

There was a night he woke with a strange pain in his chest. He looked fearfully at the clock on the stand beside the bed, as if in some senseless way he hoped to arrest time. He was about to cry out, but the pain eased almost as quickly as it had come.

Later the baby cried in his sleep, a thin wail that echoed in the silent room. Angeliki got up and brought the child to their bed and placed him between them. In another moment, her breathing eased evenly again into sleep.

Leontis turned on his side and comforted the child and fell asleep with the warmth of the child within his arms. A noise within his body woke him. His eyes opened as if his eyelids were curtains on all of life. He cried out in despair.

Angeliki sat up in bed beside the baby.

"Leontis, what is the matter?"

He was bathed in a terrible sweat, and his heart seemed to be fluttering wings like a trapped bird to escape from the cage of his body.

"Leontis!" she cried. "Leontis!"

He knew he was dying. Not fear or anxiety, as he had

known many times in the past months, but knowledge, swift and real as if seared in flame across his flesh.

"Leontis!" she cried. "You must not die before you forgive me!"

He touched the baby's face. He felt his nose, small and warm, and his eyes, and the soft strands of his hair.

"Forgive me!" she shrieked. "Forgive me!"

Her hands were on his face and then they were lost within the crest of a mighty wave that tossed his body. He tried to hug the boy with all of his soul, and the last great swell exploded from his eyes.

⟪ During my son John's senior year in Chesterton High School, I adapted three of my stories into one-act plays for his class to perform. One of those stories was "The Wooing of Ariadne," and I helped in the direction. Watching German and Irish and Swedish farm-belt youngsters coming slowly to encompass the emotional ebullience of a group of Greeks was a memorable experience. The young man who played Marko Palamas did a fine job and has never really recovered from that role. From time to time now, in his speech patterns and in the expansiveness of his gestures, I catch glimpses of the Spartan wrestler and sailor who wooed Ariadne.

The Wooing of Ariadne

I knew from the beginning she must accept my love—put aside foolish female protestations. It is the distinction of the male to be the aggressor and the cloak of the female to lend grace to the pursuit. Aha! I am wise to these wiles.

I first saw Ariadne at a dance given by the Spartan brotherhood in the Legion Hall on Laramie Street. The usual assemblage of prune-faced and banana-bodied women smelling of virtuous anemia. They were an outrage to a man such as myself.

Then I saw her! A tall stately woman, perhaps in her early thirties. She had firm and slender arms bare to the shoulders and a graceful neck. Her hair was black and thick and piled in a great bun at the back of her head. That grand abundance of hair attracted me at once. This modern aberration women have of chopping their hair close to the scalp and leaving it in fantastic disarray I find revolting.

I went at once to my friend Vasili, the baker, and asked him who she was.

"Ariadne Langos," he said. "Her father is Janco Langos, the grocer."

"Is she engaged or married?"

"No," he said slyly. "They say she frightens off the young men. They say she is very spirited."

"Excellent," I said and marveled at my good fortune in finding her unpledged. "Introduce me at once."

"Marko," Vasili said with some apprehension. "Do not commit anything rash."

I pushed the little man forward. "Do not worry, little friend," I said. "I am a man suddenly possessed by a vision. I must meet her at once."

We walked together across the dance floor to where my beloved stood. The closer we came the more impressive was the majestic swell of her breasts and the fine great sweep of her thighs. She towered over the insignificant apple-core women around her. Her eyes, dark and thoughtful, seemed to be restlessly searching the room.

Be patient, my dove! Marko is coming.

"Miss Ariadne," Vasili said. "This is Mr. Marko Palamas. He desires to have the honor of your acquaintance."

She looked at me for a long and piercing moment. I imagined her gauging my mighty strength by the width of my shoulders and the circumference of my arms. I felt the tips of my mustache bristle with pleasure. Finally she nodded with the barest minimum of courtesy. I was not discouraged.

"Miss Ariadne," I said, "may I have the pleasure of this dance?"

She stared at me again with her fiery eyes. I could imagine more timid men shriveling before her fierce gaze. My heart flamed at the passion her rigid exterior concealed.

"I think not," she said.

"Don't you dance?"

Vasili gasped beside me. An old prune-face standing nearby clucked her toothless gums.

"Yes, I dance," Ariadne said coolly. "I do not wish to dance with you."

"Why?" I asked courteously.

"I do not think you heard me," she said. "I do not wish to dance with you."

Oh, the sly and lovely darling. Her subterfuge so apparent. Trying to conceal her pleasure at my interest.

"Why?" I asked again.

"I am not sure," she said. "It could be your appearance, which bears considerable resemblance to a gorilla, or your manner, which would suggest closer alliance to a pig."

"Now that you have met my family," I said engagingly, "let us dance."

"Not now," she said, and her voice rose. "Not this dance or the one after. Not tonight or tomorrow night or next month or next year. Is that clear?"

Sweet, sweet Ariadne. Ancient and eternal game of retreat and pursuit. My pulse beat more quickly.

Vasili pulled at my sleeve. He was my friend, but without the courage of a goat. I shook him off and spoke to Ariadne.

"There is a joy like fire that consumes a man's heart when he first sets eyes on his beloved," I said. "This I felt when I first saw you." My voice trembled under a mighty passion. "I swear before God from this moment that I love you."

She stared shocked out of her deep dark eyes and, beside her, old prune-face staggered as if she had been kicked. Then my beloved did something which proved indisputably that her passion was as intense as mine.

She doubled up her fist and struck me in the eye. A stout blow for a woman that brought a haze to my vision, but I shook my head and moved a step closer.

"I would not care," I said, "if you struck out both my eyes. I would cherish the memory of your beauty forever."

By this time the music had stopped, and the dancers formed a circle of idiot faces about us. I paid them no attention and ignored Vasili, who kept whining and pulling at my sleeve.

"You are crazy!" she said. "You must be mad! Remove yourself from my presence or I will tear out both your eyes and your tongue besides!"

You see! Another woman would have cried, or been frightened into silence. But my Ariadne, worthy and venerable, hurled her spirit into my teeth.

"I would like to call on your father tomorrow," I said.

From the assembled dancers who watched there rose a few vagrant whispers and some rude laughter. I stared at them carefully and they hushed at once. My temper and strength of arm were well known.

Ariadne did not speak again, but in a magnificent spirit stamped from the floor. The music began, and men and women began again to dance. I permitted Vasili to pull me to a corner.

"You are insane!" he said. He wrung his withered fingers in anguish. "You assaulted her like a Turk! Her relatives will cut out your heart!"

"My intentions were honorable," I said. "I saw her and loved her and told her so." At this point I struck my fist against my chest. Poor Vasili jumped.

"But you do not court a woman that way," he said.

"*You* don't, my anemic friend," I said. "Nor do the rest of these sheep. But I court a woman that way!"

He looked to heaven and helplessly shook his head. I waved good-by and started for my hat and coat.

"Where are you going?" he asked.

"To prepare for tomorrow," I said. "In the morning I will speak to her father."

I left the hall and in the street felt the night wind cold on my flushed cheeks. My blood was inflamed. The memory of her loveliness fed fuel to the fire. For the first time I understood with a terrible clarity the driven heroes of the past performing mighty deeds in love. Paris stealing Helen in passion, and Menelaus pursuing with a great fleet. In that moment if I knew the whole world would be plunged into conflict I would have followed Ariadne to Hades.

I went to my rooms above my tavern. I could not sleep. All night I tossed in restless frenzy. I touched my eye that she had struck with her spirited hand.

Ariadne! Ariadne! my soul cried out.

In the morning I bathed and dressed carefully. I confirmed the address of Langos, the grocer, and started to his store. It was a bright cold November morning, but I walked with spring in my step.

When I opened the door of the Langos grocery, a tiny bell rang shrilly. I stepped into the store piled with fruits and vegetables and smelling of cabbages and greens.

A stooped little old man with white bushy hair and owlish eyes came toward me. He looked as if his veins contained vegetable juice instead of blood, and if he were, in truth, the father of my beloved I marveled at how he could have produced such a paragon of women.

"Are you Mr. Langos?"

"I am," he said and he came closer. "I am."

"I met your daughter last night," I said. "Did she mention I was going to call?"

He shook his head somberly.

"My daughter mentioned you," he said. "In thirty years I have never seen her in such a state of agitation. She was possessed."

"The effect on me was the same," I said. "We met for the first time last night, and I fell passionately in love."

"Incredible," the old man said.

"You wish to know something about me," I said. "My name is Marko Palamas. I am a Spartan emigrated to this country eleven years ago. I am forty-one years old. I have been a wrestler and a sailor and fought with the resistance movement in Greece in the war. For this service I was decorated by the king. I own a small but profitable tavern on Dart Street. I attend church regularly. I love your daughter."

As I finished he stepped back and bumped a rack of fruit. An orange rolled off to the floor. I bent and retrieved it to hand it to him, and he cringed as if he thought I might bounce it off his old head.

"She is a bad-tempered girl," he said. "Stubborn, impatient and spoiled. She has been the cause of considerable concern to me. All the eligible young men have been driven away by her temper and disposition."

"Poor girl," I said. "Subjected to the courting of calves and goats."

The old man blinked his owlish eyes. The front door opened and a battleship of a woman sailed in.

"Three pounds of tomatoes, Mr. Langos," she said. "I am in a hurry. Please to give me good ones. Last week two spoiled before I had a chance to put them into Demetri's salad."

"I am very sorry," Mr. Langos said. He turned to me. "Excuse me, Mr. Poulmas."

"Palamas," I said. "Marko Palamas."

He nodded nervously. He went to wait on the battleship, and I spent a moment examining the store. Neat and small. I would not imagine he did more than hold his own. In the rear of the store there were stairs leading to what appeared to be an apartment above. My heart beat faster.

When he had bagged the tomatoes and given change, he returned to me and said, "She is also a terrible cook. She cannot fry an egg without burning it." His voice shook with woe. "She cannot make pilaf or lamb with squash." He paused. "You like pilaf and lamb with squash?"

"Certainly."

"You see?" he said in triumph. "She is useless in the kitchen. She is thirty years old, and I am resigned she will remain an old maid. In a way I am glad because I know she would drive some poor man to drink."

"Do not deride her to discourage me," I said. "You need have no fear that I will mistreat her or cause her unhappiness. When she is married to me she will cease being a problem to you." I paused. "It is true that I am not pretty by the foppish standards that prevail today. But I am a man. I wrestled Zahundos and pinned him two straight falls in Baltimore. A giant of a man. Afterward he conceded he had met his master. This from Zahundos was a mighty compliment."

"I am sure," the old man said without enthusiasm. "I am sure."

He looked toward the front door as if hoping for another customer.

"Is your daughter upstairs?"

He looked startled and tugged at his apron. "Yes," he said. "I don't know. Maybe she has gone out."

"May I speak to her? Would you kindly tell her I wish to speak with her."

"You are making a mistake," the old man said. "A terrible mistake."

"No mistake," I said firmly.

The old man shuffled toward the stairs. He climbed them slowly. At the top he paused and turned the knob of the door. He rattled it again.

"It is locked," he called down. "It has never been locked before. She has locked the door."

"Knock," I said. "Knock to let her know I am here."

"I think she knows," the old man said. "I think she knows."

He knocked gently.

"Knock harder," I suggested. "Perhaps she does not hear."

"I think she hears," the old man said. "I think she hears."

"Knock again," I said. "Shall I come up and knock for you?"

"No, no," the old man said quickly. He gave the door a sound kick. Then he groaned as if he might have hurt his foot.

"She does not answer," he said in a quavering voice. "I am very sorry she does not answer."

"The coy darling," I said and laughed. "If that is her game." I started for the front door of the store.

I went out and stood on the sidewalk before the store. Above the grocery were the front windows of their apartment. I cupped my hands about my mouth.

"Ariadne!" I shouted. "Ariadne!"

The old man came out the door running disjointedly. He looked frantically down the street.

"Are you mad?" he asked shrilly. "You will cause a riot. The police will come. You must be mad!"

"Ariadne!" I shouted. "Beloved!"

A window slammed open, and the face of Ariadne appeared above me. Her dark hair tumbled about her ears.

"Go away!" she shrieked. "Will you go away!"

"Ariadne," I said loudly. "I have come as I promised. I have spoken to your father. I wish to call on you."

"Go away!" she shrieked. "Madman! Imbecile! Go away!"

By this time a small group of people had assembled around the store and were watching curiously. The old man stood wringing his hands and uttering what sounded like small groans.

"Ariadne," I said. "I wish to call on you. Stop this nonsense and let me in."

She pushed farther out the window and showed me her teeth.

"Be careful, beloved," I said. "You might fall."

She drew her head in quickly, and I turned then to the assembled crowd.

"A misunderstanding," I said. "Please move on."

Suddenly old Mr. Langos shrieked. A moment later something broke on the sidewalk a foot from where I stood. A vase or a plate. I looked up, and Ariadne was preparing to hurl what appeared to be a water pitcher.

"Ariadne!" I shouted. "Stop that!"

The water pitcher landed closer than the vase, and fragments of glass struck my shoes. The crowd scattered, and the old man raised his hands and wailed to heaven.

Ariadne slammed down the window.

The crowd moved in again a little closer, and somewhere among them I heard laughter. I fixed them with a cold stare and waited for some one of them to say something offensive. I would have tossed him around like a sardine, but they slowly dispersed and moved on. In another moment the old man and I were alone.

I followed him into the store. He walked an awkward dance of agitation. He shut the door and peered out through the glass.

"A disgrace," he wailed. "A disgrace. The whole street will know by nightfall. A disgrace."

"A girl of heroic spirit," I said. "Will you speak to her for me? Assure her of the sincerity of my feelings. Tell her I pledge eternal love and devotion."

The old man sat down on an orange crate and weakly made his cross.

"I had hoped to see her myself," I said. "But if you promise to speak to her, I will return this evening."

"That soon?" the old man said.

"If I stayed now," I said, "it would be sooner."

"This evening," the old man said and shook his head in resignation. "This evening."

I went to my tavern for a while and set up the glasses for the evening trade. I made arrangements for Pavlakis to tend bar in my place. Afterward I sat alone in my apartment and read a little of majestic Pindar to ease the agitation of my heart.

Once in the mountains of Greece when I fought with the guerrillas in the last year of the great war, I suffered a wound from which it seemed I would die. For days high fever raged in my body. My friends brought a priest at night secretly from one of the captive villages to read the last rites. I accepted the coming of death and was grateful for many things. For the gentleness and wisdom of my old grandfather, the loyalty of my companions in war, the years I sailed between the wild ports of the seven seas, and the strength that flowed to me from the Spartan earth. For one thing only did I weep when it seemed I would leave life, that I had never set ablaze the world with a burning song of passion for one woman. Women I had known, pockets of pleasure that I tumbled for quick joy, but I had been denied mighty love for one woman. For that I wept.

In Ariadne I swore before God I had found my woman. I knew by the storm-lashed hurricane that swept within my body. A woman whose majesty was in harmony with the earth, who would be faithful and beloved to me as Penelope had been to Ulysses.

That evening near seven I returned to the grocery. Deep twilight had fallen across the street, and the lights in the window of the store had been dimmed. The apples and oranges and pears had been covered with brown paper for the night.

I tried the door and found it locked. I knocked on the glass, and a moment later the old man came shuffling out of the shadows and let me in.

"Good evening, Mr. Langos."

He muttered some greeting in answer. "Ariadne is not here," he said. "She is at the church. Father Marlas wishes to speak with you."

"A fine young priest," I said. "Let us go at once."

I waited on the sidewalk while the old man locked the store. We started the short walk to the church.

"A clear and ringing night," I said. "Does it not make you feel the wonder and glory of being alive?"

The old man uttered what sounded like a groan, but a truck passed on the street at that moment and I could not be sure.

At the church we entered by a side door leading to the office of Father Marlas. I knocked on the door, and when he called to us to enter we walked in.

Young Father Marlas was sitting at his desk in his black cassock and with his black goatee trim and imposing beneath his clean-shaven cheeks. Beside the desk, in a dark blue dress sat Ariadne, looking somber and beautiful. A bald-headed, big-nosed old man with flint and fire in his eyes sat in a chair beside her.

"Good evening, Marko," Father Marlas said and smiled.

"Good evening, Father," I said.

"Mr. Langos and his daughter you have met," he said and he cleared his throat. "This is Uncle Paul Langos."

"Good evening, Uncle Paul," I said. He glared at me and did not answer. I smiled warmly at Ariadne in greeting, but she was watching the priest.

"Sit down," Father Marlas said.

I sat down across from Ariadne, and old Mr. Langos took a chair beside Uncle Paul. In this way we were arrayed in battle order as if we were opposing armies.

A long silence prevailed during which Father Marlas cleared his throat several times. I observed Ariadne closely. There were grace and poise even in the way her slim-fingered hands rested in her lap. She was a dark and lovely flower, and my pulse beat more quickly at her nearness.

"Marko," Father Marlas said finally. "Marko, I have known you well for the three years since I assumed duties in this parish. You are most regular in your devotions and very generous at the time of the Christmas and Easter offerings. Therefore, I find it hard to believe this complaint against you."

"My family are not liars!" Uncle Paul said, and he had a voice like hunks of dry hard cheese being grated.

"Of course not," Father Marlas said quickly. He smiled benevolently at Ariadne. "I only mean to say—"

"Tell him to stay away from my niece," Uncle Paul burst out.

"Excuse me, Uncle Paul," I said very politely. "Will you kindly keep out of what is not your business."

Uncle Paul looked shocked. "Not my business?" He looked from Ariadne to Father Marlas and then to his brother. "Not my business?"

"This matter concerns Ariadne and me," I said. "With outside interference it becomes more difficult."

"Not my business!" Uncle Paul said. He couldn't seem to get that through his head.

"Marko," Father Marlas said, and his composure was slightly shaken. "The family feels you are forcing your attention upon this girl. They are concerned."

"I understand, Father," I said. "It is natural for them to be concerned. I respect their concern. It is also natural for me to speak of love to a woman I have chosen for my wife."

"Not my business!" Uncle Paul said again, and shook his head violently.

"My daughter does not wish to become your wife," Mr. Langos said in a squeaky voice.

"That is for your daughter to say," I said courteously.

Ariadne made a sound in her throat, and we all looked at her. Her eyes were deep and cold, and she spoke slowly and carefully as if weighing each word on a scale in her father's grocery.

"I would not marry this madman if he were one of the Twelve Apostles," she said.

"See!" Mr. Langos said in triumph.

"Not my business!" Uncle Paul snarled.

"Marko," Father Marlas said. "Try to understand."

"We will call the police!" Uncle Paul raised his voice. "Put this hoodlum under a bond!"

"Please!" Father Marlas said. "Please!"

"Today he stood on the street outside the store," Mr. Langos said excitedly. "He made me a laughingstock."

"If I were a younger man," Uncle Paul growled, "I would settle this without the police. Zi-ip!" He drew a callused finger violently across his throat.

"Please," Father Marlas said.

"A disgrace!" Mr. Langos said.

"An outrage!" Uncle Paul said.

"He must leave Ariadne alone!" Mr. Langos said.

"We will call the police!" Uncle Paul said.

"Silence!" Father Marlas said loudly.

With everything suddenly quiet he turned to me. His tone softened.

"Marko," he said and he seemed to be pleading a little. "Marko, you must understand."

Suddenly a great bitterness assailed me, and anger at myself, and a terrible sadness that flowed like night through my body because I could not make them understand.

"Father," I said quietly, "I am not a fool. I am Marko Palamas and once I pinned the mighty Zahundos in Baltimore. But this battle, more important to me by far, I have lost. That which has not the grace of God is better far in silence."

I turned to leave and it would have ended there.

"Hoodlum!" Uncle Paul said. "It is time you were silent!"

I swear in that moment if he had been a younger man I would have flung him to the dome of the church. Instead I turned and spoke to them all in fire and fury.

"Listen," I said. "I feel no shame for the violence of my feelings. I am a man bred of the Spartan earth and my emotions are violent. Let those who squeak of life feel shame. Nor do I feel shame because I saw this flower and loved her. Or because I spoke at once of my love."

No one moved or made a sound.

"We live in a dark age," I said. "An age where men say one thing and mean another. A time of dwarfs afraid of life. The days are gone when mighty Pindar sang his radiant blossoms of song. When the noble passions of men set ablaze cities, and the heroic deeds of men rang like thunder to every corner of the earth."

I spoke my final words to Ariadne. "I saw you and loved you," I said gently. "I told you of my love. This is my way— the only way I know. If this way has proved offensive to you I apologize to you alone. But understand clearly that for none of this do I feel shame."

I turned then and started to the door. I felt my heart weeping as if waves were breaking within my body.

"Marko Palamas," Ariadne said. I turned slowly. I looked

at her. For the first time the warmth I was sure dwelt in her body radiated within the circles of her face. For the first time she did not look at me with her eyes like glaciers.

"Marko Palamas," she said and there was a strange moving softness in the way she spoke my name. "You may call on me tomorrow."

Uncle Paul shot out of his chair. "She is mad too!" he shouted. "He has bewitched her!"

"A disgrace!" Mr. Langos said.

"Call the police!" Uncle Paul shouted. "I'll show him if it's my business!"

"My poor daughter!" Mr. Langos wailed.

"Turk!" Uncle Paul shouted. "Robber!"

"Please!" Father Marlas said. "Please!"

I ignored them all. In that winged and zestful moment I had eyes only for my beloved, for Ariadne, blossom of my heart and black-eyed flower of my soul!

⁋ The old priest in this story is another of the Greek Orthodox clergymen I often use in my stories. I think my father's having been a priest has much to do with my fondness for them as principals. None of the fictional priests are totally my father, but fragments of him appear in them all. From time to time I have used his gentleness, patience, humor, and, from a period near the end of his life when he was battered by illness and the ingratitude of those he had served, the weariness and resignation that saturated his spirit.

The rake, Barbaroulis, offers a good contrast to the priest. In accordance with prehistoric Homeric practice, they fire insults and satirical couplets at one another, a smoking fusillade that conceals their mutual affection and respect.

This story also satisfies my boyhood expectations, when I wavered between dreams of becoming a saint and the exciting prospect of turning out to be a venerable sinner.

The Miracle

He was weary of tears and laughter. He felt perhaps he had been a priest too long. His despair had grown until it seemed, suddenly, bewilderingly, he was an entity, separate and alone. His days had become a burden.

The weddings and baptisms which once provided him with pleasure had become a diversion, one of the myriad knots upon the rope of his faith. A rope he was unable to unravel because for too long he had told himself that in God rested the final and reconciling truth of the mystery that was human life.

In the middle of the night the ring of the doorbell roused him from restless sleep. His housekeeper, old Mrs. Calchas, answered. Word was carried by a son or a daughter or a friend that an old man or an old woman was dying and the priest was needed for the last communion. He dressed wearily and took his bag and his book, a conductor on the train of death who no longer esteemed himself as a puncher of tickets.

He spent much time pondering what might have gone wrong. He thought it must be that he had been a priest too long. Words of solace and consolation spoken too often became tea bags returned to the pot too many times. Yet he still believed that love, all forms of love, represented the only real union with other human beings. Only in this way, in loving and being loved, could the enigmas be transcended and suffering be made bearable.

When he entered the priesthood forty years before, he drew upon the springs of love he had known. The warmth of his mother who embodied for him the home from which he came, bountiful nature and the earth. The stature of his father as the one who taught him, who showed him the road to the world. Even the fragmented recollection of the sensual love of a girl he had known as a boy helped to strengthen the bonds of his resolve. He would never have accepted his ordination if he did not feel that loving God and God's love for all mankind could not be separated. If he could not explain all the manifestations of this love, he could at least render its testaments in compassionate clarity.

But with increasing anguish his image seemed to have become disembodied from the source. He felt himself suddenly of little value to those who suffered. Because he knew this meant he was failing God in some improvident way, a wounding shame was added to his weariness.

Sometimes in the evening he stopped by the coffeehouse of Little Macedonia. There the shadows were cool and restful and the sharp aroma of brandies and virulent cigars exorcised melancholy for a little while. He sat with his old friend of many years, Barbaroulis, and they talked of life and death.

Barbaroulis was a grizzled and growling veteran of three wars and a thousand tumbled women. An unrepentant rake who counted his years of war and lechery well spent. An old man in the twilight of his life with all the fabled serenity of a saint.

"Hurry, old noose-collar," Barbaroulis said. "I am half a bottle of mastiha ahead."

"I long ago gave up hope of matching you in that category," the priest said.

Barbaroulis filled both their glasses with a flourish. "Tell me of birth and marriage and death," he said.

"I have baptized one, married two, and buried three this last week," the priest said.

Barbaroulis laughed mockingly. "What a delightful profession," he said. "A bookkeeper in the employ of God."

"And whose employ are you in?" the priest asked.

"I thought you knew," the old man said. "Can you not smell sulfur and brimstone in my presence?"

"An excuse for not bathing more often," the priest said.

"You are insolent," the old man growled. He called out in his harsh loud voice and a waiter exploded out of the shadows with another bottle of mastiha. Barbaroulis drew the cork and smelled the fragrance with a moan of pleasure. "The smell of mastiha and the smell of a lovely woman have much in common," he said. "And a full bottle is like a lovely woman before love."

"Your head and a sponge have much in common, too," the priest said. "Wine and women are ornaments and not pillars of life."

"Drink up, noose-collar," Barbaroulis said. "Save your sermons for Sunday."

The priest raised the glass to his lips and slowly sipped the strong tart liquid. It soothed his tongue and for a brief illusive moment eased his spirit. "The doctor has warned you about drinking," he said to Barbaroulis. "Yet you seem to be swilling more than ever before."

"When life must be reduced to an apothecary's measure," Barbaroulis snorted, "it is time to get out. I am not interested in remaining alive with somber kidneys and a placid liver. Let the graduate undertakers who get me marvel at my liver scarred like the surface of a withered peach and at my heart seared by a thousand loves like a hunk of meat in incredible heat."

"You are mad, old roué," the priest said. "But sometimes I see strange order in your madness."

"Even a madman would renounce this world," Barbaroulis said with contempt. "Why should anyone hesitate giving up the culture of the bomb and the electric chair? We are a boil on the rump of the universe and all our vaunted songs are mute farts in the darkness of eternity."

"You assemble the boil and the fart," the priest said, "from the condition of your liver and your heart."

"When will you admit, noose-collar," Barbaroulis laughed, "that the limousine of faith has a broken axle?"

"When you admit," the priest said, "that the hungry may eat fish without understanding the dark meaning in its eye." He finished his drink and rose regretfully to go.

"Leaving already?" Barbaroulis said. "You come and go like a robin after crumbs."

"There is a world outside these shadows," the priest said.

"Renounce it!" Barbaroulis said. "Forsake it! Join me here and we will both float to death on exultant kidneys."

"You are a saint," the priest said. "Saint Barbaroulis of the Holy Order of Mastiha. Your penance is to drink alone."

"What is your penance?"

The priest stood for a moment in the shadows and yearned to stay awhile longer. The taste of the mastiha was warm on his tongue and his weariness was eased in the fragrant dark. "Birth and marriage and death," he said and waved the old man goodby.

On Sunday mornings he rose before dawn and washed and dressed. He sat for a little while in his room and reviewed his sermon for the day. Then he walked the deserted streets to the church.

There was a serenity about the city at daybreak on Sunday, a quiet and restful calm before the turmoil of the new week. Only a prowling tomcat, fierce as Barbaroulis, paused to mark the sound of his steps in the silence. At the edge of the dark sky the first light glittered and suspended the earth between darkness and day.

The church was damp from the night and thick with shadows. In a few moments old Janco shuffled about lighting the big candles. The flames fingered flickers of light across the icons of the white bearded saints.

He prepared for the service. He broke the bread and poured the wine for the communion. Afterward he dressed slowly in his vestments and bound the layers and cords of cloth together. He passed behind the iconostasis and through a gap in the partition saw that the first parishioners were already in church awaiting the beginning of the service. First, the very old and infirm regarding the ornaments of God somberly and without joy. They would follow every word and gesture of the liturgy grimly. Their restless and uneasy fingers reflected the questions burning in their minds. Would the balance sheet of their lives permit them entry into the city of God? Was it ever too late to take solace in piety and assurance in sobriety?

After them the middle-aged entered. Men and women who had lived more than half their lives and whose grown children had little need for them anymore. Strange aches and pains assailed them and they were unable to dispel the dark awareness of time as enemy instead of friend.

Then the young married couples with babies squirming in their arms, babies whose shrill voices cried out like flutes on scattered islands. In the intervals when they were not soothing the infants, the young parents would proffer their devotions a little impatiently while making plans for the things to be done after church.

Finally the very young girls and boys, distraught and inattentive, secured to the benches by the eyelocks of stern parents. They had the arrogance of youth, the courage of innocence, and the security of good health.

When the service was over they all mingled together for a moment and then formed into lines to pass before him for bread. Old Janco began snuffing out the candles in the warm and drowsy church. The shadows returned garnished by incense. The church emptied slowly and the last voices echoed a mumble like the swell of a receding wave. In the end only he remained and with him the men and women standing in the rear of the darkened church waiting to see him alone.

"Father, my daughter is unmarried and pregnant. A boy in our neighborhood is guilty. I swear I will kill him if he does not marry her."

"Father, my husband drinks. For ten years he has promised to give it up. Sometimes there isn't money enough to buy food for the children's supper."

"Father, all day I look after my mother in her wheelchair. I cannot sleep at night because I dream of wishing her dead."

"Father, my child is losing his sight. The doctors say there is nothing that can be done."

"Father, ask God to have mercy on me. I have sinned with my brother's wife."

"Father, pray for me."

Until the last poor tormented soul was gone, and he stood alone in the dark and empty church. In the sky outside a bird passed trailing its winged and throaty cry. He knelt and prayed. He asked to be forgiven his sins of weariness and despair and to be strengthened against faltering and withdrawal. For a terrible instant he yearned for the restful sleep of death.

There was a night that summer when the doorbell rang long after midnight. He woke from a strange and disordered sleep to the somber voice of Mrs. Calchas. Barbaroulis was dying.

He dressed with trembling hands and went into the night. His friend lived in a rooming house a few blocks away and the landlady, a grim-faced Circe, let the priest in. She told him the doctor had come and gone. There was nothing more to be done.

Barbaroulis lay in an old iron-postered bed, a decayed giant on a quilt-and-cotton throne. When he turned his head at the sound of the door, the priest saw that dying had refashioned the flesh of his face, making the cheeks dark and tight and the eyes webbed and burning.

"I was expecting Death, the carrion crow," Barbaroulis said. "You enter much too softly."

"Did you wake me for nothing?" the priest said. "Is your ticket perhaps for some later train?"

Barbaroulis grinned, a twisting of flesh around his mouth, and the husks of his teeth glittered in the dim light. "I sent for you to get it," he said.

"Get what?"

"The bottle of mastiha," Barbaroulis said. "My mouth is parched for some mastiha."

"The custom is for communion," the priest said.

"Save it," Barbaroulis said. "There is a flask of mastiha in the corner behind the books. I have hidden it from that dragon who waits like a banshee for my wake."

The priest brought him the flask. The great nostrils of Barbaroulis twitched as he smelled the sharp aroma. He made a mighty effort to raise his head and the priest helped him. The touch of the old man's expiring flesh swept the priest with a mutilating grief. A little liquid dribbled down the old man's chin. Breathing harshly, he rested his head back against the pillow. "A shame to waste any," he said.

"Tomorrow I will bring a full bottle," the priest said, "and serve it to you out of the communion chalice. We might get away with it."

"Drink it yourself in my memory," Barbaroulis said. "I will not be here."

"Where is your courage?" the priest asked gruffly to cover emotion. "I have seen men sicker by far rise to dance in a week."

"No more dancing for Barbaroulis," the old man said slowly and the mocking rise and fall of his voice echoed from the hidden corners of the room. "The ball is over, the bottle empty, the strumpets asleep. Pack me a small bag for a short trip. Only the lightest of apparel."

"A suit of asbestos," the priest said.

"I have no regrets," Barbaroulis twisted his mouth in a weird grin. "I have burned the earth as I found it. And if word could be carried far and fast enough a thousand women would mourn for me and rip their petticoats in despair."

"Are you confessing?" the priest asked.

"Just remembering," Barbaroulis said and managed a sly wink. "When I see your God," he said, "shall I give him a message from you?"

"You won't have time," the priest said. "The layover between trains will be brief."

The old man's dark parched lips stirred against each other in silent laughter. "Old noose-collar," he said, "a comfort to the end."

"Saint Barbaroulis," the priest said. "The Holy Order of Mastiha."

"What a time we could have had," Barbaroulis said. "The two of us wenching and fighting and drinking. What a roisterer I could have made of you."

"What about you in church?" the priest said. "You might have become a trustee and passed the collection plate on Sunday. Who would have dared drop a slug before your fierce and vigilant eyes? Gregory of Nazianzus would have been a minor saint beside you."

Barbaroulis laughed again with a grating sound as if bone were being rubbed against bone. Then the laughter faltered and a long shudder swept his body. His fingers, stiff as claws, curled in frenzy upon the sheet.

The priest watched his terrible struggle and there was nothing he could do but grip the old man's hand tightly in his own.

Barbaroulis made a sign with his raging eyes and the priest moved closer quickly. A single moment had transformed the old man's face into a dark and teeming battle-

ground of death. His lips stirred for a moment without
sound and then he spoke in a low hoarse whisper and each
word came bitten slowly from between his teeth.

"I have known a thousand men and women well," he
drew a long fierce rasp of breath. "I have loved only one."
His voice trailed away and the priest moved closer to his lips
that trembled fiercely to finish. "A priest who reflects the
face of his God."

Then his mouth opened wider and his teeth gleamed in a
jagged line. For a moment he seemed to be screaming in silence and then a short violent rush of air burst from his
body.

The priest sat there for a long time. In death the old man
seemed to have suddenly become half man, half statue,
something between flesh and stone. Finally the priest rose
and closed his eyes and bent and kissed his cheek.

He left the room. The street was black but the roofs of
houses were white in the glow of the waning moon. A wind
stirred the leaves of a solitary tree and then subsided.

His friend had been a man of strife and a man of conten-
tion. But into the darkness the old man had borne the
priest's grief and his sorrow. In his final moment Barbaroulis
had fed his loneliness and appeased his despair. And as he
walked, he cried, and the great bursting tears of Lazarus ran
like wild rivers down his cheeks.

¶ We lived for about two years in Los Angeles while I worked on a couple of screenplays, including one for my novel *A Dream of Kings*. We made friends then with some Greek actors, who eagerly joined us to share my wife's tasty Greek meals. These dinners were always climaxed by some hours of vigorous dancing and singing, led by the character actors Nick Dennis and Chris Marks, with the versatile Jim Harakas playing a spirit-stirring guitar.

Late one night they performed a Karaghiozis play, the old Turkish-Greek puppet theater I had not seen since childhood. Something of their voices and gestures caught me, and several days later I began writing the story.

Since one cannot dedicate a story when it is published in a magazine, I have the chance now to acknowledge my debt to Nick, Chris, and Jim for "Dark Eye." And to let them know I don't miss Hollywood but I miss them and our salubrious parties.

Dark Eye

My father was a drunkard. Every two weeks when he received his wages from the owner of the grocery where he worked, he'd begin making the rounds of the taverns on the street. In the normal course of his journey, we would not see him for the weekend and even the following Monday. But by ten o'clock on those Friday nights he did not come home, my mother had a neighbor look after me and then went out to find my father. This wasn't a difficult search because there were only a certain number of taverns he frequented. When she located him he would be furious at her for pursuing him, would mock and deride her before his companion sots. She endured his tirade silently, until, momentarily purged by his outburst and after purchasing several bottles as hostages for the weekend, he allowed her to lead him home.

He drank steadily through Saturday and Sunday. I kept fearfully out of his way but he ignored me, hoarding his revilement for my mother.

"Tell me, woman!" he cried. "Tell me what devil's blindness made me choose a wife like you, a dried fig, a bloodless
stone, a deaf and dumb bitch!"

It seemed incredible to me, even as a child, that anyone
might wish to abuse my mother. She was a slender and
lovely woman with a complexion so pale and fine that tiny
violet veins were visible just beneath the surface of her skin.
She spoke softly and moved with a lucent grace. Sometimes,
playing alone, I felt a longing to look at her and I'd go to
find her in another room, sit close beside her for a while,
warm and nested in her presence. The moments I treasured
most were those we shared when she sat before her mirror
at night, brushing her long glistening hair that was dark as a
blackbird's wing. I watched her then with a curious tension
in my body.

My father was a tall, burly man who might once have
been regarded by some as handsome, until indulgence and
self-pity had scarred his face with weak, ugly circles.
Whether drunk or sober, he moved in a shuffling and uncertain walk, defeat and failure rising like a fetid mist from his
pores.

Although he worked at many different jobs, never able to
hold even the menial ones for very long, he regarded himself
as a Karaghiozis, the profession he had practiced in the old
country, a puppetmaster of the shadow puppets once so
popular throughout Greece. The art of the Karaghiozis was
handed down from father to son and my father had learned
his craft from his father. As a young man in Greece, he performed frequently at festivals and fairs, but the popularity
of the plays declined. Just a few years after he married my
mother, the plays were being requested only on a few special holidays. A new generation of children turned to other
pursuits and only the old and infirm lamented the passing of
the Karaghiozis.

My father must have come to America thinking that in
the new country of myriad opportunities, he would be able
to practice his craft. But the children who had never seen a

Karaghiozis had other allegiances to Laurel and Hardy, Buster Keaton and baseball. And their parents were too involved with the artifacts of home and the rigors of business to bother with an old-country art.

Once, when I was eight or nine, and this was the only time, I remember my father performing the Karaghiozis. It was in the week before Christmas and I sat in the assembly hall of the church with perhaps a hundred other children on long low benches around me. A scattering of adults sat in chairs along the walls. On a small platform in front of us was a rectangular screen of thin, translucent muslin.

When the lights in the hall were turned off, the room was totally darkened except for the radiant screen casting eerie flickering lights across the faces of the children. From behind the screen came a rattling sound, as if pieces of wood were being shaken in a sack. A few men clapped, and then on the glowing screen a palace appeared, a courtyard and gardens, and in the foreground, a fountain. The brightly attired figure of a soldier appeared. He pranced a few steps and then cried, "Karaghiozis! Wake up, Karaghiozis! The sultan is coming!"

From behind the fountain snapped a great bald head, the face in profile containing a single huge dark eye. The head drew back down for a moment and then the silhouette of Karaghiozis leaped swiftly into view. A powerful body with one arm shrunk to no more than a hand emerging from his chest, the other arm long and apelike.

The sight of the weird figure caused the children to cry out, and with a wrenching of my flesh in fear, I joined my shriek to their cries.

A frantic sequence of scenes followed, characters appearing who shouted, danced, sang, quarreled, laughed and beat one another. There were dancers and beggars, soldiers and wrestlers, fishermen and sultans, gods and devils, a rabid throng inhabiting the screen with a violent and teeming world that my father created and controlled. His nimble hands directed their leaps and jumps and somersaults; his voice delivered their cries, harsh, shrill, tearful, deceiving, demonic. Above all the players loomed the figure of Karaghiozis, his dark eye piercing the screen. It seemed to look directly at me and I screamed in terror even while the children around me shouted and shrieked in glee.

When the lights went on at the end of the performance, I sat mute and exhausted. A vigorous clapping brought my father from behind the screen, his face flushed with power and triumph as he bowed, acknowledging the cheers and the applause. He stood afterward in the center of a group of admiring men, who slapped his shoulders and shook his hands. My mother hung smiling to his arm. I went to her to be consoled for my distress, but even while she held me against her body, I felt her love directed only toward my exultant father.

He never performed the Karaghiozis in public again. In the years that followed, he kept the cardboard figures of the players, perhaps twenty-five or thirty of them, in a footlocker at the rear of his closet. Sometimes, when he was drunk, he would pull out the footlocker, open it and sit down on the floor beside it. He would bring out the mad Karaghiozis and all his companions. He'd spread them around on the floor, pick them up, move their heads and arms. They often spoke only in his head, but when he could not contain himself, he cried voices between them. In the end, exhausted and unfulfilled, he would store them carefully away and go lamenting to his bed.

My father lost his job in the grocery, worked for a while in a laundry and then lost that job as well. During this period, my mother took work as a waitress to pay our rent and food. When he could not find money on which to drink, my father spent his time brooding.

I remember a night when my mother was still at work. My father had been locked alone in his bedroom for hours until he called me in. I found him on the floor beside the open footlocker with the Karaghiozis players spread around him. He wasn't drunk then, but his face was flushed and a frenzy glittered in his eyes. He motioned for me to sit beside him and, frightened, I obeyed.

"In the old country," he said, "a father teaches the Karaghiozis to his son. In this way, it is passed from generation to generation. My father taught me and I will teach you."

I trembled and nodded slowly.

"They don't want the Karaghiozis now," my father said with bitterness, "but someday it will be revived. The crowds will gather again and cheer and laugh and cry out for Karaghiozis." He looked at me with burning eyes. "You must be ready for that time."

He motioned to one of the cardboard players. "This one is Hachivat, Karaghiozis' friend; and this is Celebit, the dandy; and Tusuz Deli Bekir, the bellowing bully; Tiryaki, the opium smoker; Zenne, the dancer . . . and this one, this one is Karaghiozis."

He picked up the cardboard Karaghiozis and held him tenderly in his hands. I had never seen him look at any living creature with the warmth and love his face held as he looked at Karaghiozis. He moved slowly to hand the figure to me. "Hold him now and I'll show you how to control his head and arms."

The huge dark eye in the profiled face terrified me and I shrank away.

"What's the matter?" my father cried. "What are you afraid of? He won't hurt you! This is Karaghiozis!"

His anger fled and he tried to speak softly to reassure me.

"It will take time to teach you all the plays," he said. "You must learn them slowly and learn them well. Then you will be able to improvise plays of your own." He stared at me with naked and earnest eyes. "Do you know that once I could continue a dialog between Karaghiozis and his friend, Hachivat, for more than fifteen hours? Do you know that once the mayor of our village, watching me perform, hearing Karaghiozis talk of politics, the mayor offered me a position in his office? Do you know . . . ?"

His voice trailed off as he looked sadly at my locked and frightened face.

"Get out, little bastard," he said wearily. "Get out of my sight. Go to bed."

I hurried from the room to undress and climb shaking under the covers. I called to my mother when she came home and she came and sat beside me, consoling me by her presence until I had fallen asleep.

That night marked a change in my father, and he seemed more furiously bent on his own destruction. His credit was dried up at the taverns on our street and he made futile pilgrimages to other neighborhoods. When he could not bully or steal money from my mother or my cousin Frosos, he begged and borrowed from friends and strangers along the street. Abandoning all efforts to find any kind of work, he whirled in a wind of drunken despair.

Any redeeming memory I had of him, any bond of blood remaining between us was demolished in the blustering, whining, raging moments when he cursed fate, the misfortune of his marriage, the madness that made him leave the old country. And in his frenzy his voice altered, becoming shrill and hoarse, taunting and pleading, demanding and denouncing, as if all the myriad tongues of the Karaghiozis players were crying through his lips.

My mother suffered as he suffered, prayed for him constantly and accepted all his curses and imprecations in silence. On those evenings when his helpless rage seemed to be tearing him apart, my mother said my prayers with me and put me to bed. She closed the doors between my room, the hall and their bedroom. I still heard faintly my father shouting and cursing for a while. Then a silence fell over the rooms, an ominous and terrible silence, although I did not understand until years later the way in which my mother took my father's rage and frenzy into her own frail body.

Once, only once, did I condemn my father to my mother. I was about twelve and it was after one of the worst of his rampages, when he had broken several dishes he knew my mother treasured, and finally, like a great beast, had collapsed in a heap on the floor. He lay sprawled on his back, his mouth open, harsh drunken snores erupting from his loose, limp face. I whispered a wish to my mother that he might die.

She had never struck me before, but she beat me then. She beat me savagely with a belt while I screamed in shock and pain.

"Listen to me," she said, her face white and her eyes like knives. "Say such a thing again and I'll have the flesh hot from your back. In the old country your father was an artist, a great Karaghiozis. They came from villages a hundred miles away to see him perform. Now nobody cares for his skill and he rages and drinks to forget his grief and loss. Do you think a man whose soul is being torn apart can help himself? We can only love him and have faith in him. He has nothing else."

But I could not understand, and for turning my mother against me, for the beating she gave me, I hated him more.

My father died when I was fourteen. During one of his drunken sprees in the coldest part of winter, he had stumbled and fallen in an alley. The snow began and the thick flakes covered him. He lay concealed for hours until he was discovered. They took him to the hospital and called my mother. For three days and three nights, while he struggled to die, she fought to hold him to life. On the morning of the fourth day, cousin Frosos took me to the hospital. We walked the long ward filled with beds and strangers, and at the end, behind a screen, my father was dying.

He was curled on his side, one half of his face hidden, one arm extended in a twisting grasp for something that seemed just beyond his reach. His cheek was unshaven, his huge dark eye open, staring straight ahead. My mother, her face worn like a river stone by tears, led me to the bed and put my hand upon my father's hand. I felt the quiver of his flesh expiring under my fingers.

He could not turn his face to look at me, but the eye stirred restlessly. He looked no different than I remembered him many times before. He was helpless, the way I most favored him, because at those times he was unable to curse or to strike my mother.

Cousin Frosos led me away from the bed, and at the screen, I stopped and looked back one last time. A fly buzzed over my father's head and the dark eye in the dying face burned in a frantic effort to escape and follow the wings' swift flight.

I awoke that night to hear my mother scream. She was still at the hospital with my father, but I clearly heard the howl of desolation and loss that came torn from her soul. I knew my father was dead.

Through the following months, my mother grieved. Only forty, she seemed to age a year with each month. Still she worked and took care of me. I took a job after school and on weekends, and when payday came, I gave my mother every dollar that I made. In addition, there was a lodge insurance policy on my father's death that provided us a small regular monthly sum. Strangely, as survivors, we lived better than we had lived when my father was alive. We might almost have been happy then, for the first time in my memory, except for the way my mother grew swiftly older, quietly, irrevocably mourning my father's death.

Sometimes late at night, when she thought I was asleep, I would see the light burning under her bedroom door. I would quietly open the door a narrow crack. She would be sitting on the floor, the open footlocker beside her, the cardboard figures spread across her lap, her hands holding, her fingers fondling the wild, dark-eyed Karaghiozis.

When I finished high school, I received a tuition scholarship to a college several hundred miles away. My mother and I accepted the separation. I wrote her at regular intervals, telling her about my classes, the news of school, and avoided letting her know about my loneliness, the ways in which the past locked me in a shell I could not break. Her letters were brief, filled with admonitions for me to study and pray and live true in the eyes of God. Each time I saw her after the separation of a few months, I marked again the ravages of premature age, her hair grown dove gray, a web of wrinkles gathering around her eyes, a gauntness at her throat.

When I graduated from college and walked to receive my diploma in a black cap and gown, my mother sat in the third row on the aisle, an old woman watching her son in his moment of fulfillment. I went to hug her afterward, holding her slim, frail body in my arms, wanting her to share the achievement she had helped make possible. Yet, in that moment, I held only a fragment of her in my arms, and with a cold chill sweeping my heart, I realized how faint a hold she retained upon the earth.

It was only a few months after my graduation that my mother died. She was less than fifty and should have had many more years to live. But she had no relish for life, and after I finished my schooling, her last bond to the earth was gone. She fell ill in the spring, lingered only a day and died as quietly as she had lived for the past eight years. It was as if the shadow she became after my father's death was suddenly brushed away by a light gust of wind.

I buried her, as she had wished, in the cemetery beside my father, one of two graves beside the stone fence. They would lie together forever, with no one to shield or console her against his abuse.

And on the same day she was buried, I carried the foot-locker to the basement of the building in which we lived, and in the furnace, one by one, I burned the cardboard figures of the Karaghiozis' puppets. Hachivat, Celebit, Tusuz Deli Bekir, Tiryaki, Zenne, the beggars, soldiers, sultans, wrestlers and devils, all consigned to the flames. Karaghiozis himself I saved for last, and when the final fragments of the others had gone up in ashes and smoke, I put him into the flames. I knelt before the furnace door and watched trembling as his arms and legs curled and writhed and darkened in the fierce fire, his limbs shriveling in a final anguished spasm, his glowing dark eye suspended for an instant of torment after the rest of the figure was gone.

My father was a drunkard, a bastard who beat and abused my mother. Yet she loved him more than she loved anyone else on earth, remained true to him for the death in life, and in the end, joined him for the life in eternity.

How strong the bonds of faith, how deep the abyss of devotion. And how terrible and unfathomable the love that welds a man and woman together forever.

ℂ This story, unhappily, is based on true experience. During the period when I owned the shabby lunchroom I mentioned earlier, harried by fear of bankruptcy and collapse I bought a crate of turkeys that had died a natural death. They cost only twelve cents a pound, and my chef, an unwilling conspirator, boiled them for a day and a night. When the wretched creatures were finally palatable, we garnished them with cranberry and a mucilaginous gravy. I served them for a full week, only varying the menu descriptions each day:

> Monday: Roast Young Tom Turkey
> Tuesday: Turkey and Noodles
> Wednesday: Hot Turkey Sandwich
> Thursday: Turkey Croquettes
> Friday: Turkey Hash
> Saturday: Chicken à la King

That was the only week in months my lunchroom showed a profit, but the fearful anxiety that one of our patrons might drop off the stool and expire on our floor has, I am certain, shortened my life.

Fortunately, we suffered no mishap that week. But every Thanksgiving since then, when I sit down at the dinner table to a succulent and butter-basted beauty, I suffer a fleeting but virulent pang of guilt.

Pa and the Sad Turkeys

Some damn fool once said that all a Greek had to do to make money in a restaurant was to enter partnership with another Greek and watch the cash register. The guy that started that rumor better stay away from my Pa.

Our place wasn't classy enough to be called a restaurant. It was a drab lunchroom in a factory district near the railroad yards. We had six tables and twenty-six stools. They were all filled for an hour over lunch, and the rest of the day and night a customer might think the place was a graveyard.

There were three of us as partners, and that was a mistake. Pa and Uncle Louie had been partners for a number of years. When the army drafted me, Pa forgave me for having left college after one year, and, in a flurry of patriotism, he and Uncle Louie cut me in for an equal share of the business. They wanted me to have something to come back to a few years later. When I returned in a month with a medical discharge for a bad knee, Pa was sorry, but by then the papers had been signed.

Not that I wanted to stay in the lunchroom forever, but I was still developing my character and had nothing special that I wanted to do yet besides make a fortune playing the horses. The lunchroom was near a reputable bookie, and I had to spend the time between races somewhere. I worked out in front as a waiter, and Pa and Uncle Louie worked in the kitchen as chefs, dishwashers, butchers, and anything else that came up.

Business was terrible and getting worse. About three in the afternoon, when we hadn't seen a customer in two hours, Pa would stamp out of the kitchen and begin. "May the fiend that sold us this place fall in a sewer," Pa said. "May his back swell with boils and his lying tongue turn black."

"Take it easy, Pa," I said. "That won't bring in any business."

Uncle Louie came to stand smiling in the kitchen doorway. He and Pa were brothers, but they weren't a bit alike. Pa was big with a barrel back and the thick neck of a bull. A heavy head of hair, iron-gray at the temples, came down over his forehead until it almost merged with his bushy eyebrows. I loved him, but I had to admit he resembled a gorilla, with a disposition to match.

Uncle Louie was an amiable idiot. I don't say that with any intended disrespect. I loved him too. He was a good-natured gentle little man who always smiled. That might seem commendable except that Uncle Louie carried smiling too far. Tell him about a terrible auto accident with the occupants smashed and bleeding, and Uncle Louie would listen carefully and smile and shake his head. Working with Pa in the kitchen would have driven a normal man crazy. Uncle Louie was insulated.

Pa fixed me with a baleful eye. "Lucky for me you went one year to college," he said. "Tell me, how did you manage four years of education in that one year?"

Uncle Louie smiled broadly.

"Cut it out, Pa," I said.

"Sure," he said and shook his head violently. "I will cut it out when you stop playing the horses and start thinking of a way to save us. This place is a graveyard. You hear me, hoodlum, a graveyard, and you are standing around with a shovel."

"Shut up, Pa," I said. "Here comes a customer."

Pa stared in disbelief as a leather-jacketed baggage handler shuffled in the door and sat down at the counter. Uncle Louie scurried back to the kitchen.

I brought the customer a glass of water. Pa elbowed me aside and handed him a menu.

"Coffee," the man said.

For a moment Pa's face twisted in a silent snarl.

"With or without a toothpick?" Pa asked, and he stood above the man with his hairy arms spread wide on his hips. The man looked up as if suspecting a joke, but Pa was grim.

"Have you had lunch?" Pa asked.

The man gaped at Pa for a moment and then numbly shook his head.

"What are you waiting for?" Pa said. "By skipping a meal you do injury to your stomach. Regular eating habits assure a sound body." He shook his head sadly. "Your appearance is unhealthy. When did you last see a doctor?"

The man nearly fell off his stool in shock and outrage. He stumbled to the door and, with his hand on the knob, turned and spoke in choked indignation. "You must be nuts!"

The door slammed behind him.

"Nice going, Pa," I said. "That should help pick up business."

Uncle Louie stuck his head out the kitchen door. "Thomas," he said to Pa. "I was waiting to hear an order. Where is the patron?"

"Coffee!" Pa said. "At a time when I am faced with eviction for nonpayment of rent, that lout comes in and orders coffee."

"He doesn't care about our troubles," I said.

"Who does?" Pa said and laughed in a show of frivolity. "Does my horse-playing son care? My educated son who spent one hard year in college and got a degree in the Daily Triple."

"The Daily Double, Pa," I said patiently. "Get it right."

"Thank you," Pa said. "I am happy you are around to correct me. I am so happy I wish I could die now in the middle of my joy."

"Don't expire yet, Pa," I said. "The Oscar Mayer man is due in for the meat order for next week."

"No order," Pa said somberly. "They have refused us further credit unless we put up cash. Not a bone without money."

"I'm sorry, Pa," I said. "I'm broke."

Uncle Louie ducked into the kitchen. He might have been simple, but he knew when to disappear. Not that he had any money either, but he didn't want to put Pa to the trouble of asking.

Pa laughed again without mirth. "In this way does it end," he said. "Next week my doors will close for good. People will whisper all across the city that Thomas Lanaras has failed. The icebox has nothing left but three small pork chops."

"One chop left, Pa," I said apologetically. "I got hungry late last night."

He fixed cold furious eyes on me.

"Can't we have a macaroni and spaghetti festival next week?" I asked.

"Do me a favor," he said slowly. "Don't think. Don't talk. Don't make a suggestion." He walked stiffly to the kitchen. In a moment I heard him wailing to Uncle Louie.

Sam Anastis came in about four-thirty. He was a renegade wholesale meatman specializing in animals that died natural deaths. He had the wide hot smile of a professional con man, a high-pitched shrill voice, and he always looked back over his shoulder at intervals as if afraid he was being followed. He carried a brown bag that he held tightly as if it contained some peerless treasure.

I lifted my nose out of the racing form. "Pa," I called out. "Sam Anastis is here."

"Tell him to drop dead," Pa shouted from the kitchen.

Sam Anastis laughed heartily. "What a sense of humor that man has," he said brightly.

"He's a riot all right," I said.

Sam Anastis walked on small quick feet to the swinging door and opened it a little. "Mr. Lanaras," he called out gaily. "It is me, Sam Anastis. I want to talk to you."

"Go to hell, Sam Anastis!" Pa roared.

Sam Anastis laughed shrilly. When he could catch his breath he shook his head at me. "What a man," he said. "Always kidding."

He opened the door slightly again. "Mr. Lanaras, please come out now," he said. "Sam Anastis has something for you at a price. I could have sold to any of a hundred restaurants, but when this golden opportunity came my way, I thought of you."

Pa said something shocking in Greek that called in question the parentage of Sam Anastis.

"All right, sir," Sam Anastis grinned slyly. "All right. I'll have to take my proposition to Mr. Botilakis. How he will laugh when I tell him I offered it to you first."

He finished and stepped back quickly. A moment later Pa came violently through the swinging door. Uncle Louie followed smiling behind him. If there was anything could set

Pa's teeth on edge, it was mention of our archcompetitor, the Olympia Lunchroom on 15th Street, run by that black-hearted Macedonian, Antonio Botilakis.

Pa pointed a big warning finger at Sam Anastis. "I give you thirty seconds," he said. "At the end of that time I personally will kick you from here into the gutter. Now begin!"

Sam Anastis wasted ten seconds trying to decide whether Pa was serious. When he realized Pa was, he hastily opened the bag he carried and drew out something long and scrawny. "Look!" he said triumphantly. "Look!"

"In God's name, what is it?" Pa asked.

Sam Anastis looked hurt. He appealed to Uncle Louie. "You know what it is, of course."

Uncle Louie furrowed his brow. He smiled sympathetically at Sam Anastis. "It looks familiar," Uncle Louie said brightly.

Sam Anastis looked heartbroken. "It is a turkey," he said. "A genuine milk-fed purebred turkey. A wonderful specimen."

"Of course," Uncle Louie said. "A turkey."

Pa looked incredulous.

"That is a turkey?" he asked.

"It is some kind of bird all right," I said. "I think I can make out a wing."

Sam Anastis laughed, and Uncle Louie laughed with him.

"Like father like son," Sam Anastis said. "Both always clowning."

"If that is a turkey," Pa said somberly, "it has been hit by a truck."

"No!" Sam Anastis exploded in protest.

"Why is it so dark?" I asked.

"I'm glad you asked," Sam Anastis said. "This turkey was raised on a farm in Florida. Healthy sunshine all year round."

He made off to hand the bird to me.

"I don't want to touch it," I said. "I don't want to catch whatever it was that killed it."

"I was in Florida once," Uncle Louie said.

"Sam Anastis," Pa said, "I have known you for ten years. I knew your father. In the old country he was arrested three times for trying to sell the Parthenon to tourists. For you to come in here and suggest I buy that bird is an action so arrogant even he would not have dared."

"What is the matter with this turkey?" Sam Anastis asked in a grieved voice.

"What did the autopsy show?" I asked.

"In Florida it was very pleasant," Uncle Louie said. "I spent much time on the beach."

"Get out," Pa said, and he waved his big fist toward the door. "Go sell that abomination to Botilakis."

Sam Anastis backed toward the door still dangling the turkey.

"You are making a terrible mistake," he said shrilly. "I have a crate of these fine birds. You can have them for twelve cents a pound. At twelve cents a pound your profit will be enormous."

Pa stopped short. "Twelve cents a pound?" he asked.

"We stayed at a big hotel," Uncle Louie said. He smiled warmly. "The windows looked out on the water."

"Pa," I said warningly. "Forget it. Serve those birds and the police will put us away for life."

Sam Anastis took a step forward.

"Any chef can fix an attractive bird," he whined eagerly. "These birds are a real test. A lot of boiling to tenderize the meat. Plenty of seasoning to lend aroma. A good thick gravy. Believe me, these birds are a challenge I would be proud to accept if I were a chef."

"Get out, Sam Anastis," I said. "I'm only a sad horse player, not a murderer."

"Wait," Pa said. "Let me examine that bird more closely."

"A turkey," Uncle Louie said. "Of course."

Pa took the bird and turned his nose away. He pressed the bony thigh. "There is meat there," he said. "And there. And there. There is considerable meat on it."

"What did I say?" Sam Anastis shrieked. "A lovely bird and for the price a steal. I make nothing on the sale, but I hope to keep you as friends always."

"How much will the crate come to?" Pa asked.

"Eighty pounds," Sam Anastis said quickly. "Exactly nine dollars and sixty cents."

"I'll give you seven-fifty," Pa said.

"I contracted for twelve cents a pound," Sam Anastis said, outraged. "I gave you the best possible price. I saved them for you. Now you make a ridiculous offer."

Pa shrugged. "Forget it," he said and turned away.

"Wait!" Sam Anastis cried. "It has been a long day. My feet hurt. I'll take it."

He started quickly to his car to get the turkeys before Pa changed his mind.

"Pa," I said. "You must be nuts. Poisoning people is no joke."

"Shut your face about poison," Pa said. "This is a miracle which has been provided to save us from bankruptcy and disgrace."

"Maybe they will let you work in the prison kitchen," I said.

"Zipper your mouth!" Pa said. "You have no faith. Uncle Louie and I will fix those birds. We will fix them so they would be fit to serve on the table of a king."

Sam Anastis came in struggling with the crate.

"Where?" he gasped.

"In the kitchen," Pa said, and there was a wild gleam in his eyes.

That night after closing, the lights blazed in our kitchen. Pa and Uncle Louie placed great pots of water to boil on the stoves. When the kitchen was shrouded in steam, they threw in the turkeys. They boiled them all night, the two of them fretting around the pots like a pair of mad chefs. The smell was awful.

On Saturday morning it was hard to get an order out of

the kitchen because Pa and Uncle Louie were working frantically over those birds. Some of the smell from the night before still lingered, and when customers wrinkled up their noses and complained, I told them a gas line had broken.

We did a light lunch business because it was Saturday, and then the place emptied again. By sometime that afternoon the first batch of turkeys had been out of the ovens a couple of hours and the second batch was in. Pa came out and sat at one of the tables with a pad of paper and a pencil, mumbling to himself as he figured out the menus for the coming week.

"Monday will be roast young tom turkey," Pa said. "Tuesday, turkey and noodles. Wednesday, hot turkey sandwich. Thursday, chicken à la king. Friday, turkey hash." He finished, pleased at his sagacity.

"You forgot chicken croquettes," I said.

"Shut up," Pa said.

I buried my head back in the racing form and wondered how I might sneak out to make a bet in the fifth race at Tropical Park.

Everything was quiet. No other sound than Pa mumbling and a mail truck rumbling past in the street outside. I heard the swinging door from the kitchen, and I looked up.

"Pa, look!" I said. "Look!"

Uncle Louie stood in the doorway. For the first time I could remember he wasn't smiling. There was a look of incredible distress on his face, and he held his hand across his stomach.

"Louie, what is the matter?" Pa asked.

Uncle Louie tried to speak, but no sound came. Before our eyes his face seemed to darken and his cheeks seemed to swell. He made another valiant effort to speak, and only a deep mournful croak came out.

"Louie!" Pa hollered. "In God's name, what has happened?"

"Pa!" I shouted. "I bet he ate some turkey!"

When he heard the word "turkey," Uncle Louie stiffened

as if he had been shot. Then he stepped forward, placing one foot down carefully, and followed it slowly with the other. He made one final mighty effort to smile. When that failed he spun around like a top, once, twice, propelled by some relentless force, and then he collapsed on the floor flat on his back.

"He is dead!" Pa wailed and ran to him. "Louie is dead!"

"A stomach pump!" I shouted. "His stomach must be emptied!" I rushed to the phone.

Pa knelt weeping beside Uncle Louie. "Speak to me, my beloved brother," Pa beseeched him. "Speak to me, companion of my youth. Speak!"

Uncle Louie stared in anguish at the ceiling.

I got Doctor Samyotis, who had a little office on the boulevard about a block away, and he promised to come at once. I rushed over to where Pa cradled Uncle Louie's head just in time to hear a terrible rattle rise out of Uncle Louie's throat.

"His death cry!" Pa shouted. "Get a priest!"

"Take it easy, Pa," I said. "The doctor will be here in a minute."

"Too late," Pa wailed. "My brother will be gone."

"Don't give up hope, Pa," I said. I opened Uncle Louie's collar. He sure looked awful.

The door banged open, and Doctor Samyotis came in. He took one look at Uncle Louie. "In the kitchen," he snapped. "Carry him back there."

Pa and I picked up Uncle Louie and carried him into the kitchen.

"Put him on the table," Doctor Samyotis said. "Get a pail. The ambulance is coming."

We set him down, and I felt a little sick myself. I left Pa to help the doctor and walked back to the front. A truck driver had come in and was nonchalantly sitting at the counter.

"We are closed," I said.

"I just want a bowl of soup," he said.

"We are closed," I said. "Get out."

"Whadyumean closed?" he said. "I just want a bowl of soup."

From the kitchen Uncle Louie wailed a terrible cry of anguish and doom.

The guy made it to the door in a single leap. I locked up and sat down to wait. I was worn out.

In a few moments the ambulance pulled up in front of the store. I unlocked the door, and two white-coated guys came in with a collapsible stretcher. I waved them into the kitchen.

In another few moments they came out carrying Uncle Louie. He was covered with a blanket to his throat, and a towel was wrapped around his head. All that showed was his mouth, and poor Uncle Louie wasn't smiling.

Pa came out with Doctor Samyotis.

"Doc," I asked, "will Uncle Louie be all right?"

"He will be all right," Doctor Samyotis said. "Just sick for a while."

The attendants loaded Uncle Louie in the ambulance. A small crowd of railroad workers gathered around outside and peered in through the plate-glass window.

Pa started to get his coat. Doctor Samyotis stopped him. "You stay here!" he barked. "Go bury those turkeys!"

Pa stared shamefaced at the floor.

The doctor walked out and slammed the door. The ambulance pulled away.

A few guys still stared through the window. Pa made a fierce face through the glass, and they scattered. He came back and sat despondently at one of the tables.

"What have I done?" Pa said, and he rocked back and forth like a mourner. "What have I done?"

"It wasn't entirely your fault, Pa," I said.

He shook his head somberly. "He might have died," he said. "Poor Louie might have died."

"It would have been worse if it was a customer," I said. "We might have gotten sued."

"Shut up!" Pa said. "You have no family feeling."

I didn't say anything more because I knew how stricken he was about Uncle Louie.

At that moment the front door opened and Sam Anastis came in as if he had sprung out of the earth. He stood beaming his hot wide smile at us. I was afraid to look at Pa.

"Greetings," Sam Anastis glowed. "I was passing by and thought I would stop and inquire how went the turkeys? Are they roasted yet?"

I finally looked at Pa, and his face was impassive, but there was a blue vein swelling in his forehead and his cheeks were gathering red with blood.

"Welcome, Sam Anastis," Pa said in a strangely gentle voice. "What a friend you were to bring those turkeys to me."

"What did I tell you?" Sam Anastis trumpeted. "I made nothing on that sale, but for friends like you I don't care."

He saw Pa approaching. For a moment a cloud of uneasiness swept his face. Then it was too late. Pa reached him, and I held my breath. But Pa just clapped him softly on the shoulder.

Seeing Pa close enough to feel the heat shaking off his cheeks made Sam Anastis realize something was wrong. He tried to smile away his fear, but by that time Pa had his arm and began to walk him back to the kitchen.

"Come and see the turkeys, Sam Anastis," Pa said. "I will make you a little sandwich."

Sam Anastis looked shocked. He had an iron-clad rule against eating anything he sold. "I have just eaten," he laughed weakly. "I am not a bit hungry. I never eat this time of day."

By the time they got to the kitchen door, Sam Anastis was dragging his heels. Pa graciously all but lifted him through the door and turned back to me. "You!" he barked. "Call Doctor Samyotis!"

I went quickly to the phone and dialed the doctor's office. He wasn't back yet, and I left urgent word with the nurse

for him to come. For Pa's sake, I hoped he would make it in
time.

As I hung up, a terrible cry of lament and despair
sounded from the kitchen. I got my coat and hurried out the
door. I didn't want to go all through that again. Besides, if I
hurried, I might still get a bet down in the last race at
Jamaica.

¶ This was a painful story for me to reread, reminding me of a period in my life when everything seemed unfocused and unbalanced, when love aborted and helplessness wielded power.

Yet even in such bleak intervals a writer has a recourse denied most other human beings. By refashioning the memories of suffering into fiction, he lyricizes and softens them and, in this way, renders the pain a shade more bearable.

Homecoming

On the way into the city, Alex picked up a hitchhiker, a seedy youth about nineteen or twenty with long, thick hair and shaggy sideburns. He wore a faded leather jacket and carried a worn duffel bag.

They rode in silence for a while, Alex thinking about seeing Miriam again after almost three years. The youth stared out of the window. They entered the perimeter of the city, the highway burgeoning through a landscape of small shacks and stunted houses, wrecked and partially dismantled cars littering the weed-tangled yards.

"You live in Chicago?" Alex asked.

The youth shook his head.

"I'm catching a bus for San Francisco," he said.

"Got a job there?"

The youth was silent for a moment and then he turned and looked at Alex.

"I'm 1 A," he said. "I'm going to refuse induction. I heard the judges in Frisco give lighter jail sentences."

The words were spoken with such finality there seemed nothing to add. Alex nodded and didn't speak. The houses began to cluster more thickly on the land, old frame dwellings with decrepit, unpainted porches. Here and there a few solitary trees with tinted leaves formed a bright fresco of autumn.

"I was in Korea," Alex said. "No war makes sense. But I

wouldn't have had the guts then to do what you're doing now."

"If you had," the youth spoke quietly without turning his head, "maybe we wouldn't have to go through this now."

"Maybe you're right," Alex shrugged wryly. "Seems so long ago I can't remember what I felt like then."

They rode in silence again along one of the expressways tracking into the heart of the city. The roofs of buildings gleamed below, their windows masked and blurred, concealing the men and women who lived inside. Only when they descended a ramp to the street did the inhabitants suddenly become visible. Alex dropped the youth a block from the bus depot.

"Good luck," Alex said.

"Thanks," the youth said. "Thanks for the lift too."

The light changed and Alex drove off. In the rearview mirror he saw the youth crossing the street against the light, the duffel bag bouncing against his leg as he walked with a certain and defiant stride.

The midday sun, waning with the glitter of October, shone across the expanse of Grant Park as he turned onto the outer drive and followed the curve of the lake. A boy and girl sat close together on one of the slopes of grass. He recalled the spring morning three years before when he and Miriam had lain against one of the same slopes, feeling the scales of winter peeling from their flesh. In the jubilation of the season and the sun they had danced a wild abandoned little dance together, an old man on a bench a hundred feet away staring at them as if they were mad.

Afterwards Alex kissed her and tasted on her lips the sweetness of the orange juice they had drunk a while before. Then, wordlessly, possessed by desire, they had hurried to the car and driven to her apartment a few miles away to make love.

The white caps of breakers rode the waves toward the shore. He felt a curious surge of hope, unlike the resignation he had endured driving across the country. He knew even

before he had started, the probable futility of any effort
to recover the love he and Miriam once had. But he had
come doggedly anyway, driving instead of flying, preparing
his words and at the same time perhaps delaying the foun-
dering of the dream. Now, suddenly, between the surf and
the sky he was no longer convinced he would fail.

Miriam had moved from her apartment to another place
but she still worked for the same agency. He had phoned
her from California on the day he left but when the operator
rang her department he panicked and hung up, afraid she'd
tell him not to come.

He pulled over to a wayside telephone and got out and
dialed the number. A woman in her department told him
Miriam was still out to lunch. He left no message and hung
up.

He thought of waiting downtown on the chance she
might leave work to see him before the end of the day. He
knew that was unlikely and then, despondently, he decided
to go and see his mother.

He followed the drive south and turned off at 67th Street.
A few blocks later he pulled up before his sister and
brother-in-law's house, a narrow, high stucco dwelling, a
few sparse evergreens before the porch, the grass in need of
cutting. As he emerged from the car a cluster of small black
children on the porch next door fell silent and stared somberly at him. He waved to them, smiling, and one boy of
about four started to wave back. An older girl snapped him
as immobile as a tiny ebony statue.

He crossed the walk and ascended the stairs, bracing himself for the meeting with his mother whom he had not seen
in the three years since his departure. In one of the few letters exchanged with his sister, she had told him the old lady
was failing, senility, illness and old age combining to push
her closer to death. In the last letter his mother had written
him herself he could barely decipher her illegible scrawl.

He stood for a moment before the front door, seeing
through the sheer curtains into the hallway and the small

kitchen beyond. He recognized his mother's short, stocky body sitting at the kitchen table, bent over tea or a bowl of soup. He felt a strange cracking of the shell of the past, remembering all the times he had stood before this door and in the instant before inserting his key in the lock, seeing her at the table in the kitchen.

He rang the bell. He watched her head turn slightly, and then, slowly, heavily, she rose. She came shuffling toward the door, one shoulder lowered slightly because of the arthritis in her arm. He saw her fingers fumbling to pull aside the curtain and he bent toward the rim of the glass. She could not discern him clearly, continuing to peer fearfully through the window.

"Mama," he said loudly. "It's Alex. Alex."

He saw the tremor sweep her cheeks and she flung both hands toward the knob of the door. She struggled and tugged, unable to coordinate her fingers. He heard her crying out his name and, finally, she jerked the door open. For one spectral and terrible moment he saw how she had changed. Then he bent and embraced her, assailed by the familiar scents of incense, rosewater, sweat, and that peculiar, indefinable odor he remembered from childhood, an odor of spice locked in a container a long time and when finally opened, mingling pungence with a thin asthenic staleness.

They sat in the small parlor, side by side on the old worn sofa, the afternoon sun raising a wraithlike mist in the corners of the room. She clutched one of his hands between her thin-fleshed fingers. Whenever he looked at the ravages of illness and age marking her face he felt compelled to turn away.

"Your sister and Chester are both gone in the morning before I wake up," she said in a soft plaintive voice. "Before I open my eyes I hear the emptiness of the house and know I got to be alone all the day till they come home at night. I pray to God, then, for him to let me die."

"Don't you have coffee with the neighbors anymore? What about Mrs. Garfakis?"

"She moved with her son to Glencoe," his mother said. "A lot of people moving now. The Felton house next door was sold to colored about six months ago. Pretty soon the whole neighborhood will be black."

"They've got to live someplace."

"They don't bother me," his mother said. "They wouldn't bother with an old lady. I stay in the house and keep the doors locked. But Chester worries about your sister." She paused and stared at him with her eyes frightened and pleading for reassurance. "Do I look very bad?" she asked slowly and raised her hand in a feeble, mournful gesture to her cheek.

For a moment they sat in silence. He was forced to look without flinching at the dark, withered lips, the webbed, ashen cheeks, the pulp of flesh at her throat. He searched her eyes for a vestige of the vigor he remembered but saw only the querulous lids, the pupils peering in terror from the prison of her body.

"Your hair is whiter," he said, "but you look fine."

She shook her head.

"I'm not well," she said drearily. "I can't eat anymore and can't hardly walk."

"Chester still at the mills?" he asked to divert her attention from herself.

"He's doing what he'll always be doing," his mother said. "Working in the mills and with your sister entering contests to win new cars and washing machines and t.v. sets. When they come home they eat and watch some t.v. and go to bed. They don't have a dozen words to say to each other or to me."

He recalled the lean and weary frame of his sister and the stolid, gentle man she had married. In the years he had lived with them he marveled at the unchanging pattern of their days, work, food, sleep, television, and occasionally, love. From his attic room early in the morning he could hear the creaking of the springs of their bed in the room below, his sister's muted moaning and sometimes a single hoarse cry from Chester. Only in their moment of union did he hear either of them utter a cry to indicate they were alive.

He felt an urgency suddenly to leave, get out into the air, abandon the tight, dismal house as he had fled from it three years before. He rose and his mother reached up to him with a spasm of anguish.

"Not yet!" she pleaded. "Don't leave yet, Alex!"

"Listen, Mama," he said gently. "I've got some important business, one of the reasons I came to town. But I'll be back first thing in the morning."

"I've got some bologna and cheese," she said. "Have a sandwich first and Chester has beer in the icebox."

"I can't now, really, Mama," he said. "I've got to go."

She looked up at him with her naked, glistening eyes. "There are vesper services at church tonight, son," she said. "I don't get to church much anymore. Marika and Chester sleep late Sunday mornings and I can't stand on my feet too long anyway. Can you take me to church tonight?"

He started to refuse, thinking of Miriam, and then his mother's wretched face muted his rejection.

"If the meetings finish early," he said, "and I can get away, I'll take you to church."

"Services start at eight o'clock," she said. "But if we're a little late, it's all right."

"Okay, Mama," he started restlessly for the door. When his hand touched the knob he heard her voice, thin and in the grip of some nameless fear.

"Alex?"

"Yes, Mama?"

"You try, my boy. You try to come and take me to church."

"I'll try, Mama."

He drove back downtown, anxious suddenly and impatient. He parked the car and walked to the small bar a block from Miriam's office where the two of them used to meet.

He had a couple of drinks and about four o'clock he phoned her office. He waited in turbulence while someone called her.

"Yes?" Her tone was pleasant and unsuspecting.

"Miriam, it's Alex."

There was a moment of startled silence.

"How are you, Alex?" He sensed her wariness.

"I'm fine," he said. "I'm just passing through town on business and thought I'd call. How are you?"

"Oh, I'm fine," she said.

He heard a voice close to her raised in inquiry and she muffled the phone for a moment and answered. He heard the receiver moved back to her ear.

"Miriam," he spoke her name with a sudden urgency. "I'm at the Zebra down on Michigan. Remember? I wanted to see you, talk to you for a few moments. Can you come over after work?"

"Oh, I'm sorry," she said. "I can't, Alex. Some of us are going out to dinner tonight. I've got to hurry home and dress."

"Listen, Miriam," he said, and felt his throat harsh and dry. "If you could come down for just a few moments . . ."

"No, I . . ." he heard an irritation and hardness enter her voice.

"I've got to leave late tonight," he said. "Just one drink, please."

Someone in the office spoke to her again and she left the phone. He waited in a growing unrest until she returned.

"All right," she said. "I'll be down a few minutes after five. Just one drink."

"One drink," he said, and felt a leaping in his blood because he was going to see her again. He held the phone tightly in his fingers long after she had hung up.

He went back to the shadowed booth and drank a third scotch, feeling his spirit reinforced. He fashioned an eloquent structure of words to tell her why he wanted and needed her.

At five o'clock the door opened, letting in a burst of light, and he tensed. Two secretaries entered, laughing and excited, their miniskirted legs visible for an instant before the door closed. He signaled to the waitress to bring him another drink.

He tried to sort out the memories, the months that he recalled now with nostalgia. Those nights when he'd knock on her apartment door and she opened the door on the chain and peeked out at him, her short taffy-colored hair framing her adorable face.

It's your lover, he would say.

I have no lover, she would say. My husband and five children are asleep. Go away.

I promise not to wake them, he would say. Let me in and I'll give you a present.

What present, she would say.

My hands and my lips, he would say, my body and my heart.

My darling, she would say, and she'd open the door and he'd walk in and they'd embrace, their bodies pressed tightly against one another.

They would eat dinner together, the juicy steaks and the sparkling wine, the two of them seated across from one another at her small table, laughing, touching each other with their eyes, the wine glistening wetly on her lips.

She'd laugh and in a great torrent of words would tell him the events of her day, with the magic to make something special of each ordinary occurrence. She'd use her hands and body and eyes to pantomime the scenes. And he had to laugh with her laughter that came deep from her slender body. Afterwards she'd come and sit on his lap and rest her cheek against his cheek and whisper her words of love.

"Alex?"

He looked up with a start and Miriam stood beside the booth. He started to rise and nearly upset his glass.

"I'm sorry," he said. "I was daydreaming. Sit down, Miriam. I'll get the waitress."

"I don't really want a drink," she said and she sat down in the booth across from him. "Let's just talk a few moments."

He stared at her face, seeing the remembered brightness of her eyes even in the shadows, the fine sensual curve of her lips.

"You're still lovely, Miriam," he said.

She stirred restlessly and looked down at the table for an instant. Then she looked back at him.

"How are you, Alex?" she said.

"I'm okay," he said. "I'm just in, like I told you, for a little while. I stopped by and saw my mother and thought I'd give you a ring."

"That's fine," she said.

The front door opened again and several men and girls entered, filling the bar with their shrill and boisterous voices. Miriam looked after them as they slipped into booths across the way.

"Did you get my letters?" he asked.

She looked at him surprised.

"No," she said. "Did you write?"

"No," he said. "I started letters many times and never could put down what I wanted to say. I decided finally I had to come and tell you myself."

She looked down for a moment at her hands, the marvelously gentle hands that made every touch seem a kind of caress.

"It was just as well you didn't write," she said. "There wasn't anything really to say."

"Are you sure?"

There was an instant of strained silence.

"Listen, Alex," she said quietly. "Let's not suffer through one of those nostalgic here-we-are-once-again reunions between old lovers. I'll always be grateful to you. The year we had together was one of the loveliest of my life. But it's over now. The way you wanted it over three years ago."

"I didn't want it over, Miriam," he said. "Not really. But there were all the other things. My mother waiting for me to

marry so she could live with us. You don't know what that
would have been like. I lived with her and my sister for the
ten years after my father died. It got so I couldn't breathe. I
had to get away and think things out."

"Whatever the reason," she said. "It's over. Let's just talk
for a little while now as old friends."

"Are you happy, Miriam?" he asked.

She laughed her melodic little laugh.

"Dear Alex," she said. "Have you come back to salvage
me from misery and spinsterhood?"

"I didn't mean it that way," he said, and felt his face
flushed.

"I know you didn't," she said gently. "And I didn't mean
to sound cynical. I was miserable and unhappy for a long
time after you left. I cried a lot waiting for the phone to ring
or for the mail to bring a letter from you. Little by little I
began to mend the broken seams of my life."

"Are there different boyfriends or just one?"

"For the last year, just one," she said. "It's not the way it
was with you and me, not nearly as crazy and wild. But he's
good and gentle and loves me very much. And I love him."

"Do you, Miriam?" he heard the harsh urgency in his
voice and was ashamed.

"Yes," she answered quietly. "I love him very much. I
know what you're thinking. All the times we told one another that our love would endure forever. But that kind of
love exists only in the poems of lovers. Most of us have to
make an accommodation with loneliness and with life."

"Does he bring in your tree on Christmas Eve?" he asked.
"Do you trim it together with the ornaments we bought?
And do you sit in the glow of the lights and drink Lancer's
wine from the little long stemmed glasses?"

"It's almost like that," she said calmly. "But not the
same." She sat back in the booth, her head erect, watching
him.

He was conscious suddenly that the bar had filled, all the

stools taken by shadowed forms, a surging clamor of voices and laughter sweeping the room.

"Have you found anybody else?" she asked.

"There have been a few girls," he said. "No one I care about." No one I loved as I loved you, he wanted to say.

"It's good to have someone you really care about," she said. "You know the way I am. I need someone." She raised her arm to look at her watch. "Listen, Alex," she said. "I've really got to go. I'll be late."

"Go ahead," he said.

She started to rise and then stopped and slowly sat down again.

"Don't be angry," she said gently. "If I could stay longer, I would, for a little while anyway. We could have a few drinks together and share all the old memories. But it really doesn't make any sense."

"Nothing much does these days," he said.

"That's true," she said, her voice low and suddenly somber. "When they murdered Bobby Kennedy too, I cried not only for him but for all of us."

"I've felt like that lately," he said. "Nothing makes much sense. I feel that I'm drifting with no port in sight. Because I can't seem to look ahead I think I've begun to look back."

She was silent for a long moment and he had a curious sense of a period being placed carefully at the end of a page he had kept without punctuation.

"I'm sorry," she said. "Alex, I'm sorry. I have to go."

She rose slowly to her feet. He rose to stand beside her.

"That's all right," he said, and shrugged wryly. "Are you going to marry this fellow?"

"We talk about it once in a while," she said. "Neither of us feel anything urgent about it. We live in the same building, different apartments on the same floor. We can be together, and alone when we want to be."

"Convenient," he said. "I had to drive for miles."

She smiled. "You slept over many nights," she said.

"You cooked fine eggs for breakfast," he said.

She laughed. "You mean burned fine eggs. I was a terrible cook and I'm not much better now."

She put out her small, slim-boned hand.

"Goodby, Alex," she said. "When you're back in the city again, phone me and maybe you and Paul and I can have a drink together." She paused. "I've told him about you. I think you'd like him too."

"I'll phone next time," he said.

She hesitated and then she laughed.

"I was going to kiss you," she said. "But it seems foolish. We've shared so many wonderful kisses, you and I, what use is a little peck in public?"

He smiled against the stiffness in his cheeks. "I'll reach into my memories and pick one more fitting," he said.

She reached out and touched his arm in a fleeting, soft caress. Afterwards she turned and walked to the door, holding her lovely head as high and proud as she always walked. He was reminded of the young hitchhiker of that morning, the same calm, certain step. They both accept life, he thought, and I retreat from it.

The door opened and he saw the glitter of the setting sun mantle her head. He felt an urgent longing to run after her, to cry out that he had returned because he still loved her, still needed her. Instead, he walked unsteadily to the men's room, past the stools and booths filled with laughing, drinking men and girls.

The interior of the church glistened with candles, the air drifting slow and warm scents of incense and melting wax. The priest in his gold and brocaded vestments stood before the altar and raised his long pale fingers toward the cross of Christ.

Alex looked down at the bent figure of his mother standing beside him, a twisted form that might have been carved from the trunk of a gnarled tree. She pressed her hands tightly against the railing before them.

In the pews around them he recognized men and women

he knew, looking older, more resigned. He had a strange feeling of the years falling away, standing in the church between his mother and father, memories of coffins closed, candles flickering, elegiac chants, and the sweet taste of communion wine.

The choirmaster's voice rang somberly across the church, the chorus of girl's voices following behind. The priest turned and motioned for the congregation to be seated. His mother leaned against him, her hand gripping his arm for support, and lowered herself slowly to the bench. He sensed her watching him and he turned and caught her with a curious tender joy on her scarred cheeks.

When the collection tray came out he reached into his wallet and brought out a couple of dollar bills. He felt his mother tug at his arm.

"Don't put in too much," she whispered. When the tray reached them he dropped in a dollar and she put in a nickel and a dime.

At the end of the service he took his mother's arm and led her slowly into the stream of people moving toward the portico. She peered anxiously around her for familiar faces.

"Hello, Mrs. Savalas, you're looking fine. How's your family? I'm not so good, you know. I'm sick. Remember my son, Alex? He's come from California to visit me."

She repeated the same message loudly to several different people, pleased when strangers heard and looked toward her and Alex. In the portico as he tried to lead her from the church, she pulled back.

"We've got to see Father Valoris," she said. "He'll want to see you."

They waited in the rear of the church and he shook hands numbly a number of additional times with people who greeted his mother. She stood close beside him, one hand resting upon his arm, a warm pleasure rampant within the slow, stiff movements of her head, absorbing the exultant moments to be recalled countless times later.

When there were fewer than a half-dozen people left in

the portico, the priest came from the nave of the church, his long black cassock swirling about his ankles. Alex's mother tugged at his arm, moving them into the priest's path.

"Father, you remember my Alex?" she said with her voice trembling. "He's come all the way from California to see me."

The priest put out his hand and smiled. Alex took it and mechanically, as he had done a thousand times in the past, bent and kissed the back of the palm.

"A long way," the priest said, "but worth it to bring such pride and pleasure to your mother's face."

"All the way from California, Father," his mother said and there were tears in her eyes.

They shook hands once more, and then as the sexton began snuffing out the candles to darken the church, they left.

The four of them sat and drank coffee around the old walnut, diningroom table. His mother, his brother-in-law, Chester, eyelids heavy and mouth twisted in an effort to remain awake, and his sister, Marika, pale lean-fleshed cheeks, and a sullen curl to her lips.

"Well, I think I'll hit the sack," Chester said. "We got a rough rolling schedule tomorrow." He rose and smiled at Alex, extending his hand. "Maybe I'll see you in the morning."

"I'll be leaving tonight," Alex said. "I have to get an early start to make New York by day after tomorrow."

"No, Alex!" his mother said with dismay. "Not so soon!"

"I can't, Mama, I'm sorry," he said.

"At least sleep here tonight," his mother pleaded, her voice whining and distressed. "You can start early in the morning."

He shook his head slowly.

"Let him go, Mama," his sister said. "He says he's got business, so let him go."

"I'd stay but I'm a day late anyway," Alex said.

"Well, if I don't see you, Alex, good luck," Chester said.

He smiled at him again and stood for a moment thinking of something else to add. He gave up and said good-night and started wearily up the stairs.

His mother rose heavily from her chair and began fumbling at the plates.

"Leave the dishes, Mama," his sister said sharply. "I'll pick them up."

"I just wanted the rest of the cookies," his mother said and she raised the small platter and held it trembling in her palsied fingers. "I'll wrap them so Alex can take them with him. I know they're his favorite."

"Thanks, Mama," he said. He watched her shuffling weary and slow-gaited toward the kitchen. He looked back to see his sister's eyes fastened in his flesh.

"Can't you even stay with her for one night, you bastard," she said in a low, hoarse voice. "You bastard, do you think the lousy fifty bucks you send each month buys you off everything else?"

He looked at her and recognized the marks of her suffering.

"Has it been that bad?" he asked.

She was silent for a moment, her anger fleeing as quickly as it had come.

"What's bad, what's good," she said with a cold grunt. "She's dying slowly, day by day, falling apart. And I have to watch her dying, listen to her whimper and cry when she thinks no one hears. She can't do more than walk a few steps and can barely dress herself anymore. One of these days she won't be able to get out of bed and I don't know what we're going to do with her then."

"Maybe you can find a woman to come in and look after her," Alex said.

"A woman costs money," his sister said.

"I'll try to send more," Alex said.

"Sure," his sister said. "You send some more."

He rose then and walked into the kitchen where his mother stood packing the cookies in a small box. He reached around her and picked one up and popped it into his mouth. He whistled in pleasure to please her.

"Delicious, Mama!" he said. "I'll finish them before I'm out of Chicago." He paused. "Listen, I think I'll stay tonight. I'll sleep up in the attic if it's okay but I'll have to leave first thing in the morning."

Her face crinkled like paper, each fold trembling with joy.

"Marika!" she called to his sister. "Marika! Alex is staying tonight. Get sheets for his bed upstairs." She looked back at him. "For one night," she said softly. "It'll be like it used to be. I'll hear your steps and close my eyes and sleep better because you're here."

He lay in his bed in the darkness of the attic, listening to the silence of the house. A branch brushed against the roof and he felt the familiar almost forgotten sound deep in his body. On the street below a car passed and the headlights swept the ceiling of his room with a beam of light. A car door slammed and a dog barked.

Somewhere on the road to San Francisco, the young hitchhiker who was 1 A sat awake or slept in the dark, rocking bus. In their bedroom below the attic Chester and Marika lay together in heavy, burdened sleep. In the small corner bedroom, his aging, dying mother lay comforted by his presence for a single night. And across the city, Miriam's warm, naked body consoled the body of her good and gentle Paul.

The trees made a dry, soughing sound. He settled himself deeper in the covers, turning into himself, remorseful about his mother. He might stay for a little while and try to comfort her. Then he knew he could not stay. We only love those who can still save us, he thought. He turned and faced the wall, thinking of Miriam, wishing it were dawn so he could rise and leave.

¶ Even in my early, unpublished stories, I showed a preoccupation with aging and death. From my reading of Jack London's *Martin Eden*, at age thirteen, I also gained an awareness that a time might come in any life when sleep would not provide the needed rest and death could be a liberation. That was the theme of this story.

For reasons that escape me now, I also named the character of Death in this story Matsoukas. In my later novel *A Dream of Kings* I used the same name for the forceful, life-loving, and sun-possessed Leonidas Matsoukas, operator of the Pindar Master Counseling Service, who always acted as if he were immortal.

There may not be a contradiction here. Without life, there could be no death. Without death, life would be endless and meaningless. So life and death may not be polarities, but an integral, undivided whole.

Matsoukas

On Saturday evening Lambos kept his small grocery open an hour longer than his usual closing time. This enabled his regular customers to buy a carton of milk or a loaf of bread for Sunday morning when he did not open until noon.

That Saturday evening near the end of November was a cold and desolate night, the black and mottled streets deserted of all living things except a prowling tomcat gliding furtively through the glow of a street lamp before disappearing again into the dark cave of an alley.

Only a fool would brave the wind and the cold, Lambos thought, and his legs ached as they always did by the end of his long day. He yearned suddenly for his bed in the quiet small room above the store. He turned the key in the door and snapped off the main lights leaving only a tiny bare bulb above the window and another dim light in the rear of the store.

Across the street a tattered awning flapped in the wind. A patch of moonlight broke abruptly upon a sheet of newspaper floating over the curb. The beam of a passing car swept the pyramids of cans in his window. A corner of a wrapping-paper sign on which he had lettered with black crayon and taped to the window had come loose and he bent and pressed the tape back into place, feeling the glass cold beneath his fingers.

He was startled by the figure of a man watching him from the sidewalk outside his window. Lambos peered through the glass to identify him but the small bulb did not allow sufficient light. Deciding unhappily that he was a customer expecting the store to be open, Lambos snapped the lock back and opened the door.

The small bell tinkled as the man entered, a gust of icy wind swirling about his legs. Lambos shivered and closed the door quickly. When he turned around the man was standing almost concealed in shadow. Lambos could only make out that he was small of build wearing a gray topcoat too light for the weather and a battered felt hat pulled rakishly to one side.

"I was just closing," Lambos said in annoyance. He turned to open the overhead lights.

"Don't bother," the man said and it seemed to Lambos the words came flippantly from his mouth. He turned and peered over the counter at the shelves of canned goods. "Do you carry Meyer's clam chowder?" he asked.

"The supermarket in the next block," Lambos said brusquely. "They carry everything. I carry what my customers buy."

The man walked past the glass counter that contained several varieties of cheese. He halted before the small barrel of briny pickles. "These are my favorite," he said with a pleased wave. For a moment the light shone full across his face that was shaped like a total moon with small bright eyes above the pinches of scarlet where the cold had marked his cheeks. His mouth was so wide when he smiled the corners cut almost to his nostrils giving him a droll and absurd appearance. Almost midnight, Lambos thought bitterly, and I get a clown.

"One pickle," the man said. "Mark it down." He reached into the barrel and raised a single dripping pickle and with measured relish bit off the end.

"I will remember," Lambos said. "Something else?"

The man chewed the pickle slowly punctuating each bite with a loud smacking of his lips.

"A man shouldn't eat pickles this time of night," Lambos said. "They cause heartburn."

When there was still no answer, Lambos felt a sudden uneasiness. He looked toward the battered register in which he kept change and a few bills. As if understanding, the man laughed softly. "Don't worry about that, Lambos," he said.

"You know my name?" Lambos asked in surprise. He peered more closely at the man again.

The man finished the pickle and drew out a handkerchief to wipe his fingers. "You have never seen me before, Lambos," he said with a jaunty wink, "but you and I have had an appointment for a long time."

"Maybe you are right," Lambos said soothingly, "but it is late now, friend, and I wish to close up. If there is nothing else . . ."

Instead of moving toward the door, the man walked to the end of the counter. He sat down on a wooden crate and indolently crossed his legs. "That supermarket has ruined you, hasn't it?" he asked cheerfully.

"My business is no concern of yours," Lambos bristled, forgetting his decision to humor the man. He turned his back on him and picked up the broom and began sweeping a patch of floor in agitation. He heard no sound but the whisking of the strands of straw against the bare wood. He ceased sweeping and turned to stare helplessly at the man who had not moved.

"My name is Matsoukas," the man said and his mouth twisted in a weird and expansive grin.

Lambos saw a glimmer of hope. "Are you Greek?"

"What else?" Matsoukas said.

"If you are Greek," Lambos said, "you know it is not polite to enter a man's store at closing time and eat a pickle and sit around like you are in a coffeehouse."

"Think of me as a friend," Matsoukas said, "who has come to help you find rest."

"Five minutes after you are gone, friend, I will be in bed," Lambos said.

"You need a much longer rest," Matsoukas said. "A rest sleep for a single night cannot provide." He lifted his shoulders in a wry shrug. "Actually I've been putting this visit off. I should have come a year ago."

"Who are you?" Lambos said. "What do you want?"

The cold eyes measured him and the great mouth taunted him silently.

Lambos loosed a hoarse cry and walked as quickly as his legs would allow behind the counter. He reached into the box where he kept a hammer and raised it violently above his head.

"You are a crazy man!" he shouted. "Now get out of my store!"

Matsoukas pointed to the hammer and shook in a spasm of silent and sardonic laughter. "Cuckoo, cuckoo, cuckoo," he snickered when he could get his breath.

Lambos lowered the hammer slowly to the counter. "I don't understand," he said helplessly.

Matsoukas leaned forward and his face entered the ray of light. The mask of the clown was strangely altered, as if the surface were a dried and wrinkled crust stretching over something more ominous beneath.

"I will make it clear," Matsoukas said with disdain. "Your heels are run down, your cuffs shabby, your pants so stiff with odors even the moths ignore them." His voice was the jagged edge of a broken mirror. "Your veins are scurvy roads that run through the ruins of your body. You endure a solitude reserved for beasts and saints. It is time to throw in your soiled towel."

Lambos stared at him numbly trying to find some sense in

what was happening. "Are you sure you are Greek?" he asked finally.

"My name is Matsoukas."

"A name means nothing."

"Mine does," Matsoukas chuckled.

"What does it mean?"

"What I want it to mean."

"I don't want to listen to you any more," Lambos said.

"You are not listening now," Matsoukas said harshly. "Protoplasm is a sticky business. Better to have it over and done with."

"Are you a doctor?" Lambos shook his head fitfully. "You want to take my temperature and give me a prescription? I have a cabinet full of powders and pills."

"It is too late for pills," Matsoukas said. "I am here to unchain you from your barrel of pickles. Wise up."

"Who are you?" Lambos cried. "Tell me who you are?"

"Who I am doesn't matter," Matsoukas said loudly. "It's who you are that counts."

"Who am I?" Lambos asked loudly.

"I can sum up your life in one breath," Matsoukas said. "First a suckling baby, then a child answering his name, a youth with pustules on his face, a man searching for love, a husband in the misery of unhappy marriage, a father dreaming of eternity and resurrection," his baleful eyes flayed Lambos with scorn. "Now you are a sick and spindly-legged old man, wife and son dead, and not a single reason why you shouldn't be too. Wise up."

"Leave me alone." Lambos put his hands desperately to his ears.

"Admit what I say is true," Matsoukas said. "Is there anyone left to mourn you? Is there anyone left to love you?" He made a gesture of impatience. "I can't waste much more time here." He rose from the crate and walked in agitation to stand at the window staring silently into the street.

"Listen to me," Lambos pleaded. "Will you listen to me?" When Matsoukas did not turn around, Lambos began to pace the store. "How can you know what I am?" he said. He started around the counter and turned and walked back, dragging one foot slightly behind him. "Twenty years I was married," he said, "and then long after I had given up hope I could ever be a father, we had a son. All my life seemed different then." He passed beneath the light and bumped the edge of the counter and nearly fell. "I saw him growing into a fine man, raising a family of his own, my grandchildren. I saw my old age as green and warm. But from his tenth year he had a sickness in his body. For two years they kept him alive by giving him blood. He grew thin and his flesh bruised and blue and then he died. For two years I watched and measured each pulse of his dying. Not a day or night when I would not have died in his place." He paused and stretched his arms to the ceiling of the store and spread his dry stiff fingers, and then he cried out, a terrible cry of loss and despair. At the window Matsoukas stirred uneasily.

Lambos walked wearily to the same crate Matsoukas had used a short while before. He sat down and let his face drop slowly against his cupped hands. He closed himself into the nest of his palms, alone for a moment with the heavy beating of his heart. "I am afraid," he said softly. "I am afraid."

Matsoukas turned then from the window. He walked to Lambos and then slowly and awkwardly put out his hand and touched Lambos gently on the shoulder.

"Listen, Lambos," Matsoukas spoke in a strangely altered voice. "Your heart is scarred by loneliness and sorrow. Your body is a wound from which your life falls like drops of blood. Your burden is hopeless and it will grieve no one if you lay it down."

Lambos closed his eyes tightly for a long moment. When he opened them he noticed that moonlight had entered the store. It shimmered across the worn wood of the floor and swirled mist in the corners.

"It is easy to accomplish," Matsoukas said. "Merely believe and say, I want to die. Think of night eternal across your body." He paused and drew a fitful breath. "I'll tell you something I don't ever bother to tell anyone. Grief and despair belong to life. False dreams and vain hopes belong to life. Death is peace."

It seemed to Lambos in that moment as if the sharp and mournful world around him began to soften. The edges began to dissolve, shelves and counters and walls fading slowly away.

Lambos nodded slowly and rose. He hesitated for a moment and then reached again for the broom. He swept the last of the litter into a pile and picked it up with a piece of cardboard that he threw into the basket in the corner. Then he fumbled at the apron that bound his waist.

"When I was a boy I had such dreams," Lambos said. He looked sadly around the store. "Now at the end there is so much I do not understand," he sighed, "perhaps if I had not been such a simple man . . ."

"Only the simple and the great may be sure of dying in their own way," Matsoukas said. "The rest die in imitation."

Lambos folded his apron and placed it upon the counter. He stood uncertainly for a moment as if there were something he had forgotten to do. "Will you stay with me now?" he asked and tried not to show his fear.

"Each man must enter death for himself," Matsoukas said. "But do not despair, Lambos. Go up to your bed and lie down and close your eyes and you will sleep as you have never slept before. I promise you that."

Lambos walked to the foot of the steps. He looked once to the door at the top and then turned back to Matsoukas.

"And God?" he asked softly. "Where is God in all of this?"

"If you have not found the answer to that in all your years on earth," Matsoukas said gravely, "how can you expect to have the answer now?"

Lambos placed his hands on the railings for balance and started slowly up. He heard the tinkling of the bell above the door and felt a sudden gust of wind about his legs. He looked back and beyond the glass of the window saw the arm of Matsoukas raised in a shadowed farewell.

He walked up a few more steps. The chill of stone crept into his body and he thought of tombs and the comfortless earth. He remembered his son and tried to go higher but his one leg trembled so badly it would not hold him.

"Matsoukas!" he cried.

There was no answer from the store below him. The steps he had passed were shrouded in darkness. He looked once more up to the door and felt himself suspended on a frail bridge over the void. He slipped to one knee.

"Matsoukas!" he cried in anguish. "Help me!"

Then he remembered. Grief and despair belong to life, Matsoukas had said, false dreams and vain hopes belong to life. Death is peace.

He pulled himself to his feet and holding to the railing with both hands began to drag himself up. Strangely his fear was gone and he felt a strength such as he had not felt in many years. He smelled the fragrance of his unmarked youth, the childhood of his life. He felt with certainty that he was going home, mind and body and heart back to his beginning.

His voice echoed in a long joyous cry down the stairs. Below him the shelves and pyramids of cans, the racks of bread and the paper banners, snapped squarely and forever into darkness.

¶ This story also relates to the elements of aging and death I wrote about in "Matsoukas." An act of infidelity may not always stem from a lack of love between a husband and a wife but be a product of the anxieties that develop in us as we grow older. Feeling life slipping irrevocably past, one reaches out in panic for additional moorings.

I was not trying to justify the husband's unfaithfulness but to make it a little more understandable.

End of Winter

The first snow fell early in November. Almost at once the weather turned cold. Winds howled in the night and shook the house. The oil furnace ran from dark to dawn almost without stopping, but the rooms were still cold. Della and I got up several times during the night to make sure the boys were covered.

In the morning I was the first one up and shaved and woke the boys for school. While they dressed, Della made their lunches and cooked breakfast. We ate together and I left for work about the time the boys headed for the school bus. Della waved to us from the door and the dog next door barked as she always did.

The boys were eight and six years old that winter. Della was pregnant again, we had found out for sure from the doctor just after Labor Day, so we had the winter to go with the baby to be born in the spring.

The pattern of our lives ran much the same as it had for years. In the evening we ate supper and then watched a program on TV—Disneyland or one of the better western stories. I enjoyed them, too. Then, while Della finished the dishes, I put Tom, the six-year-old, to bed. I washed him and tussled with him on the bed. I read him a story and took pleasure in his wonder at the world opening before his eyes. Ralph would come up and wash himself and then the three of us would lie together in the darkness for a few moments recounting the events of the day.

Once a week Della and I went out. A baby sitter came in and we went to a show or a play. Sometimes friends visited us. We drank Martinis or Manhattans and played charades and laughed about many things I could not remember the next day. After they had gone Della and I went to bed and made love.

I know that winter my job in advertising was no more beset by aggravations than it had been in other years. I had been promoted in the summer to brand manager and while it increased my responsibilities it allowed me more freedom as well. I enjoyed my work most of the time and still looked forward to the evenings at home. If the routine of supper and baths and stories weighed sometimes on my back, much more often I was aware of the warmth and laughter.

So in a way I find it hard to understand why that winter, after almost twelve years of marriage, I should have been unfaithful to Della for the first time.

A girl who worked in our offices. Not a girl obviously suited to infidelities the way Norma was, tall and blonde with lithe long legs that gleamed like satin, or elfin-eyed little Dolores who worked in the art department and was always smudged cutely with paint and whispered promises to all the men at the office Christmas party.

Pat had shining black hair the color of Della's. Both had large dark eyes and clear skin. They looked alike except Pat was about 24, the age Della was when we were married.

I remember that afternoon in November when I first suggested to Pat that we have dinner together. She had brought some copy into my office for my approval and stood waiting beside the desk. She had been with the firm about a year and I knew little about her except that she had been married young and then divorced. She had high small breasts and fine ankles. I was conscious of her as attractive, but I swear more than that drew me to her. There was a

dream of candlelight and lost springs about her. A fleeting
memory of youth as a time of promise. The shadow of some
unfathomed sadness about her eyes. Suddenly I felt the stirrings of desire, but not of the flesh alone. A wish to see
behind the mask of her face, to share her laughter, and
know her well enough to push back the dark errant curl of
hair fallen across her forehead. I mentioned dinner to her
then, my tone jesting, to provide a retreat if she seemed
offended. She was silent for a long moment and I knew she
understood the truth. In the way she watched me, coolly
appraised me, I knew she had decided to accept.

She met me that night at a small café on the edge of the
city. I waited at a table by the window as the snow fell
softly across the bare trees in the park across the street. I
thought of the years with Della and of the children at home
preparing for bed. I thought of the unreality of the moment
sitting in a strange café, miles from my house, watching the
snow fall and waiting for a strange girl.

When she came to the table she startled me. The snow
glistened in her hair and her cheeks were bright, flushed
with night and cold.

"I'm late," she said, and her voice was low and husky and
her red lips moved easily about her teeth as she spoke.

"I was watching the snow," I said.

I took her coat and saw the soft pale skin of the back of
her neck. The waiter came and we ordered wine and then
sat watching one another.

"When I walked up," she said, "you looked as if you had
forgotten I was coming."

"I was watching the snow," I said, "and fell into some
kind of trance."

"Were you hoping I would not come?"

"I'm glad you did."

"I wanted to," she said. "I am not much good at poses. I
can't show outrage if I don't feel outrage."

"I guess you thought I was like the rest," I said. "Another

married man with problems looking for a young shoulder to cry on."

She watched me silently for a moment.

"I have no problems," I said. "I love my wife and my children. I am not unhappy in my job."

"Then why are you here?" she asked softly.

That stopped me for a moment.

"I don't really know," I said. "I thought of a lot of things when you came into my office today. Maybe I fooled myself. Perhaps I'm here because you are very pretty and I want to touch you."

"That is why I came," she said quietly.

She must have read something in my eyes and she laughed softly.

"I told you I was no good at poses. Does that shock you?"

"A little," I said.

The waiter brought the wine and seemed to give us a look that implied censure. She raised her glass and the wine gleamed red.

"There are many wolves," she said, "behind every office door. They leer and pinch and pat. I don't think you belong among them. You are unaware of all the frantic machinations that go on in the office by men trying to get girls to go to bed."

"How can you be sure I'm not like all the others?" I said.

"I can't be sure," she said. "I think I am right. I think that's why I came. To be made love to by a man who has been faithful to his wife for twelve years is like love-making in a strange land."

So we ate a little and drank more wine and left the café. I sat with her in the front seat of her car with the heater going. We watched the snow falling around us in the deserted park. The scent of wine was about us, aroma of walnuts and richly laden tables. I kissed her lips and tasted ripe sweet fruit.

I touched her body, gently, almost shyly at first and then more rudely as the warmth became flame and still unlike the

passion I remembered in the first years with Della. Because
even in desire I could not forget those years or the children
that waited at home. So there was this sadness as we made
love, a sweet and burning sadness, and all the while the
snow kept falling out of the darkness.

In the next few months I saw Pat several times a week. I
lied to Della of meetings with customers after hours. Of ac-
counts in jeopardy and old college friends in for a few hours
between trains. The trust built through our years together
helped her believe. After the first night it was easier and I
did not think as often of the children.

Pat and I went dancing sometimes in little cafés outside
the city and afterwards made love in the car. Other evenings we would spend in her small apartment with the glistening lamps and the Pullman kitchen and the bed that
came out of the livingroom wall. We made ham sandwiches,
thick with lettuce and tomatoes, and listened to her hi-fi as
we ate them and afterwards went to bed. Sometime after
midnight I had to get up and dress to leave. She would be
warm and sleepy within the sheets and her lips soft as I
kissed her goodby. Then I drove through the dark midnight
streets to my own dark house. I undressed quietly in the
bathroom and looked in on the boys and climbed gently into
bed beside Della. She stirred restlessly and moved against
me in the bed, warm as Pat had been warm, flesh that was
mine where Pat's was borrowed. I would lie awake for a
long time listening to the stillness of the house, hearing
Della breathing softly in sleep beside me, finally falling
asleep myself for a few moments and waking with a start not
sure in whose bed I really was.

There were nights when my life of lies and deception
bred anger in me at Della and the children. I put the boys
brusquely to bed, quick to slap or reprimand. Again there
were nights I made love to Pat roughly as if to revenge myself for the injustice upon my family.

The weeks passed into months and the swell of Della's body curved like the arc of the moon. In awareness that her flesh would soon become sluggish and shapeless, she demanded love more fiercely than she had in years. Afterwards we lay together and she would be pleased and feel in some way we were drawing closer together.

"I'm storing up love," she said. "For the baby. I'm taking love from you and holding it for the baby."

I would touch the warm flesh of her throat and stroke the slight swell of her body and feel a strange pain in my chest.

"I am scared about this baby," she said. "I wasn't with the others, but I am scared with this one."

"You will be all right," I said.

"I think I will," she said. "But I am older now. It must be harder when you are thirty-six, not as easy as when you are younger."

"It will be all right," I said.

"Tom was coughing today," she said. "I want to take him to Doctor Vaughn on Friday."

"All right," I said.

"Flora Seaman called today," she said. "They want us for dinner on Sunday. I called Nora. She can come to stay with the children, if you want to go."

"We'll see," I said.

She rose from the bed and went into the washroom. I watched her, not sure of just what I felt, but something bred of remorse and a shattering of my flesh.

There was a night in March I spent with Pat. She cooked supper for us in her apartment and then barefooted in slacks and a blouse came to lie at my side across the bed. The music from the record player in the corner drew together the small warm room.

"Almost two weeks since you last came," she said. "In a little while you will not come at all."

I touched her ear, the delicate lobe I had gotten to know so well.

"I have been busy," I said. "One of the boys has had a bad cold that keeps hanging on. He waits for me to come home in the evening." I paused for a moment under great tenderness and moved closer to her on the bed. "I miss you when I do not come," I said.

"I miss you too," she said.

We were silent for a while listening to the music.

"I can see it ending," she said. "The little love that kept us warm this winter. There is something sad about love when it is over."

"Why do you say over?" I said. "Nothing is over yet. We will have the spring and the summer. Things will be the same."

She shook her head.

"For a little while you feel a part of you has been lost," she said. "You look into faces on the street to find someone, something that is gone."

"Was your first love like that?"

"That was different," she said. "That hurt in a way terrible to remember. I was seventeen when I married him."

"Where is he now?"

"He is remarried," she said. "To a woman in Dallas who had three children." She laughed softly. "I would tell him he could not accept responsibility, so he showed me. But before that I wrote him long letters. Shameful letters in which I begged him to take me back. He never replied."

She uncoiled off the bed like a cat with warm and supple grace and came to sit on my knees. I put my arms around her waist and felt the warmth of her flesh through the thin cloth of her blouse.

"We should not stay in," she said. "It is not good for you and not good for me. You think of your children and your boy who is waiting for you to come home and I think of my first love and how far he is from me now. We should go somewhere far out of the city and dance and kiss each other in the shadows of a booth and make our love in the car."

"Tuesday night," I said. "Next Tuesday night we will do that. Tuesday night for sure."

I stood up and tucked my shirt in my trousers. She came once more into my arms, her dark eyes searching my face.

"In a little while it will be spring," she said. "And in the springs to come will you remember this winter?"

"I will," I said. "I will."

When I got to the street I seemed to smell from far off the faint early scents of spring. The shade of her window was pulled slightly to the side and she stood there with her body shaded against the light. I waved and could not be sure she waved back or not.

When I got home I knew something was wrong. I came in the front door and hung my hat and coat in the hall closet. I saw light in the kitchen and felt a quick sense of dread.

Della sat dressed at the kitchen table. I stood for a moment in the doorway. She knew I was there, yet for a long moment she did not look up. I walked to the table and sat down and saw her cheeks pale and still moist and knew she had been crying.

"Wally," she said, and she spoke softly in almost a whisper. "Wally, don't lie to me now. I promise not to cry anymore or become angry. I want to talk to you. I can take almost anything, but don't lie to me now."

I sat there and did not answer.

"There was no meeting tonight," she said. "Lawrence called for you. And then I thought of all the other meetings late at night that you have attended the last few months. All the other things that suddenly fall into place. Then I knew it was a girl."

Her face was naked and her flesh tight across her cheeks.

"Yes," I said. "Tonight and all the other nights. Yes, there is a girl."

She must have expected to hear me say that, but still her face loosened as if the bone beneath the skin had suddenly broken. I was sorry I had not lied, that for a little while I had not indulged all the heated denials.

"Do you want a divorce?" she asked.

"Del," I said. "It was just a girl. I don't want a divorce. It didn't mean that much to me."

"It means that much to me," she said. "Maybe I want the divorce." Her voice rose just a little. "Do you think you are a rooster who can come swaggering back from another henhouse and find everything in order in his own roost?"

"Del," I said.

"Do you think because I'm pregnant now," she said, "and because I have the children that I'm helpless? Do you think you can make me swallow your dirt because I'm helpless? Do you think that?"

"Del," I said. "I don't think that."

"Why?" she said. "I've been sitting here for almost three hours frantically trying to reason why, why? Is it that I'm not a good wife? I don't wash enough clothes or do enough dishes? I make too many demands? I nag too much? I don't keep myself neat? Why?"

"Del," I said, and struggled for the right words. "My God, Del, it was none of these things. Something happened to me. A bad and restless winter. It wasn't right, but it had nothing to do with you."

She laughed a hard little laugh that echoed strangely in the kitchen.

"Has she been the first?" she said. "Has this one been the first or have there been others?"

"I swear the first," I said.

She watched me then.

"What are we going to do?" she said. "What is it you want to do now?"

"I don't know," I said. "I mean there's nothing to be done. I will not see her again. I would have stopped soon anyway. I want you to believe that."

We sat silent for a long time.

"Like a telegram with word someone close has died," she said. "A world suddenly coming apart. I was angry, but I'm not angry now. I am bewildered and confused. I don't know what this means to us." She put her hands across the full swell of her abdomen. "I don't know what this means for this one in my body or for the boys upstairs. I don't know just how to go on or how to turn back. I'm scared and I should still be angry, but I'm only scared and mixed up."

"Del," I said and got up from my chair. I went to her but she shook her head.

"Not now," she said. "Don't touch me yet. I want to believe you. I want you to tell me you still love me and we can go back to the way it was. Then I'm ashamed because it means I have no pride. I'm ashamed and scared and alone."

She stood up and walked out of the kitchen. After a moment I turned off the lights and followed her upstairs.

We undressed in the dark bedroom and did not speak. I went to the bathroom and when I came out she was lying still under the sheets.

I walked to the boys' room across the hall and checked them and came back. I sat on the edge of the bed and moved slowly beneath the sheets careful not to touch her.

"I know what you want," she said softly. "I know what you want."

The house about us was quiet and the room shadowed and still.

"You want the love we had," she said. "You want us young as we used to be."

She moved helplessly beside me and I felt the length of her leg along my own flesh. I took her into my arms and held her tightly against the trembling that swept us both.

There was a sound of coughing from the boys' room. I got out of bed and went to them and Tom coughed again, harshly in the darkness. I pulled his covers about his throat and felt the flesh of his cheek flushed and warm.

I went to the window and closed it a little. The night was cool and all the earth was still. Far off in the dark huge sky the timeless stars glistened.

In that moment a great sadness burned my body.

⁋ I tend to resist the category "ethnic writer," since it is often used in a pejorative sense or to suggest that the work is limited in domain. Since most of my material is based on a Greek background, the heroes and the history of Greece are important to me. From that past I move to the immigrant descendants of those heroes, small merchants and shopkeepers, who look back with longing toward a golden, seemingly inviolate landscape and time.

If I were a writer of American Indian origins, I would draw upon the rich social patterns and cultural mores of the great tribes. Studying their myths and histories, I know I would unearth the same passion for the perpetuation of a tradition, the same nostalgia, I find now in the Greek. I wrote "The Victim" as an example of what I mean.

A writer must write about the things he knows, utilizing those inherited resources of the generations that produced him. That is only a beginning, however; from there he must contend with love, hate, vengeance, betrayal, and death, those emotions bridging the barriers of race and tongue. In the end, whether the stories involve Greeks, Indians, Jews, Poles, Germans, or the black and white Southerners of Yoknapatawpha County, those things that alone can make good writing, as William Faulkner said, "are the problems of the human heart in conflict with itself."

The Victim

Standing in the shadow of a pillar beside the tracks on which the steaming train had just come to a stop, Lenny watched the travelers descend from the coaches and then saw his father. From that distance Charley Hawk did not appear changed at all in the seventeen years since Lenny had last seen him. His hair was white and straight as it had been and he looked just as tall and lean. For a moment he was lost behind a rack of baggage and then he reappeared walking with a grave and unhurried gait up the ramp. As he neared the pillar where Lenny waited, he passed beneath a bright terminal light and for the first time his son saw his face clearly, an ancient mask modeled by death for very old age.

His skin was dark brown and tight across the bone and etched with a web of coarse wrinkles. There were pits at his temples that ran along gullies into the shriveled hollow of his mouth. His nose, always big, loomed now like the great scarred beak of an eagle above the crag of his jaw. He was dressed in a shabby and shapeless gray suit, a heavy cotton shirt buttoned at his throat, a pair of battered work shoes on his feet. His only baggage was a shoe box under his arm, tied with a piece of rope.

Lenny stepped out of the shadow of the pillar. The old man stopped and recognized him without a sign of greeting. Lenny saw that his eyes had not changed, they were still dark and savage and unafraid in the shadow of death.

"How you been, Pa?" Lenny made an effort to smile before the austere face and then abandoned it as useless. The old man answered with a brief, barely visible nod of his head.

"I got my car just outside the station," Lenny said. "I thought we could go to my house first and give you a chance to rest."

"Where's Jim's body?" the old man asked and his voice came in a low harsh rumble from his throat.

Lenny tried to meet his eyes and failing, turned away in irritation to smooth a wrinkle from the sleeve of his dark tailored blue suit. "He's at the Indian Center," he said. "We'll have him cremated in the morning the way you want and you can take his ashes back home."

"Take me to him now," Charley Hawk said.

He turned and began walking again up the ramp. Lenny came a step behind him, sneaking glances at the scarred and stony profile, the erectness of the body attached to the old and withered head. Lenny remembered him back on the Dakota reservation incredibly agile and lithe even in his sixties. He had to be close to ninety now, probably one of the last Sioux alive who could remember having hunted buffalo and fighting in the last Indian Wars against the cavalry. Even now that he showed his age he was still the damn stoic Indian, Lenny thought resentfully, more like the useless legends than the legends themselves.

He swung open the door of the car. The old man bent and moved in without a trace of stiffness. Lenny walked around to the other side and got in behind the wheel. He turned the key and with a roar the motor kicked over.

"Two hundred and sixty horsepower," Lenny could not refrain from a defiant show of pride.

Charley Hawk grunted. They drove in silence for a while. Lenny gave up expecting that the old man would ask any questions.

"He died in the hospital," Lenny said finally. "When I got word he was there I went over with my own Doctor but it was too late. He had been drunk and fallen asleep or passed out in some alley. The rain fell on him most of the night. By the time they found him, he was near frozen. He died a day later and that's when I sent you the wire."

Lenny paused and stared with irritation at the face that might have been chiseled out of stone.

"I know you blame me," he said defiantly. "He was always your favorite. You never cared what happened to me. But there was nothing I could do any more. I got him a job, two, maybe three times in the past three years. He couldn't stay sober long enough to hold one more than a week. I didn't even have to help him that much but I did. He didn't want to help himself."

"I knew he was dead," Charley Hawk said and he spoke quietly as if he were talking to himself. "I had a dream that night. A horde of black-tailed magpies attacked a sick and weak gelding. The gelding screamed. He raised his head straight up. The magpies dug in with their claws, picking at his eyes, gorging upon him until they pulled him down."

"Jesus Christ, Pa," Lenny said impatiently. "Your dreams had nothing to do with it. He drank himself to death and there was nothing anybody could have done to save him."

Charley Hawk was silent for a moment and then he made a harsh spitting sound with his mouth. Lenny gripped the wheel tightly between his fingers and pressed his foot down harder on the gas pedal. The car spurted forward and swept swiftly along between the terminals and factories on either side. The old man stared straight ahead, looking neither to the right or left.

"I had the same beginning as him," Lenny said bitterly. "I grew up on the reservation too. I went to the government school and when the war came I went into the army same as he did. Why couldn't he make his way like I did?" He curled his heavy lips and the words flared from between his teeth. "They told us both, 'Big Chief Wampum good only to sit by his tepee on U.S. 66 selling beads to tourists,' or 'keep whiskey away from an Indian, they go crazy on it,' or 'the only good Indian is a dead Indian.'" He drew a hard shaken breath. "He would always lash back, always fight, and that made them torment him more. I laughed with them and made a place for myself. I got a good job and a nice house and a car and money in the bank."

"He was your brother and of your tribe," Charley Hawk said. "You looked out only for yourself."

"Why not?" Lenny said savagely. "The tribe did nothing for me. It meant nothing to me but poverty and hardship, scrawny cattle and barren land. The dingy shacks and the ceremonies that made no sense and the old men living in the past and the old women always mourning. It was different for you. You remember a time when you were free. But I had nothing and had to fight to make a place for myself in the white man's world. I am respected here. People call me Mr. Carey. They don't even think of me as an Indian anymore."

It came out in the rush of words and the moment he had spoken he clamped his teeth together tightly. They drove along residential streets with well trimmed lawns and lights gleaming in the windows of the houses.

"My house is just a mile or so from here," Lenny said and

spoke more softly. "You have known only the reservation and the farm. You don't need anyone close to you. But I want to live like a human being and raise my children and see they have shoes on their feet and hear them laugh when their little bellies are full." He looked into the glass of the windshield, seeing the old man's unmoved cheeks reflected in cold planes and circles.

They rode then in silence until the car pulled up before a two story building on a street of shops. Charley Hawk sat in the car until Lenny had gotten out and came around and opened his door. Then he swung his long legs to the curb and rose swiftly. They walked up to the building entrance and Lenny knocked. After a moment the door was opened by a well-dressed man with a brown glistening face and dark black hair.

"This is my father, Charley Hawk," Lenny said. "This here is Bill Cloud who is in charge of the Indian Center. He has made the arrangements for the services and cremation tomorrow."

Charley Hawk nodded. "Where is my son?" he asked.

"He's in the north parlor," Bill Cloud said. "We laid him out there so that any friends who wished could pass and pay their last respects. We got a couple of nice wreaths already. We notified his American Legion post and although he hasn't been an active member for some years they're going to have a rifle squad at the services tomorrow." He waited smiling for the old man to show some approval and after a moment he looked at Lenny. "That's all right, isn't it?" he asked.

"Why not," Lenny shrugged. "Let them give him the full treatment."

Bill Cloud looked uneasily at Charley Hawk once more and then turned and led them down a narrow hall. From some other part of the building came a loud scatter of voices and a burst of laughter. "Some of the younger boys in the recreation room," Bill Cloud said in apology. "I'll ask them to quiet down."

He paused before the entrance to a room that had long drapes hanging from the walls. A few armchairs and a table with a small potted plant and in the center of the room on a low platform, a square plain casket with a candle burning at the head. Charley Hawk stared for a moment at the casket and started slowly into the room. Lenny moved to follow and the old man looked back at him with eyes like knives.

Lenny faltered. Then he shrugged. "I'll wait for you out in front," he said.

"There is no need to wait," Charley Hawk said. "I will stay here until morning."

"That's all right," Bill Cloud said quickly. "There won't be anybody to bother you. I'll just tell those fellows to quiet down." He moved off down the hallway.

Charley Hawk turned again toward the casket. Lenny watched him for a moment from the doorway. "How can you feel anything?" he called harshly after his father. "How can a Sioux whose heart is made of stone feel anything?" He pulled the door closed behind him.

Charley Hawk stood above the casket. The face that lay within the shapeless folds of white cloth was that of a stranger, the rouged cheeks looking like jagged patches of color on stiff canvas. The body lay stiff and straight in death, the wrists springing like broken stalks from the sleeves of his shiny black suit, and the long brown fingers of his hands folded together over his chest.

The old man tried to remember the face of this son as a young man. His skin had been deep rose-brown, his hair so black a blue sheen glinted over it. He had strong cheekbones and a high arched nose and sinewy arms and strong legs.

Now the face seemed muted and blurred, the mouth marked by dissolute circles, the cheeks and throat more grimly scarred than the old sun dance scars on Charley Hawk's chest. He reached out and smoothed a fold of cloth away from his son's cheek and then sought vainly to rub away the stains of rouge. The flesh felt like coarse stone and would not yield to his touch.

He sat down in a chair beside the casket. He could see his son's face in profile and he studied it in wonder for a long time. He closed his eyes and for a moment he dozed, and in his sleep heard a mare whinny and a stallion answer with a great shrilling. He rose with a start and leaned over the casket. After a moment he spoke with his lips close to his son's face.

"I tell you again, my son," he said. "This land belonged to our people long before the white man came plundering and seeking gold. There was nothing in your blood of which to be ashamed."

He moved away and returned, his eyes holding to the dead man's face as if they were teeth.

"You were impatient with the tribe and the land," he said. "You scorned the plow and the seed. The world of the white men drew you and like your brother you tried to become white yourself. But not all eagles can become ravens."

He stood motionless then for a long time, the flame of the candle sweeping shadows across his face.

"There are no drums to beat for you now, my son," he said. "No painted shields and lances to wave for you in the air. No songs to be sung at your pyre."

He sat down again beside the casket. He stared at the great veins in the backs of his hands, dark and hard, smoke-dried like old meat.

"If I had been born thirty years before," he said, "and you had been born my son then, you might have become a warrior, one of the great men of the tribes like Black Moon or Crow King or Spotted Eagle. You might have ridden a fine buckskin yearling and followed the winter frost cloud of a buffalo herd."

He leaned his back against the wood of the chair. He stared at the white cold ceiling overhead.

"You might have known the scent of sweetgrass and sage burning in the council lodge," he said. "You might have hunted the swift antelope showing their white rumps in flight and heard the fall whistle of the mating elk. You might have taken as a wife a daughter of a chief with bracelets of copper and silver on her strong arms. She would have borne you many sons who would have grown up with deep chests and sinewy arms and they would have ridden the prairies at your side. All this you might have known."

He rose then and slowly went to open the small box he had carried in with him. There were ashes in the box and a long glistening eagle feather and a slim handled knife. He scattered the ashes across his own head and shoulders and he carefully placed the eagle feather beside his son's head so that it rose like a warrior's plume from his hair.

He picked up the knife and ran the blade around his left forefinger until it drew a thin line of blood. Then he sat down and put his hands over his son's folded hands. He leaned his head against the rim of the casket and closed his eyes. He began to chant softly, a chant that became a low terrible wail.

¶ I knew a blind girl once, and although we were not lovers, she helped me renew a delight in touch and a wonder in life. Many readers have written me they found this story moving, but a dear friend, whose son has been blind almost from birth, who taught herself Braille and who teaches classes to the blind, felt the story was not totally realistic. She told me the blind are not as graceful as I portrayed the girl to be, and she should know.

If my portrait of the girl is not as authentic as it might be, the writer is a genuine and impeccable creation. He is the fool I was, the fool I am, and the fool I will always be.

The Eyes of Love

Autumn came and passed quickly that year. Almost overnight the last dry, brown leaves burned in the twilight street fires. The nights began to turn cold, and in my basement flat the steam sputtered and hissed through the overhead radiators. I pushed my bed away from the window in the bedroom and pulled a woolen blanket from the shelf in the closet.

I didn't really mind the winter. I preferred it to the false faces of spring and summer, the ephemeral masks of buds and flowers that concealed the desolation underneath. The season I liked best of all was autumn, when the air smelled definably of death, and the declining days wore their proper raiment.

I was a writer of stories and a couple of novels that had been reviewed well in the *New York Times*. They produced a small spasm of activity in the book-review columns and a sparse display with my picture in one of the downtown book stores. Then, like the tide coming in across a beach littered with debris, the cut-glass fragments of my fame were once more submerged in anonymity.

But writing was still the only thing I wanted to do, even though I had realized years before how senseless was a writer's dream that he could, within the pages of a book, cultivate a garden beyond the darkness of his death. In addition, the stories provided me a meager living and saved me from forty hours a week in another man's vineyard.

Each day I rose early in the morning and slipped into worn sneakers and old pants. I enjoyed a pot of hot, rousing coffee and then wrote at my typewriter till afternoon, when the children broke loose in squealing joy from school.

There was a basement flat similar to my own across the narrow court, and it was occupied by a piano teacher I had never seen. Each day after school her students banged out a shrill and discordant series of scales. To evade their wretched hammering I walked down to the corner tavern and lingered for a couple of hours over beer.

In the twilight I returned to my flat and shaved and dressed in more formal clothes. I ate a steak in a neighborhood restaurant and marinated it with a glass or two of red wine. When I sold a story and had a new check in my pocket, I treated myself to a full bottle of good wine. Then, with my normally somber nature submerged beneath the laughter of the grape, I would ardently search out some young lady in a tavern and tempt her to join my celebration. This was a kind of gaiety that could not survive the sober dawn, and in the morning I had a mountain of a head and a tongue like the moss on a rock.

It was on such a night in that autumn, preparing for a small celebration because the check for a sale had been meager, that I passed the piano teacher's flat. Through a partially raised shade I saw that she was a young woman with dark, long hair sitting on a bench before an upright piano.

Later in the evening, after I had consumed a half-bottle of wine, I thought of her again. She had been attractive and young. Each afternoon her talentless students drove me from my rooms, and that seemed a legitimate grievance on which to base a visit. I took along what was left of the bottle of wine.

When I reached her apartment, the shades were all drawn closed. I thought she might be asleep or out and then I saw a shadow of movement along the rim of a shade. I rang her bell.

In a moment the door opened just a few inches and I heard the jangle of a chain.

"I beg your pardon," I said, and couldn't see her face. "I live in the basement flat across the court. I was just passing and felt it was time to introduce myself."

She was silent and wary for a moment. "It's a little late, isn't it?" she asked.

"We are artists," I said amiably. "You a musician and I a writer. We understand that time is the greatest irrelevance of all."

I couldn't be sure in the shadows but it seemed to me she smiled. "I have heard you typing for hours at a time."

"I have heard your students at their lessons," I said. "An unusually talented group."

"I'm sorry if they disturb your work."

"Not at all," I said, "but I would be interested in knowing whether they use hammers on the keys?"

She laughed a pleasant sound that dispersed some of the wariness.

"My name is Pete Zachary," I said, "and perhaps we could visit for a few moments."

She hesitated a moment longer and then made up her mind. She closed the door and drew off the chain and then opened the door again. With a triumphant swagger I stepped inside her apartment.

I followed her into the living room. There was only a small lamp burning on a table in the corner, and most of the room was draped in shadow. The upright piano took up almost one entire wall, and on a couch across from the piano reclined a gray, furry cat that regarded me with ominous yellow eyes.

Off the living room was a small kitchen similar to my own with a table and two chairs and an assortment of plates and glasses in an open cabinet. There was a large shelf along the wall decorated with several heads of sculpture, carved and polished heads of men and women, that seemed suspended without bodies on the wall.

"My name is Andrea," she said, "and the cat is Emily." At the sound of her name the cat rose and stretched indolently and then leaped with a sinister warning to the floor.

"Pleased to meet you both," I said and sat down.

Andrea sat down on an ottoman across the room from the lamp so that she was darkly concealed in shadow. From as much as I could discern, she was an attractive girl, slender-bodied with good legs. Her hair framed her face and the skin of her cheeks gleamed pale in the shadows and gave an impression of ghostly beauty. But the most striking thing about her were her hands. They were pale, paler than the hue of her face, and the fingers flowed from her slim wrists as if they were long-petaled flowers.

"What kind of things do you write?"

"Short stories mostly," I said. "A couple of novels that did nothing. My creations disappear into the water like small pebbles or finish on a table of remainders at forty-nine cents apiece."

"Are you a beatnik or an angry young man?" she asked with a trace of humor in her voice.

"I'm not revolting against a thing," I said, and the wine loosened my tongue. "All is vanity and vexation of the spirit. Nothing is worth fighting about." I shook my head. "What about you? What makes a young, attractive girl become a teacher to a bunch of piano butchers?"

"That is the way I make my living," she said, "and they're not all butchers. One or two are even very good."

"Things are tough all over," I said and then realized I was still clutching the half-full bottle of wine. "I was taking some wine home. Would you like a small glass?"

"No, thank you," she said, becoming wary again. "But you have a glass if you like."

I walked toward the cabinet. "This place is laid out exactly like mine," I said. There was a lamp on the cabinet and

I switched it on to locate a glass. I poured an extra glass and carried it to her.

"You really should try a sip," I said. "It's good sauterne." She raised her head as I reached her. The lamp I had turned on glowed light across her face. She stood staring at a point just beyond my shoulder, not looking at the glass or me, and I realized that she was blind.

I was fiercely shaken and, as if she understood, she spoke quickly to cover my disorder. "I will try a sip," she said and raised her hand to take the glass from me without a trace of fumbling.

"I'll have a glass myself," I said, "and then I'd better leave. It is late, and I shouldn't really have disturbed you." I drank my wine quickly.

I hesitated a moment and then walked toward the door. She rose from the ottoman and followed me. We stood for an instant by the door. "I am sorry about the students," she said softly. "I'll make sure my windows are closed."

"That's all right," I said quickly. "Don't worry about me. I'm through writing by then anyway."

I opened the door and walked out. She was a dark, slender figure against the light, her face concealed again in shadow.

"Goodnight, Pete," she said in a calm and pleasant voice.

"Goodnight, Andrea," I said. She closed the door quietly.

Instead of returning to the bar, I went home. Coldly sober by that time, I mourned the impulse that had sent me to her door. If the world were full of grief and affliction, there was no need for a man to search it out. I felt sorry for her, but there was nothing I could do. I went to bed.

In the first total snap of darkness as I closed the lamp, I wondered what her life was like, denied the sight of faces, figures, fruits, and flowers, the red of a sunset, and the green of grass. After a while I was grateful when I could make out dim familiar objects in my room. But there was also a strange serenity about her that I found moving in recollection, the loveliness of her pale, slim fingers and the softness of her voice. It took me a long time to fall asleep.

The rain started the following Friday night and kept falling all day Saturday until late afternoon. I wrote for a while and then sat by the window smoking a cigarette, watching the water strike the streets and sweep in swift currents to the sewers.

I was hungry, and there was nothing in the place to eat. I put on a raincoat and an old felt hat and ran to the corner to a Chinese restaurant. I ordered a large carton of chow mein and carried it straight to Andrea's door as if I had meant to do that all along.

She answered the door in slacks and blouse, a thin yellow ribbon holding back her fine, black hair. I had the feeling even before I spoke that she knew it was me.

"Andrea," I said, "I've got enough chow mein for two. You interested?"

She smiled and motioned me in quickly out of the rain. I hesitated. "I'm dripping wet," I said.

"Give me your things," she laughed. "I'll hang them in the bathroom to dry."

While she took my wet things inside, I unlaced my sodden shoes and stepped out of them.

"Bring the chow mein in here," she called from the kitchen. I crossed the room, and on the couch Emily somberly turned her head and looked at me with her baleful yellow eyes.

We carried two plates of chow mein back to the living room.

"If you don't mind sitting on the floor," Andrea said, "we can use the coffee table under the window."

"I always eat better on the floor," I said.

She sat down, folding her legs lithely beneath her. I sat down across from her. The window was a square of gray light, and the rain cracked against the panes of glass.

I watched her as we ate. Now that she was visible in a

better light, I saw that she was very lovely. The ribbon held her hair, but a single strand had come loose and hung down across her cheek. Even as I noticed, she raised her hand and swept the fallen lock back into place.

"This is wonderful," she said between swallows. "Much better than the hamburger I was going to fry."

Emily came slowly from the couch to sniff the plates. She rubbed her furry back in silent appeal against Andrea's leg.

"Do you think it would bother her?" Andrea asked.

"She may never drink milk again," I said, "but forever after demand pekoe tea with fortune cookies."

"I'll chance that." Andrea laughed and gave her what was left in her plate.

"I'm sorry about the other night," I said, "busting in here like I did half-tanked."

She smiled slightly and bent her head to conceal the smile. "You were so surprised," she said. "You came in here like a jolly bulldog and left like a remorseful Chihuahua."

"I was full of wine," I said ruefully.

She drew up her legs and clasped her arms around her knees. Her face changed under a pensive and solitary withdrawal.

"People are always much more sensitive about blindness than the blind," she said. "When you are blind you get used to it."

"How long has it been for you?" I asked.

"About twelve years now," she said. "I spent eight of those years in an institute for the blind. I came out four years ago and took some college work back home and then came to Chicago and started giving piano lessons to support myself."

"What do they teach you in an institute?"

She smiled pensively again, and her nose twitched in recollection as if she had bitten on a sour plum. "You learn to find the end of a piece of meat with your fork and cut it off with your knife. You learn about social graces and adjustment to society. You learn to try never to fumble because any fumbling you do will make people pity you and remind them you are blind." She paused and grimaced. "But all that sounds very scientific and orderly. What it comes down to is that you learn what it is to be a donkey in a world of horses."

"The things most people take for granted," I said, "must be the things you have to learn all over again."

"The beginning is the worst," she said and she seemed to be listening to the sound of the rain against the glass. "It happened to me when I was ten years old after meningitis. Emily Dickinson wrote of dying, and years later when I read her poems I understood that is the way it is; as if a fly came with an uncertain, stumbling buzz between the light and you, and then the windows close, and then you cannot see." She shifted her body slightly on the floor. "Do you know Emily Dickinson's poems?"

"Some of them," I said.

"I have all her poems in Braille," she said. "They don't consider her too fashionable anymore, but she does well for me." She stroked the cat, who raised her head and stared ominously at me. "Emily here is named after her." For a moment she did not speak. "Now what about you?" she said. "Have you been writing long?"

"Since the Korean War," I said. "I was going to do a great war novel, better than Shaw and Mailer, but it never worked out. I worked on a newspaper for a while and wrote stories at night. About four years ago I sold my first story and published my first novel about a year later. I've managed to make enough by writing to eat and pay the rent and get drunk every once in a while."

"On wine?" she asked.

"On wine," I said. "It's more genteel than Scotch or gin."

"Don't you have a girl?" she asked.

"I was engaged to a girl right after the war," I said. "She broke it off because her parents felt I was indolent, lazy, and shiftless because I wouldn't take a steady job. She agreed with them, and they were all right."

"Where is she now?"

"Who knows? Married to another poor slob and making his life as happy as she would probably have made mine."

"You sound so old and weary," she said.

"In this gilded age," I said, "you don't have to grow old to feel weary. Even the young perch on their ash heaps and wait like Job for the next disaster." I paused to light a cigarette. "Where you from?" I asked.

"A little town in Kansas," she said. "My father was a pharmacist there and lived with my mother in a frame house with a long porch that I was born in."

The room had grown darker, and I could barely make out the white fabric of her blouse. The rain grew faint and left only the sound of water gurgling in the gutters.

"How did you happen to come here alone?" I said.

"Whenever my mother kissed me I could feel the tears on her cheeks," she said. "And every time my father walked into my room I could sense his grief and despair. They loved me very much, but they were full of pity and wouldn't let me live. I write them that I am living with three other girls, gay and friendly girls, who take good care of me."

"You've got guts," I said.

"I'm not at all brave," she said with a trace of scorn for herself in her voice. "I'm not always cheerful either. I left home simply because I couldn't bear their pity. There was even a boy who took me to dances, and his nobility rose like wind from his pores, and everybody in town praised him for dating a poor, blind girl."

"You're a good-looking girl," I said. "Maybe you weren't fair to him."

"There have been a few others like him," she said defiantly. "Men intent on a quick moment of pleasure and willing to concede that sometimes a woman has no need of sight. But I don't need that kind of love."

A silence settled between us. The room was completely dark by then. I felt a vague unrest and moved to rise.

"Let me turn on a light," she said. "You'll stumble and fall."

She rose and crossed the dark room swiftly and switched on a lamp. The light hurt my eyes for a moment. She stood there, slender in her slacks and blouse, her face a pale oval within the frame of her hair.

"Will you read me something you've written?" she asked.

"Sure," I said, "but don't expect Emily Dickinson."

She brought me my coat and hat, and we stood a moment by the door.

"You're tall," she said slowly. "You have a strong voice, a little weary sometimes, but with a good tone. What do you really look like?"

"You'd never mistake me for a movie star," I said. "My face is what a pulp writer would call weatherbeaten."

"I can imagine you any way I wish," she said. She smiled and extended her hands toward me. Her fingertips made a soft and subtle contact with my cheeks. I had never known that a woman's hands could be that gentle. They touched my temples and moved across my eyes and slipped down my cheeks. "Your eyes are set in deep hollows," she said, and there was a look of waiting and listening on her face. "I think your nose is too broad. Your upper lip is full, and you have a sharp cleft in your chin and you need a shave."

The touch of her fingers carried a pressing warmth through my body, and I felt an urgent longing to touch her. I bent and kissed her then, first on the forehead, lightly and with gentleness, and then with urgency, hard on her lovely lips. When I reached out to hold her, she pulled away.

"What do you want?" she asked, and a strange hardness had entered her voice. "What do you want?"

"Andrea," I said, "listen . . ."

"Do you love me already?" she said, and there was no mistaking her baleful mockery. "Is it desire you feel without love, or just pity for the poor little blind music teacher?"

"I just wanted to kiss you," I said. "Emily Dickinson would have understood."

A shadow of remorse swept her face, and then she shook it off. "Thanks anyway for the chop suey."

"Chow mein," I said.

"All right," she said and relented slightly with a trace of a smile.

"Some day this next week," I said, "I'll borrow a car and we'll go for a drive."

She was silent for a moment. "Maybe," she said finally. "We'll see."

I had never put credence in the myth that love might begin at first sight, by a look or by the touch of a hand. And I had always mocked those sonnets of passion that mediocre poets wrote in flame. But that winter, those days and nights of cold and snow, I woke in the morning without a sense of burden in the beginning of another day. For the first time in years I could endure the twilight becoming darkness without a wavering of my spirit.

Andrea and I took long walks together in the park. We sat closely together on a bench beneath the black trunk of a cold, bare tree. When she listened raptly to the scurrying of a squirrel, or ran her hands along the hard, frozen bark of a tree, or felt a change in the wind I could not hear, it was as if we were both young again, on an earth that still retained its magic. When I was with her it was strangely true that all things recaptured their edges, became sharp for me where they had been blurred.

"Andrea, do you believe in God?" I asked her one day in the park.

"Yes," she said quietly.

"Blindness has not made you bitter?"

"If I had not become blind," she answered softly, "I might have lived my years taking the earth for granted. My blindness has made me search again to discover all things anew. Is not God somewhere in this search?"

There were the evenings in her flat when I lay on the couch while she played a melancholy sonata or a gay song that echoed the wild whirling of figures in a lovers' dance. We ate and drank together, and the stain of wine glistened upon her lips, and it was true that she came upon the desert of my days as if she were a flower.

But there was always a wariness in the hours we spent together, an evident fear in her at what was growing between us. When I tried to kiss her she drew back in guarded restraint, so that I grew apprehensive, too, and all that winter did not speak of the way I felt. Until one night, one night when I could not contain myself any longer, I broke the silence that held us apart.

She had moved from the bench of the piano and had come over to where I lay on the couch. She sat on the floor with her head near my knees, and the moon fell across her face, a white and glistening vision. I touched her hair, felt the fine strands tingle beneath my palms, and understood how aware she had made me of touch. The thought of having her as my wife suddenly possessed me with a wild sweetness such as I had never known.

"I love you, Andrea," I said.

She withdrew her head from near my knees. Her open fingers which had been lying on the cloth near my hands flew back to her lap.

"There is an old folk legend," I said, "that speaks of a blind man joined with one who is lame. They journey together until they find the healing waters and are both restored."

"I don't want to talk of love," she said. She rose from the floor and went to stand beside the window.

"Are you going to spend the rest of your life alone?" I asked. "In this little flat, in these dark rooms, teaching piano to unhappy children?"

"I can look after myself," she said. "I don't need anyone to look after me."

"We all need somebody," I said.

"I can look after myself," she said, and the words came ripped from her flesh. "I don't need pity."

She moved away from the window, away from me, into the darkness at the other end of the room. She sealed herself against me, retreated into silence that she wore as if it were armor. And I was left alone in the beam of the futile and bright moon that seemed to be hanging just above the roof of the building across the street.

I did not see Andrea for several weeks after that night. I wrote hard, harder than I had in years, and drank much more, and spent a good deal of time walking alone in the desolate park. I felt her everywhere, and yet pride and anger kept me from her door. In the afternoon, when the children played their scales at her piano, it filled me with a fierce melancholia. Sometimes walking past her flat at night I paused in the darkness and waited for a quick, furtive glimpse of her within the basement rooms.

The first traces of spring appeared in the city. Great winds swept the streets at night, and in the parks and gardens the earth stirred and waited. I listened to the wind shake the panes of my windows and knew Andrea must have been listening to the wild wind as well. In the morning the sun felt a shade warmer. Then, one day in early April, a sparrow perched on my sill and in the quick flutter of its jubilant step I knew the spring had come.

Near the end of April on an afternoon, while leaving my flat to go for a beer, I passed a small moving truck parked outside in the street. As it pulled away I noticed an upright piano secured with rope and cloth. Under a sudden apprehension, I looked at Andrea's windows, and the shades were up and the curtains were gone. I went down the stairs and tried the door. When it opened I walked inside. I called her name, and there was no answer. The furniture was gone, and the rooms were empty. I turned in despair to leave, thinking of ways to pursue the truck, when a small, furry body moved beside the stove in the kitchen and caught my eye. Emily came slowly over to look at me, and I knew that Andrea would be back.

I waited until twilight fell. The street lights went on and threw sharp beams of light through the uncurtained windows across the bare wood floor. I found some milk in the icebox and poured a saucer for Emily, but she rejected my offering.

It must have been some time later when I heard the car outside. I looked out the window and saw the taxi from which Andrea had emerged. A moment later she entered the apartment. I made no sound, and yet she knew at once I was there.

"Pete," she said, and I couldn't understand whether there was sorrow or gladness in her voice.

"You were running away," I said bitterly. "You were going to leave and say nothing to me."

She made a helpless motion with her hands.

"Then go, damn you," I said. "I understand you now. When you say you don't want pity it is really pity that you want. You want to remain alone because then people will always pity you."

"You have no right," she said, and her voice was a thin, tight whisper, "no right to say that to me."

"Emily has more courage than you," I said savagely. "She at least goes prowling in the midnight alleys and comes back in the dawn with her fur ruffled and shreds of skin under her claws. But you are afraid of love."

She twisted her body as if to flee, and then something made her turn back, and the sight of her cold white cheeks swept the anger from my body.

"When I found you my life was nothing," I said. "You taught me a new way of seeing a tree and a flower. A new way of understanding the earth and hearing the wind. You taught me that all life is connected by the touch of a hand. Don't take that from me now."

For a long moment she did not move. She seemed to be holding her breath. Then she walked slowly to where I stood and raised her face to mine and lifted her hands to my cheeks. Her breath came out in a long shaken sigh. She did not speak, but for the first time touched me in a fierce caress. She touched my eyes and touched my lips and her hands trembled with love. And for the first time since I was a child, I cried again for the great wonder and beauty of life.

¶ On rereading, this story doesn't impress me. I have allowed it to remain in the collection because if critics are looking for weakness and fallibility in my work, they might fruitfully probe this story. On the other hand, if they are enthusiastic about all the other stories in the collection, then, in the name of decency and through a recognition that no human being is unflawed, they might simply ignore it.

The Return of Katerina

In April of that year, Paul Brademas had been dead two years. His widow, Katerina, lived with his father, Lycurgus, in a small apartment above their tavern.

After his son's death, Lycurgus wished to sell the tavern. He was almost sixty himself and wearied of the long hours on his feet. In addition he did not think it proper that a young attractive woman such as Katerina should work in the smoky room of boisterous men.

But Katerina insisted they keep the tavern which brought in a good profit. When she worked hard there was little time left to brood upon the death of her husband. She also felt it provided Lycurgus a meeting place for a few old friends with whom he could sit in the evening.

In the beginning Katerina's grief for her husband was a wild despair. For a while the memory of their lovemaking was something she could recall at will. At those times she felt her breath become short and her breasts grow taut. And so strong was the love she held for him that she could almost feel again his hands across her body and the strength of his arms about her waist.

But time passed and the seasons changed. In the winter the snow piled in drifts before the tavern. Katerina would rise early to clean the walk before the old man rose. When he came downstairs he would grumble that shoveling was man's work and take the shovel from her hands.

In the spring of the second year after her husband's

death, a strange restlessness possessed Katerina. She was no longer satisfied to recall her husband in dreams. She walked in the glittering twilight and felt envy growing in her heart at the sight of lovers in the park.

She visited her husband's grave and placed fresh flowers upon the mound of earth. In those moments under the sighing trees she wept and swore eternal love. She waited for some sign that he had heard and understood but the earth made no gesture of redemption.

In the evenings in the tavern she no longer took pleasure in the wild laughter of the men. She became snappish and cross. Her temper flared quickly and she acquired a reputation for an acid tongue. Lycurgus was concerned for her and tried to ease her labor in different ways thinking that perhaps she was working too hard.

After closing he sent her to bed at once and swept the floor himself and locked the door. The only person left inside was his old friend, Zakinthákis, veteran of ten thousand drinking bouts and three wars. A wise rascal of a man who counted his life of fighting and wenching well spent. Lycurgus disapproved of his friend's morals but enjoyed his company.

After counting the cash Lycurgus took a final glass of mastiha to the table for himself and another for Zakinthákis. They toasted each other solemnly.

"I am troubled over Katerina," the old man told Zakinthákis. "Nothing seems to please her. She has grown as peevish as an old woman."

Zakinthákis looked into his glass of mastiha and a faint zestful smile curled his thin lips. He admired the fine lush body of Katerina and knew the reason for her distemper. He wished he could still have been the one to comfort her.

"When Paul was alive," Lycurgus said sadly, "she was not like that. They loved each other dearly." He wiped a stray tear from his eye. "It must be her grief," he said. "She still mourns for him."

Zakinthákis sipped at his mastiha and marveled at how a

man could have lived as many years as Lycurgus and still understand so little about women.

"Grief is a terrible thing," he said somberly, and within him he laughed because he knew that when he died a thousand women would grieve for him . . . but not for long. Then because the long evening of drinking had dulled him slightly, he spoke without thinking. "She needs a lover," he said.

Lycurgus sat shocked and rooted to his chair. His lips moved and no words came. Then he found his voice and let out an angry roar.

"Devil!" he shouted. "Lecher and animal out of darkness! Have you lost your mind?"

Zakinthákis realized his mistake and sighed. He rose heavily to his feet to leave. Lycurgus followed him raging to the door.

"You dare speak of my son's wife in that way!" he cried. "Get out, you stepson of some unholy devil!"

Long after Zakinthákis had left, Lycurgus still paced the tavern and hurled curses upon his friend's head. Each time he considered the outrage, his blood flamed anew.

Finally he turned off the last lights and went upstairs. Outside the bedroom of Katerina he listened for a moment at her door. There was no sound from her room and he went to bed.

For a long time he could not sleep. The murmur of the night came through his window. He was restlessly aware of his age and his inevitable death. The years had swept by so quickly. He had never traveled, never cared for cards or drink, and had been shy with girls. A day came when he married because he could not bear his loneliness any longer. His wife had been a dark and thin woman who wore black for mourning all her life. Rarely would she suffer Lycurgus to caress her and from one of these uncertain, unsatisfying unions their only child had been born. But the child was little comfort to Lycurgus because of the domination of the mother. In the boy's seventeenth year, his mother died, accepting death as gratefully as a suppliant. Lycurgus could not grieve for her and accepted joyously the return of his son. When Paul married Katerina he wept for their happiness and for his own good fortune. He envisioned the day that grandchildren would scamper around him. But then the young man had fallen sick, and after a short shocking illness had died. As if his mother, dark and brooding from the grave, had called to him to join her.

Lycurgus tossed in helpless despair. Then he remembered Katerina in the room beside his own. Her nearness was a comfort to him, and he slept.

Spring passed into summer. The heat came early in the day and twilight brought no relief. Along the street on which they lived men and women sat before the stores, fanning themselves until long past midnight. The boys and girls ran by squealing to slap one another's bottoms in the dark alleys.

After closing the tavern Lycurgus and Katerina walked for a while in the park. On the grass in long uneven rows, men, women and children slept under the sky. A great sound of whispering, like the drone of countless crickets, rose from the dark and hidden groves.

Back in their flat with the open windows providing no relief from the heat, Lycurgus lay awake in the dark listening to Katerina in her room. He heard her talking to herself, and though he could not make out the words he heard the bitterness in her voice. Once he thought he heard her weeping, and because he felt she wept for her dead, he cried with her, silently, so she would not hear.

On a night in August a group of strangers came to the tavern. They were loud and bold young men, blond Norsemen, and they drank great quantities of beer. Countless times during the evening Katerina carried trays of beer to their table. They laughed and teased her and a bright flush of pink appeared in her cheeks. They finally left, holding one another up, and the bawdy sound of their voices could be heard rioting from the street.

The next night one of them, a blond young giant with big hands, returned alone. He sat in a corner and did not sing or carry on. Katerina served him several times and lingered at his table.

From that night on the blond stranger came every evening. Whenever he could, Lycurgus served the man whose light pale eyes seemed full of menace. Lycurgus was reminded of tales he had heard as a child of the villages raided by the pillaging Turks. The burning of houses and the screaming of women.

An evening came when several hours before closing, Katerina told him she was not well. He suggested she go at once to bed but she wished to walk alone for a while and he let her go. It was not until she had left that he noticed for the first time in several weeks that the blond stranger was not at his table in the corner. A cold fear enveloped him but he remembered Katerina's sacred allegiance to her dead and suppressed his apprehension.

Summer passed and the first winds of autumn swept the scent of burning leaves along the street. The days grew shorter and there was a strange still beauty in the crisp nights.

With the passing of summer, Katerina took on a new grace. Lycurgus marveled at the change. She had thrown off the terrible melancholia and once again enjoyed the laughter in the tavern. Her black hair gleamed lustrous and alive and her body once more appeared lithe and supple. He heard her sing in her room at night.

In the morning as she cooked him breakfast, he basked in her radiance and marveled at how beautiful she had become once again. He watched her eat with pleasure, the ripe soft lips parting slightly and the small pieces of food going between them. Her cheeks were as soft and unblemished as those of a child and the color of her flesh was the cool, transparent whiteness of the foam on new milk.

When they had finished she rose from the table and carried the dishes to the sink. She spoke softly with her back to him.

"Papa, I am going away," she said. "I am going to the country for a little while. Now when the leaves are changing and the earth is so beautiful."

"Going away?" Lycurgus said in alarm. "Katerina, you cannot go away alone!"

"For just a little while," she said gently. "I am weary suddenly of the city and the noise and the disorder."

"It is not right that you go alone," Lycurgus said. "We will close the tavern. We will go away together so that I can look after you."

"I wish to go alone," she said, and then she added quickly, "You do not like to travel. You would come only because you are concerned for me." She bent over the dishes in the sink. "Zakinthákis can help you in the tavern. I will be gone only a little while."

"Zakinthákis!" the old man cried. "I would sooner ask help of the devil!"

"Then find someone else to help you," she said and there was a firmness in her voice.

She left the following Friday and was gone for almost two weeks. Lycurgus missed her terribly. At night he could not bear to go to their rooms and stayed downstairs in the tavern long after closing. In loneliness and desperation he accepted the return of Zakinthákis and drank with him for hours.

"She could have waited until I died," he complained bitterly to his friend. "She could have taken her vacation then."

Zakinthákis merely sighed.

At the end of the second week Katerina returned. On a night after Lycurgus had closed the tavern and sat drinking with Zakinthákis.

He had turned off most of the lights and when he heard the door he thought he had forgotten to lock it and that some patron had entered. Then he heard her voice speak his name and a great gladness leaped in his heart. He rose quickly from the table.

"Katerina!" he cried. "Katerina!"

It was not until then that he saw she was not alone. Only when his eyes became accustomed to the shadows about the door, did he recognize the tall blond stranger.

A terrible distress ran riot in his body. He wanted to cry out but no sound passed his lips. He stared at the silent figure beside Katerina. Never had he hated a man more. He would not let himself think but only let the hot flow of hate sweep over him in waves.

"Papa," Katerina said, and her cheeks gleamed pale in the shadows. "This is my husband, Edwin Larsen."

Then Lycurgus cried out. A cry of pain and anguish. A cry for his dead son and for deceit and the fiendish heart of a woman. He burned suddenly under a white hot flame.

"Thief!" he said to Edwin Larsen, and smoke and fury curled off his tongue. "Vandal, bastard out of darkness!" His voice rose. "I should have killed you the first night I saw you!"

"Papa, try to understand," Katerina said. "I loved Paul very much. You know I loved him." Her voice rose and broke. "But you cannot love the dead forever."

"Not forever!" Lycurgus said and he spoke to her in angry bitterness. "Only two years and you forsake his memory."

"I loved him," Katerina said. "When he died I could have died with him. But I lived and in the summer I saw the new buds spring to life on the trees and heard the lovers whispering in the dark groves."

"Silence!" Lycurgus cried. "I do not wish to hear your shame!"

Katerina turned and reached back for her husband and brought him into the light. "Papa," she said, "Papa, do you want me back? Tell me now. If you want me back I will come back."

Lycurgus looked from her to the stranger. "Alone," he said. "I want you back alone."

"I cannot come alone," she said. "I am married now."

"You are married to my son."

"He is dead," Katerina said.

"I do not want you then!" Lycurgus cried. "I do not want you then!"

Through a mist of grief he saw her turn. Slim beside the tall Norseman, she walked to the door. Her steps made a slight fading sound as she reached the street.

When he could hear her no longer he turned fiercely on Zakinthákis. "Get out," he said. "Leave me alone."

Zakinthákis moved slowly to the door. He paused with his hand on the knob. "I am going," he said. "I will tell you something first, old friend."

"Leave me alone!" Lycurgus cried.

"You do not weep for your son," Zakinthákis said, and his voice was filled with pity and sadness. "You weep for yourself."

And in that instant after the door closed and he was left alone, in that moment of dark revelation, he heard his voice cry her name in the silence. "Katerina!" and only the raven-winged vision of his wife heard and returned to comfort him.

¶ When this story was published, in 1958 in *The Atlantic*, the magazine received a batch of outraged letters from indignant readers who felt the esteemed periodical had abandoned a tradition of respectability by publishing such indecent trash.

How times have changed! Through a bloody war, three assassinations, the immorality of Watergate, boundaries of taste have been expanded to include the powerful books of Henry Miller and the films of the flexuous Linda Lovelace. Against this climate of almost total freedom as to what can be read and seen, the assault of Mike Larakis on the formidable ramparts of the Widow Angela creaks with the shuffle of a Victorian romance.

Yet I think the humor in the story saves it from being dated. Laughter, since the plays of Aristophanes, has a timeless and durable quality.

Courtship of the Blue Widow

Something happened to me the first time I saw the Widow Angela in the grocery of old Mantaris. More than just the restless stirring of flesh a man feels in the presence of a lovely woman. I was bothered as I am often bothered when I see a woman I like I cannot at once touch. After she walked out with the bread and cheese she had bought, I asked old Mantaris about her.

He rubbed his big knuckled fingers across the leathery skin of his cheeks. He shook his head sadly. He drew a long breath and sighed.

"She is a woman, that one," he said. "She was born and reared in the mountains of the old country. A grown woman at fourteen. She came to this country and married a giant of a man who worked in produce. Then her man died."

"How long has her man been dead?" I asked.

He shook his head slowly, trying to remember.

"Two years ago," he said. "Maybe a little longer. He was a Spartan. A big man with the arms of a wrestler. She has been in mourning ever since."

Two years and maybe longer. Too long for a woman built

as the Widow Angela was built to set a seal upon her heart.

Then I understood what had bothered me about her. She was tall and dark with dark hair pinned back into a prim bun. Her face was pale and clean of powder or rouge. Her lips were full but untouched by lipstick. The black dress she wore was a plain dark folding of cloth high across her breasts and full across her thighs. She was without any of the artifices women use to point up their womanliness. In some strange way this made her more beautiful than any woman I had ever seen.

"She sleeps in a widow's bed," Mantaris said, and his voice shook with woe. "Her good husband sleeps in the cold earth." He paused and licked his thin dried lips. "I saw her once at a picnic with him some years ago. She danced in a line of women, taller than any other. That day she was not pale-cheeked as she is now but hot with life. Not one of your withered city women but a mountain woman wild with the flow of heroic blood."

"You are a patriarch now," I said. "A recorder of history and a recounter of legends. Stop bagging your bread and slicing your cheese long enough to advise me where she lives."

Suddenly one of his big long fingers pointed straight at my head like a gun. His leathery cheeks quivered and his eyes burned. "I know who you are," he said. "You are a Turk bent upon pillage and rape!" He clenched his fist and beat his chest. "You do not see the tragic nobleness of her grief. To see her now and remember her as she was hurts me here." He touched the region of his heart. His voice sharpened with contempt. "You are touched much further down."

"My friend," I said gently. "You do me an injustice. I too believe in the nobility of grief. Remember, I too am a Greek."

He shrugged and rippled noise through his lips. "It is true you are Greek," he said. "But there are Greeks and Greeks. Some are the descendants of lions, and others . . ."

I put my finger expectantly to my nose.

"Others come from goats," he said.

"She is a lovely woman," I said.

The hard lines of his face softened. "Yes . . ." he said.
"Yes."

"A face like Helen to launch a thousand ships," I said.

He shook his head approvingly. "Yes," he said.

"She has breasts like great cabbages," I said.

He almost leaped to the ceiling. When he came down
with his face flaming he slammed his open palm upon the
counter. "Your head is a cabbage!" he yelled. "You have no
respect!"

"You are right," I said. "My old dried-up friend, you are
right."

He looked at me scornfully.

"What can you know," he said. "What can a young goat
know of dignity and beauty?"

"A woman is going to waste while you call me names," I
said. "I leave you to your cabbages."

"Then leave your head!" he shouted. "I'll weigh it with
the rest."

I waved back from the door.

The next day was Sunday. All the night before I had
tossed restlessly with dreams. I dreamed of the pale-faced
Widow Angela whose body looked long asleep. There were
fine cabbages in my dreams and an old toothless lion who
guarded the gate to the patch.

In the early morning I shaved carefully and dressed and
left my rooms. I crossed the square past the closed stores. I
went to the church beside the Legion hall. I waited outside.
From within I could hear the full deep tones of the organ
and the chanting of the priest.

I waited there until the services ended. Until the doors
were opened and the first men and women came out. When
I saw Mantaris I called to him. He looked about and blinked
in the sunlight and then saw me and came closer.

"Watch for her," I said. "Watch for the widow."

He looked at me in shock and surprise. "You are a crazy man!" he said. "Is your head on straight or do I call for help?"

"If you don't introduce me," I said, "I will accost her myself, here in front of the church."

"You would not dare!" he said, and then breathing hard he shook his head slowly. "You would. You are part Turk."

Then I saw her and my fingers tightened again around his arm. She came out into the sunlight and the black dress she wore saddened my heart. She wore a small dark hat over her dark hair and her cheeks were still pale and she walked stiffly without notice of those who walked around her.

The old man trembled at my side.

"God help me," he said, and he crossed himself quickly and I gave him a little push and we started through the crowd. A short way down the stone steps we caught up to her and he called out her name and she stopped and turned. He looked around once more desperately as if thinking of escape and then spoke quickly. "Good morning, Mrs. Angela," he said. I stood close behind him, a somber look upon my cheeks. "It is a bright morning," he said.

"Good morning, Mr. Mantaris," she said. "Yes, it is a bright morning."

I punched the old man in the back and he jumped. "Mrs. Angela," he said, and he seemed to be having trouble getting the rest out. "May I present Mr. Larakis."

"How do you do, Mrs. Angela," I said, and I was very careful not to smile. One does not laugh before the watch fires of grief.

She looked from the old man to me and her face darkened slightly. The old man shifted in some sort of agony from one foot to the other. Then she nodded an acknowledgment slowly and turned to walk on.

I punched the old man in the ribs again to follow her. He turned on me snarling like he was going to take a chance and clout me. He would not budge. He stood like one of the pillars of the Parthenon. I left him spitting at me under his breath.

I had to run several steps to catch up to her. "Excuse me, Mrs. Angela," I said. "May I walk with you to the next corner? We are going the same way."

She turned again and looked at me darkly. I think what saved me was the cool and impersonal expression on my face. A shadow of a smile would have whipped me right there. She nodded without speaking and I fell into step beside her.

We walked silently for a little way and the cars passed in the street and the spring sun shone brightly in the sky.

"Forgive me, Mrs. Angela," I said. "I knew your husband. I was grieved when I heard of his death. I have been out of the city a long time."

She looked at me with those deep dark eyes and there was nothing I could understand on her face. Then her cheeks loosened just a little. "Thank you," she said quietly. "It was a terrible loss."

I spoke softly and sympathetically. "A fine man," I said. "Did he ever wrestle? I do not remember ever seeing a man with stronger-looking arms."

She shook her head slowly. I was sorry for the remembered pain returned to her cheeks. I am not a sadist. But this initial surgery was necessary. "He was not a wrestler," she said. "But he was very strong."

"I believe he once mentioned to me he came from Sparta?" I said.

"Yes," she said. "Kostas was a Spartan."

"Of course," I said. "Where else? Sparta stands for strength and courage."

We had reached the corner and she stopped and looked at me again. "He would have been pleased to hear you say that," she said. "Thank you, Mr. . . ."

"Larakis," I said. "Mike Larakis."

"Thank you, Mr. Larakis," she said. "Now I turn here."

I took a deep breath. I had to proceed carefully. Whoso

diggeth a pit might fall therein. "Mrs. Angela," I said. "Please do not think I am disrespectful. It is only I have not been back in the city very long. My old friends are moved and gone. Can you understand what it is to be lonely?"

That one was a beauty. I could see the shaft of the arrow sticking out of her wonderful chest.

"I know what loneliness is," she said. She spoke those words with real feeling.

I pushed my advantage. "Would it be too forward of me to think you might permit me to have dinner with you?" I asked. "Some quiet restaurant where we might sit and talk?"

She looked at me closely and I felt unrest under the intensity of her gaze. Those big dark eyes were more than ornaments on the Widow Angela. Her soul poured through them. "I do not go out socially," she said. "Not since my Kostas died."

"Forgive me," I said. "I was too forward. I have offended you. I am sorry."

I apologize very well. Frankly, it is not an easily acquired skill.

She shook her head. "Please," she said. "I was not offended. Just that it has been so long."

"A little food," I said. "A little quiet talk with a friend. Surely to allow yourself that is not to show disloyalty to a sacred memory."

I could see her making up her mind. Her skin without make-up gleamed cleanly. I felt a smarting in my fingers. Sweet is a grief well ended.

"All right," she said.

"Thank you," I said humbly. "You are kind to a lonely man." I paused and looked thoughtfully into space. This needed a clincher so she would not change her mind. "I regret I cannot make it tonight," I said. "There is a meeting of one of the church organizations I have just joined." I paused again. "I would rather sit and talk with you," I said.

"You must attend your meeting," she said firmly. "We will make it another night."

"Tomorrow night," I said. "If you are free."

"Tomorrow night," she said.

"I will call for you," I said. "Do you live close by?"

"The brownstone house," she said. "That one across the street. I have the first-floor apartment."

"At six?" I said.

"At six," she said.

"Thank you," I said.

She turned and walked away and I watched with intense interest the fine great sway of her marvelous thighs and savored my small pleasure like a general who had won the first skirmish but needed yet to win the war.

On the following afternoon I stopped for a moment in the grocery. Mantaris was bagging warm bread from the oven in back of the store. As I walked in he raised his head and sniffed as if an animal had entered.

"Good evening, old man," I said.

He stood glaring at me.

"I merely stopped by to let you know," I said. "Tonight I dine with the Widow Angela."

"You lie!" he said.

"This is a serious matter," I said. "I never lie where love is involved."

"Love!" The old man looked as if he might strangle on the word. "You would not know love if it had teeth and bit you in the ass."

"I will let that pass," I said. "Tonight I dine with a Queen and feel kindly toward the peasants."

"Get out, boofo!" he cried. "Go and drop dead!"

I left the store smiling and went home to dress.

At six that evening I rang the bell of the Widow Angela. She opened the door and she was ready and we said good evening to one another and commented on the fine spring weather. She went to put on her hat and came back and we walked down the stairs. I led her toward the car. She shook her head.

"Such a lovely evening," she said. "Let us walk. There is a little restaurant a few blocks from here that I often pass and have never entered. May we go there tonight?"

"Certainly," I said.

The restaurant she had spoken of was a small one off Dart Street. A little bell rang over the door as we entered and we walked down a few stairs into a small room with a row of booths and candles on the tables. I could not have picked a better atmosphere myself.

A small dark man with a heavy mustache greeted us and ushered us to a booth. We sat down. I ordered a glass of wine. She hesitated, and finally nodded. We ordered another glass. I sat back and looked at her. Her face in the candled light of the booth was a page from an Old Testament psalm. David to Bathsheba. And Solomon's song.

"You are very kind," I said, "to take pity on a lonely man."

She shook her lovely head. "You must not say that," she said. "I have been lonely too. It was generous of you to ask."

I am fearfully and wonderfully made. I caused the Widow's heart to sing with joy.

"You are shy," she said. "I understood that yesterday when we walked from church. You must try to make friends."

I was trying to make friends. Angela, Angela, you have no idea how hard I was trying.

"I cannot help myself," I said. "As a child I was shy. I have never fully gotten over it."

The waiter brought the bottle of wine. He poured from it into our glasses. The wine gleamed dark red. "In wine there is truth," I said.

She raised the glass to her mouth. When she lowered it the stain of wine glittered wetly on her lips. "What is the truth?" she said.

"That you are lonely," I said. "That you mourn golden days that can never be again."

A sob seemed to catch in her throat. "Never again?" she said.

"Not in the same way," I hastened to add. "The past has its place. Memories remain sacred, but one must somehow live."

I filled her glass again with wine. For a girl out of circulation for over two years she knocked off that wine like a champion.

"There are nights I cannot sleep," she said. "Nights when I lie awake and hear strange noises in the dark."

"Loneliness," I said. "There is nothing more terrible than loneliness." As an alternative, Larakis offers himself as chosen comforter. Lucky Angela.

We ordered a little food. I poured another glass of wine. In a little while bright patches of red adorned her cheeks and her teeth gleamed even and white when she smiled.

"It seems so long ago," she said, "since I have sat like this and tasted wine and talked a little."

"You are still young," I said. "You have your life ahead of you."

"And you?" she said. "You are young and have known loneliness. Is your life still ahead of you?"

"For both of us," I said.

She paused and took another sip of wine and held her head a little to the side watching me intently. "I am glad," she said.

There was a bright spring moon high over the city as we walked home together past the houses and the stores and I did not even try to hold her hand.

After she had opened the door to her apartment she stood in the doorway weaving just a little. The scent of midnight tables was about her body. Aroma of walnuts, wine, and fruit. "Will you come in for coffee?" she asked. Her face was hidden in the shadows and I could not see her eyes.

I was tempted. But as an expert in such matters I knew it

was too soon. Timing in these things is the principal thing. Therefore if thou would emulate the master, get timing. And with all thy getting, get understanding.

"It is too late for you," I said. "You have been kind and I will not impose further upon your kindness."

"You are a good and gentle man," she said.

She was right. Only fools make a mock at sin.

"Tomorrow night?" I said.

"Tomorrow night," she said. She closed the door.

A week passed. A week in which I saw the Widow Angela every night. Twice we ate in the little restaurant with the candles. Once we drove to an inn outside the city and ate beside a tree-shaded lake. Once we went to a movie and it was a sad love story and she cried. Several times after taking her home I stopped in for a little midnight coffee. She showed me an album of family photographs. She had been a remarkably well-developed child. In later photographs I could not help being a little glad that I was not conducting this raid for plunder while her husband was alive. He looked a real brute of a man. I had no doubts, however, of my ability to equal or surpass his capacities in the main event.

All that week I never once tried to touch the Widow Angela. Several times in the past few nights I had the feeling she would not have objected too strongly if I had kissed her good night. I refuse to match for pennies when a chance for a gold piece is involved.

Late Saturday afternoon it began to rain. I stopped in the grocery with two bottles of dark wine that were wrapped as gifts. Mantaris stared at the bottles.

"Won't be long now," I said.

He glared at me and pulled fiercely at his nose. "Why don't you leave her alone?" he said. "Why not a woman of the street or some other wench? Why the Widow Angela?"

"She is the Rose of Sharon," I said, "and the Lily of the Valley."

"You are a goat," he said. "You hold nothing sacred."

"You are a poor loser," I said.

"In the end you will give up," he said. "You will get nowhere with her."

"I will not give up," I said. "I am getting somewhere very fast."

"Get out!" he said. "You are a Turk! I spit back to your father's father!"

I looked around. "You have no fresh cabbages today?" I said.

He got red in the face and started to splutter.

"It does not matter," I said. "Tonight I think I pluck my own. Tonight, old man."

I heaped the coals of fire upon his head. He stood there and did not say another word.

On my way to the Widow it began to rain again. I ran from the car to the stairs making sure not to drop the wine. She stood smiling, waiting in the doorway. "Let me take your wet things," she said.

I gave her my raincoat and my hat. I carried the wine in myself. "A bad night," I said.

"It is very bad," she said.

"A good night to sit inside," I said. "The rain has chilled me."

She stood for a moment without answering and the light of the lamp shone across her face. Her lips were red with a touch of lipstick and there were marks of rouge upon her cheeks.

"I don't mind," she said.

She brought a corkscrew and little decorative glasses for the wine. I opened one of the bottles. We sat together on the couch. We heard the whipping sound of wind and rain against the window.

"It has been a nice week," she said.

"I have enjoyed it very much," I said.

I refilled our glasses of wine. We sat without speaking for a little while with only our hands moving our glasses to our lips. The room seemed guarded like a valley between great mountains.

There was a record player in the corner. I got off the couch and walked to it and snapped the switch. The turntable revolved and the needle lowered upon a record. An old country mountain dance. Angela sat watching me from the couch.

"Come and dance," I said. "I have seen you dance before."

"Where?" she asked.

"At a picnic," I said. "You were taller than any woman in the line. You were beautiful and full of fire."

She stood up. The music rang the quick shrill melody. She came slowly to the machine. "I do not dance any more," she said.

"Why not?" I said.

"It is not right," she said.

I reached out and very gently touched the hair of the Widow Angela. I might have waited until she had more wine but I was not made of stone. Besides, there was something about that moment, something in the way she stood. I knew this was it.

She turned her head slightly and my hand fell away. For a moment I saw her face with the sad dark eyes and the full lips like moist fruit before a hungry man. "You must not touch me," she said.

I touched the nape of her neck, feeling the slight teasing softness of her hair across my fingers. "I want to touch you," I said, and I really meant that line. "Angela, Angela, all my body wants to touch you."

I saw the first press of uncertain breathing stir her breasts. She knew I had seen and the moment tightened under her disorder. "It is not right," she said. Her hand moved uneasily to her cheek. "It is not right that he should lie in the cold ground and that I should be warm and flushed."

"You are not dead," I said. "Angela, you are not dead.

You are a living breathing woman. When you are dead you will be cold forever. Till then you must live."

She turned from me as I spoke. She stood with her back to me, her face to the wall, and her hair glistened darkly.

I snapped off the phonograph. The dance died sharply and a quick silence took its place. There was wild anticipation in my belly. I knew I had her then. I knew by the way she stood and would not look at me. Weeping may endure for a day, but Larakis cometh in the evening.

I reached for her and when she felt my hands she wantonly turned to meet me. I heard her breathing as if breathing were a punishment. Her eyes were closed and hollowed above her rouged cheeks and as I pulled her to me she opened them and they were frenzied and uncaring.

I kissed her full lips. My mouth hard upon her caught breath and the brazen scent of wine between us. The kiss broke and we shakenly drew breath and she stepped away for only a moment and then came back into my arms fiercely. I felt her fingers upon my face and on my throat and across my eyes. I quit goofing around. I started to pull her to the couch.

The buzzer rang a sharp shrill sound.

I felt her stiffen and I tried to catch my breath.

"We won't answer," I whispered. I caught her again. I reached for the great flowing hills of her breasts and felt them like fire beneath my hands.

Somebody pounded on the door.

We looked at each other. Her face, pale and shaken, reflecting my own.

"We must answer," she said huskily. She stepped away pulling weakly at her dress.

If I had had a gun in my hand at that moment I would have emptied it through the door without caring who it was. Instead I stumbled to it, cursing under my breath.

I flung it open and caught old Mantaris with his hand raised to pound again.

He looked startled and his mouth dropped open. The fierceness of my face must have scared blood out of him.

"What the hell do you want!" I roared.

He raised his hands in trembling defense. He stepped back and then looked around me quickly to where the Widow Angela stood. He spoke pleadingly to her watching me from the corner of his eye.

"Good evening, Mrs. Angela," he said and he reached down beside the door and brought up a large bag. "I am delivering your groceries."

I looked at him speechlessly. The Widow came closer to the door.

"Mr. Mantaris," she said, and her voice was still shaken. "I did not order any groceries."

The old man tried to look surprised and in his excitement and fear bounced up and down in the doorway.

"I was sure this was your order," he said. "Mrs. Angela, maybe you forgot about this order."

"Are you nuts?" I said, and a strange unrest bit at my belly. "She said she didn't order any groceries. Now get the hell away from here."

"Mike," the Widow Angela said reprovingly. She had regained her composure.

"I am very sorry, Mr. Mantaris," she said quietly. "There has been a mistake. I did not order any groceries."

The old man stopped bouncing and the sweat crouched in little beads across his brown cheeks and forehead. "I am sorry. I am getting old," he said. "I became mixed up. Forgive me."

For the first time I looked at the bag of groceries. I almost choked. Right on the top as bold as you goddam please was a cabbage! That did it. I gave him a shove and slammed the door in his face.

I turned back to the Widow. I was confused but not discouraged. I had come so close I refused to believe I could not make up the lost ground. I went for her again.

She greeted me with her elbows and a tight dark face.

"Angela," I said. "My darling, don't turn me away."

She shook her head. She stood like a stranger in the room. "It was wrong," she said. "If that old man had not accidentally come at the moment he did, it would have been wrong."

I watched her moist lips move as she talked and remembered them soft under my own.

"You can't go to bed alone forever," I said harshly.

She shook her head and her eyes were deep and clear. "Not forever," she said. "When I find a man to love and marry who will love me, we will go to bed."

I heard her with the hearing of my ear and saw her with the seeing of my eye. There was a roaring beginning in my head and a sense of outrage in my loins. "You are crazy," I said.

"I was for a little while," she said. "I am all right now."

"I won't give you up," I said.

"I will not see you," she said.

"I will make you see me," I said.

"We can be friends," she said.

That word nearly strangled me.

Her face was set into hard firm lines. She wore her virtue like a coat of armor.

I had enough. A man's heart deviseth his way but the Lord directeth his steps. While I was missing from the couch, the fire burned out.

"Goodby," she said.

I stood there a moment. Nimrod, the mighty hunter, returning with an empty pouch.

"My hat and coat," I said haughtily.

She turned to get them and I took one last mournful look at her strong fine thighs and the slender turn of her trim ankles. She brought me back my things. She walked to the door and opened it. I walked past her and turned in the doorway standing in the same place that sneaky old bastard had stood a few moments before.

"Angela," I said. "You are doing us both wrong."

She turned and walked out of the room and left me in the doorway with the door still open. If she had at least closed the door or pushed me out, but she left me standing there with the door still open.

With what dignity I could muster I reached in and closed the door in my own face. I turned and walked down the stairs.

In the car I debated between throwing a rock through the window of the Mantaris grocery or going to Crotty's bar. I decided on the bar. If I hurried I knew a cigarette girl there that I might talk into taking the night off. She had a squeaky giggle and an unfortunate tendency to cold feet, but any port in a storm.

An ass is beautiful to an ass and a pig to a pig.

To hell with the Widow Angela.

⁋ My mother was a compassionate woman who devoted a considerable portion of her life to serving needy families and unfortunate individuals. One of those she aided was a lonely little seamstress in her late fifties suffering from a terminal illness. After we had finished a holiday dinner at our family table, my mother would fill a small basket with food for the seamstress, who lived in a furnished room some miles away. I resented having to leave the party and deliver the basket.

Later I found myself reluctantly involved with driving the woman back and forth to the hospital for treatments. When she required drugs for which she could not pay, I used my own money, begrudgingly again, because a free lancer's income was precarious.

When I complained to my mother about the time and expense involved in caring for someone who was, after all, a stranger, she reprimanded me. "You want to write about life," she said. "This dying woman is life."

Of course my mother was right. When the seamstress died, a few weeks later in a ward at the county hospital, moved and remorseful I wrote "Zena Dawn." When I sold the story I recouped many times over whatever that poor woman had cost me in money and time.

Zena Dawn

There was a sound Zena Dawn heard early in the morning before daylight. In the beginning she thought it belonged to a dream but afterwards there were many nights she lay awake and heard it too. As if a strange wind, restless and cold, swept fleetingly through her room. But her door was closed and a ventilator locked in her single window. There was no opening through which a draft might enter.

Once she heard the sound she could no longer sleep. She drew the spread tightly to her throat and held herself aware of each long and silent minute.

The night is so long, she thought. The night is so quiet. Even a sudden fall of rain against the window comes as a relief. Even the murmur of the pigeons mourning in the cornices and the cry of a prowling cat help me remember I am not alone.

She was grateful for Mrs. Cohen's husband, a baker who rose early, a heavy-bodied man who tried to walk quietly. But his bulk and the absence of carpeting on the stairs defined his steps. His passing raised a shade on the night and soon the first in a series of alarm clocks ruffled the silence with a thin and agitated humming. A baby in the flat above hers wailed a hungry cry for food. Zena Dawn was able to sleep again knowing that the long night was over.

She woke to full daylight and the strong loud voice of Clara calling to her from the basement landing of the building next door. She rose from her bed and slipped into her robe feeling the stiff twinges of pain. She walked unsteadily to the window and raised the shade and waved.

Clara was a rampart-breasted Black woman in her late fifties who owned the junk shop in the basement of the building next door. She lived in three rooms in the back of the store with a half-dozen children she raised alone since her husband deserted her.

"Good Lord!" Clara hollered and her voice carried clearly through the ventilator in the window. "Woman, you going to stay in bed all day? I'm on my third pot of coffee and the sweet rolls from Jenny is dripping sugar. Now put out the cups and I'm coming."

Zena Dawn turned eagerly from the window anticipating the visit which was a morning ritual for them both. She went to the mirror over the dresser and combed her hair. As she swept the strands back from her cheeks she saw how illness had ravaged her face and hidden her eyes in dark and solemn pits. She turned quickly from the mirror and walked to the small table that she covered with a clean cloth. From the shelf above the table she took down a pair of decorative cups and saucers. She had only a moment left to fill a pitcher with milk when she heard the heavy step of Clara on the stairs.

Clara entered like a wild woman clutching a pot of steaming coffee in one hand and a bag of sweet rolls in the other.

"Gangway!" Clara cried. "On the way up here I run over two hags and burned hell out of a third!" She laughed boisterously and went rapidly to the table and poured the hot black coffee into the cups. She set the pot down on the small hot plate. "Get it while it's hot!" She waved Zena Dawn to the table and briskly opened the bag. "And wait till you taste them sweet rolls."

Zena Dawn sat down and placed the napkin carefully across her lap. "It smells good," she said. "Clara, the coffee certainly smells good this morning."

"You say that every morning," Clara said.

"I mean it every morning," Zena Dawn shook her head earnestly. "But this morning it smells especially good."

Clara tore a sweet roll in half with her big hands and took a large bite. She chewed vigorously and swallowed with pleasure. "Course it smells good," she said. "Clara Sullivan makes the best damn coffee in the city."

From the sidewalk below the window came a shrill cry.

"Can't leave me alone a minute," Clara said in a vexed voice. She walked from the table and flung open the window impatiently.

"Ma," the voice of her eldest boy called. "Ma, a man here wants to buy the iron eagle. I told him it was two dollar and he say he not going to give no more than one dollar."

"One dollar!" Clara hollered. "You tell that man that eagle belonged to a lady so rich and elegant I be ashamed to sell it for cheap pickings like one dollar. You tell him I rather throw it away or give it to one of you kids for a wedding present when you old enough to marry."

"He hear you, Ma," the boy called. "He putting on his hat."

"Wait!" Clara shouted. "Tell him if he pleased to pay a dollar and a half he can take that fine eagle home right now."

"He going, Ma," the boy said. "He got one foot out the door and the other in the air."

"Tell him to leave that dollar!" Clara screamed and her broad rump shook in agitation. "Get that dollar and give him the eagle. Clyde, you hear me! You make that sale or I beat your seat with a barrel stave. You hear!"

An anxious moment of silence passed and then the boy's voice floated up in triumph. "I got the dollar, Ma. The man got the eagle."

Clara drew her head back in and closed the window down to the ventilator loudly.

"That boy be my death," she said and returned to the table. "I try to teach him all I know and make a trader out of him but he don't know which end is up." She motioned at Zena Dawn's plate. "All that time," she said grievously. "You make only one chintzy little bite into that delicious sweet roll. You got to keep up your strength, honey, you all bones now."

"I'm not hungry," Zena Dawn said. "I love the sweet rolls but I'm just not hungry." She looked anxiously at Clara wishing to please her but unable to make the food go down her throat.

"You had much pain again?" Clara asked in a softer voice. "Did you pass another real bad night?"

"The pain wasn't bad at all last night," Zena Dawn said, and tried to speak cheerfully. "When I fell asleep I had a dream. I was somewhere in the sunshine, Clara, and could smell fresh flowers just as real as if I stood in a garden."

"The way you dream," Clara marveled. "And the things you dream."

"When I was a little girl I used to dream of flowers too," Zena Dawn said. "My father would kiss me goodnight and I would smell the flowers of his shop on his clothes and our house was always full of flowers." She paused and looked shyly at her pale fingers on the cloth of the table. "I've told you so many times before."

"Tell me again!" Clara said. "I like for you to tell me again!"

"Our house was full of flowers," Zena Dawn said. "Roses and sunflowers and chrysanthemums. Clara, it was always so beautiful."

"I bet it was," Clara said in awe. "You were lucky." She clucked her tongue. "Flowers all the time. Imagine that."

"I loved my mother," Zena Dawn said, "but my father was more dear. He picked out my name. He called me Zena Dawn because it sounded like the name of a flower."

"It sure does," Clara agreed earnestly.

"He said my name would always be a charm," Zena Dawn said, "I would have many friends and people to love and I would never be lonely." She grew suddenly pensive. "That was so long ago. Mother died when I was still living at home. But when my father died I was far away and I rode a train for two days and a night to go to his funeral but when I got there they had buried him. And all the flowers were wilted too."

"Eat some of that sweet roll now," Clara said vigorously. "You listen to me and eat some of that sweet roll."

"Bawl me out, Clara," Zena Dawn smiled. "It makes me feel good when you bawl me out. When I get better and can sew again I will make you a dress, a beautiful red dress that you can wear to church on Sundays. I promise you that."

"A red dress?" Clara said pleased. "It's been a long time since Clara had a new dress." She winked at Zena Dawn. "That's the way to talk," she said. "Think on tomorrow instead of what happened years ago."

"It's hard sometimes," Zena Dawn said. "How different we expect things to be. I was married to Theron for only three years when he was killed. He will be dead nineteen years this September. We had so short a time together. And the years have passed so quickly since then."

"We both lost our men," Clara said. "But your man went to heaven and my man just went." She paused and shook her head. "I married a real prize. I waited and thought carefully and then I picked the laziest, most no-count man I could find and I married him. He was big and sassy and loved to slap me across the seat." She laughed huskily in spite of herself. "But he was no good out of bed. He was an evil man that done every sin you can think of and even made up a few more." She sighed with pleasure in the recollection. "One day he up and left me. He left me with six kids. That man was evil and no good but for a long time I missed him. To this day whenever I smell cheap gin I think of him."

She rose from the table and carried the cups and saucers to the small sink. Zena Dawn rose to help her and a sharp quick pain in her body made her cry out.

Clara watched her in concern. "When is the doctor coming back?"

Zena Dawn sat down again and placed her hands with the fingers open squarely upon the cloth of the table. She breathed slowly and fearfully against the pain rippling within her. "He won't be back until the day after tomorrow. He told me to keep taking the pills."

"That's right," Clara said firmly. "Keep taking them medicines. They help you get better and keep the pain from becoming too bad." She peered closely at the assortment of bottles on the shelf. "You got any of them red pain killers left?"

"I've got some left," Zena Dawn said.

"When you run out I send Clyde to get you some more," Clara said.

"I won't let you spend any more money on me!" Zena Dawn said. "You have your own family and all the other things you do for me is enough."

"You just shut up," Clara said with rough tenderness. "When you well enough to begin to sew, you can pay me back." She stared sharply at Zena Dawn. "Any of the relief money left?" she asked. "Now don't tell me no lie."

"Only the rent money," Zena Dawn said. "Mr. Mitchell is coming for that tomorrow."

"Then he be here tomorrow," Clara said grimly. "He come on his black horse and with his black pocketbook open as wide as a whale's mouth. He come blowing his rent-horn like a wild jackass out of hell." She stopped pleased as Zena Dawn began to laugh. "It's true!" Clara cried vigorously to encourage the laughter. "If the Lord took it into his mind to wipe out the earth with forty days and forty nights of rain, just before we all drown, that bastard come swimming by for his rent."

Zena Dawn laughed so hard she had to hold her ribs. Clara watched her with pleasure. "Laugh!" Clara said fiercely. "Laugh! When you most feel like crying, that's the time to laugh!"

"Clara, Clara," Zena Dawn said in wonder as she caught her breath. "How can you laugh when you've got the children to worry about, to feed and to clothe, and the store to run, and me to look after?"

"I got a few more things even than that," Clara said with a tight edge to her voice. "I got a boy whose teeth coming in so crooked they look like they belong in two different mouths. Doctor says he needs wires around them and for the price I swear I could buy ten miles of fence. And I got two feet, two damn feet that raise corns and calluses quicker'n the landlord can raise the rent. And I just got a letter from my daughter, the growed-up one, that married the iceman. He beating her up every Saturday night now and she want to bring her baby and stay with me."

"O Clara," Zena Dawn said in quick compassion. "I'm so sorry for her."

"That's all right," Clara shook her head with a savage resolve. "I told her to come. We make room for her and the baby. Always room for a few more." She brushed the crumbs from the bodice of her dress and looked sternly at Zena Dawn. "Now you do like you're supposed to," she said. "I'll see you a little later."

Zena Dawn was silent for a moment. She struggled for words to encompass the measure of Clara's devotion. Clara cut off her need to speak with a quick wave of her broad-palmed hand.

"There ain't no need to say nothing," Clara said. "As for looking after you, I do that because I want to. Maybe," she shrugged, "maybe because you're a white woman and there ain't no white man nor white woman showed up to help you." She smiled in a gentle jest. "Maybe it's just your fancy name. Zena Dawn. Maybe that's it. You got to live fifty-seven years with a washerwoman name like Clara to understand that." She picked up the coffee pot and started briskly to the door. She paused with her hand upon the knob. "You call me now if you get bad pain," she said. "Just holler by the window."

When she had gone, Zena Dawn felt as if all the light and life in the room had fled as well.

At lunch Clara sent her a bowl of soup and some crackers which she barely managed to finish. Later Clyde brought up the afternoon paper. Zena Dawn read for a while and in the late afternoon the sharp stabbing pain returned. She went quickly to the bed and pressed her arms tightly across her stomach. She held her breath because she could feel the walls crumbling again, the tissue-thin walls that gave way before the bleeding. She felt her life draining out with her blood. She managed to rise from the bed and with a faint cry of despair stumbled to the ledge above the table and took down one of the bottles of pills. With a flare of panic she saw only one was left. She filled a glass with water and flooded it down. She went back to the bed and lay down and pressed her face into the pillow.

She felt a pounding in her forehead, an ache behind her eyes. Her breath rose in little bubbles to pop in her ears.

How lightly I lie upon the springs, she thought, how fragile is my hold upon the earth. A gust of strong wind could blow me away. She turned on her back and stared gravely at the ceiling. It was blue by day but in the twilight all color seemed bled from it, and it loomed over her head as if it were the cold stone of a tomb.

She tried furiously to form the images of memories. Once

when I was a child, she thought. But she could go no further. One memory fell upon another. One tumbled quickly upon the next. They would not assemble into any order.

A minute passed and then another. Or was it an hour? She fell asleep. A great starburst of pain woke her. She shrieked and pulled at the sheet. Despair flooded over her. She cried out to her father. The room door opened and Clara stormed in.

"Damn you," Clara said. "I told you to call me. Damn you, white woman, with your fancy name!" Then in quick remorse she raised the slim frail body and held her fiercely to her own great breasts and rocked her gently back and forth.

"Clara!" Zena Dawn cried and she looked in terror at the ceiling. "I want to go to the hospital. Maybe they can help me there."

"Just hold up," Clara said. "There ain't nothing the hospital can do for you that old Clara can't do."

"Don't leave me alone," Zena Dawn whispered. "Clara, don't leave me alone. I am dying and don't leave me alone."

"Only a minute, honey," Clara said in a soft and shaken voice. "Only one minute to phone the doctor and I'll come back and I won't leave you again."

The doctor came a few hours later. He sat beside the bed and briefly examined Zena Dawn. She watched him from her eyes that were crusted by pain. He filled a syringe and gave her a shot. He closed his bag and rose to leave. Clara followed him to the hall outside the door.

The doctor looked tired and out of sorts. "Something might keep her alive a few more days," he said. "But it's better if she goes fast." He turned away and Clara caught at his sleeve.

"She wants to go to the hospital," Clara said. "She thinks they might help her there."

"That won't do any good," the Doctor said quietly.

A sudden anger flared in Clara's voice. "They don't want

her to die there," she said. "They want poor folks to do their dying at home."

"Everybody is dying, mother," the Doctor said. "The rich and the poor and the weak and the strong. Everybody is dying a little all the time."

"I know," Clara said and her anger left as quickly as it had come. "God knows that is the truth."

She sat with Zena Dawn through the night. In the dark still hours after midnight she rose at intervals from her chair beside the bed and stretched against the stiffness cramping her body. She went a number of times to the window and listened for a sound from the basement next door.

Zena Dawn stirred uneasily on the bed and Clara took her a little water and moistened her lips. Her face was loose and dark, changed somehow, and her lips trembled in drugged and uneven sleep.

The hours passed slowly. Standing by the window Clara heard the cooing of the pigeons in the cornices. Somewhere a dog barked a sharp sound upon the night. She sat down in the chair and closed her eyes and dozed. Mrs. Cohen's husband woke her as he left for work, his steps heavy and clear upon the stairs. An alarm clock hummed down the long corridor. A baby raised a plaintive cry.

Clara walked to the window and raised the shade. The first faint gray of morning hung across the roofs of the city. A pigeon took flight with a harsh beating of its wings. She peered down at the back of her store to make sure everything was still quiet. She went back to the bed to cover Zena Dawn and saw how still she lay within the folds of sheet. Clara shook her head gratefully and pressed her hands tightly against her breasts.

The back door of the store downstairs opened and the voice of one of her children rose to her. She walked to the ventilator and called that she was coming. She turned for a moment back to the bed.

"You don't worry no more now, Zena Dawn," she said

quietly. "You got a place all set for you. Old Clara been paying on a burial plot for you too, right next to me, and you don't worry no more now." She wiped fiercely at her eyes with the back of her hand. "There ain't going to be no more pain and no more bleeding and no more white folks not caring whether you live or die. Ain't going to be no more stale sweet rolls and no more landlord beating on the door come the first of the month. Ain't going to be no more relief checks that run out the end of the second week." She paused and struck her breasts violently with her fists. "You got a place next to me and they ain't going to put you in no pauper's grave nor cut you up. You got a place to rest and long as I live I see there is a flower on your head." She finished and shook her head in despair. "You the lucky one now," she said. "The rest of us got to go on living."

From the store another child wailed for her and a second took up the chorus of complaint. She turned and walked to the door. She looked back once and made a mute final gesture of consolation toward the body of Zena Dawn.

¶ When I consider all the Greek coffeehouses and Greek ta-vernas I have eaten and drunk in, all the evenings I have spent listening to the singers and watching the dancers through the viscid vapors of saganaki, gyros, and the resinated wine, I am surprised I have not used this background in much more of my work.

If I often use priests as narrators in my stories, I also show an affinity for bartenders. Making the bartenders Greek also gains a dimension. In addition to the philosophical outlook on life they gain from their profession, they are also steeped in the blood-stream of a fertile past. Like the leader in an old tragic chorus, they can draw attention to the parallels and the forebodings.

This story was published in *The Saturday Evening Post* and retitled "A Knowledge of Her Past." When I complained about the change in the title to an editor on the magazine who was also a good friend, he advised me to shut up and cash the check.

I took his advice. . . .

The Ballad of Daphne and Apollo

You would not have thought, to look at him, that my friend Apollo was a subject for tragedy. He had none of the great mournfulness of countenance that must have marked Mac-beth and Oedipus. But calamity is not the divine right of kings alone.

Apollo played the guitar in the tavern of Ali Pasha, where I worked as a bartender. He was in his middle thirties and of average height. He appeared taller because he had a lean and hard body and moved with the grace of a flamenco dancer. He had strong white teeth that flashed in a warm and engaging smile.

In the evening, when the tables in the tavern filled with patrons, he would ascend the low platform in a corner of the large room. He played bright Greek mountain dances that made any feet but my swollen and aching ones itch to leap into the air. He played bucolic love songs of Zakynthos and

Thessaly, and old-country island melodies that I remembered hearing as a boy.

Late at night as the smoke grew thicker and the mastiha ran freely down eager throats, a line of wild old men would rise to dance. They would circle and weave among the tables in a brisk Hassapiko or a martial Tsamiko that provided the leaders a chance for precarious leaps and hazardous jumps.

It was on an evening near the end of summer that Daphne first came to the tavern. She entered alone sometime after midnight wearing a raincoat and a strip of silk scarf across her head that she untied as she approached the bar. Her hair as it tumbled free was the rich black shade of fine Calamata olives.

"I would like to see the boss," she said in a husky voice.

I walked to the door at the end of the bar and called for Ali Pasha. In a moment he came lumbering out of the office. He had a great, gross body, the disposition of a hangman and a range of facial expression from bitter to bleak. He also fancied himself a bit of a rake and sported a handlebar mustache with curled and pomaded tips that he pulled fiercely when he grew excited.

"I'm looking for a job," the girl said.

"Only men serve the tables," Ali Pasha said brusquely. "The kitchen staff are men as well."

She swept her hair back impatiently with one hand, exposing a long jeweled earring glittering on her ear. "Do you take me for a kitchen flunky?" she asked. "I am a singer."

"A singer," Ali Pasha said, and a rude leer settled around his mouth. "Where have you sung?"

"Plenty of places," she said. "My last job was at George Spartan's in Cleveland and before that the Hellas in Detroit. Business improves wherever I sing."

He gave her a long, appraising look. She was a handsome young woman with a certain sensual boldness that made me uneasy. He motioned her to a stool. "Sit there," he said. "I will listen to you in a minute."

He walked toward the platform where Apollo sat. I wiped the bar briskly with a cloth. "Would you like a mastiha?" I asked.

"Thanks."

I poured her a glass, which she raised to her lips and drank as swiftly as any man.

"Is that guitar player any good?" she asked.

"He plays a beautiful guitar," I said firmly. "When he plays the songs of the old country, he returns old men like me to our mountains and our islands."

"If he could just make you forget the brandy and cigar stink of places like this," she said with a taunting little laugh, "he would still be the best I have ever heard."

In another moment Ali Pasha returned with Apollo. "This is Apollo Gerakis," he said to the girl. "He plays the guitar for me." He motioned to Apollo. "This girl is a singer."

"Daphne," she said. "Daphne Callistos."

"Daphne," I said. "Apollo and Daphne." The old legend came to my mind.

"What's that?" Ali Pasha asked.

"Nothing," I said. There was no use explaining anything classical to him.

"I suppose we can use a singer," Apollo said as he looked carefully at the girl. "Can you sing the songs of Pontus and Epirus and Crete?"

"I know them all," Daphne said. "The lullabies and the love songs and the laments."

"One thing you should know," Apollo said. "The salary here is next to nothing. I exist on tips which are tossed into a box while I play. We would have to share what tips we get."

"I've worked that way before," Daphne said.

"Never mind salary and tips," Ali Pasha said. "Let's hear her sing first."

She gave him a final amused look and walked with Apollo toward the platform, removing her raincoat on the way. She was sheathed in a black dress that fitted her body tightly. Ali Pasha uttered a low, hoarse curse.

When they reached the platform, they stood talking a moment, and then Daphne moved alone into the beam of muted light. Apollo struck the first chords of a lament and the men at the tables quieted slowly.

A lament is a morose and melancholy song, and Apollo played them with feeling. But as she sang I had the strange sensation I was hearing a quality of despair I had never heard before. Her voice, haunting and mournful, led us down the path where the stream of woe pours into the river of lamentation. At the tables men stirred, and a wind of pleased muttering swept the room.

When she finished the lament, Apollo changed the tempo to the lilting melody of a festive mountain dance.

Daphne placed her hands on her hips and threw back her head, and her voice, suddenly bawdy and vibrant, assaulted the room. At one of the tables near the bar an old man sleeping off too much to drink raised his head like a startled bird. Her ardor paid homage to the woodland spirits of fertility and abandon. In such a way must the wild nymphs have sung in the festivals of Dionysus before the satyrs playing their pipes made of reeds.

When she finished, a storm of applause rose from the roomful of men. She walked with a careless insolence past the tables, and many called to her and blew her kisses. She came back to the bar, and Ali Pasha showed his teeth in hungry admiration. "You sing all right," he said grudgingly. "The truth is, I don't really need a singer. It is an expense I might not be able to afford."

In another moment Apollo joined them. "You are very good," he said.

"The boss doesn't think I'm good enough," she laughed.

"Never mind the lousy salary," Apollo said. "I think you will fill the box."

"Out of which you'll take your half," Ali Pasha snarled. He spoke to the girl with a crooked attempt at a winning smile. "If you want to work, you can start tomorrow night at eight."

She nodded calmly as if the outcome had never been in doubt. She turned to leave, and Ali Pasha spoke slyly. "A good-looking woman like you will be a pleasure to have around."

She looked at him as if her eyes were knives severing little hunks of his flesh and made a motion of good night to the rest of us as she pulled on her raincoat. We watched her as she walked to the door. Ali Pasha tugged fiercely and silently at the tips of his mustache, and walked back into the office.

I dimmed the lights in a signal to the customers that we were preparing to close. Apollo sat down on a stool at the bar.

"I wonder where she comes from?" he said slowly.

"She is from disaster," I said, "and on her way to catastrophe." Then, because he did not seem to be listening, I reached across the bar and shook his arm. "Forget her," I said. "Don't get involved with her."

"She is not all that brass she puts on," he said. "When she sings, she sets dreams to weeping. I remembered that it has been a long and lonely summer. I am tired of playing my songs alone." He pushed off the stool. "Hurry and clean up, Janco," he said. "I'll buy you a cup of coffee on the way home."

He walked toward the platform for his coat and guitar. I snapped off the lights above the bar. The waiters were beginning to clear the tables, and customers were moving in reluctant groups to the door. An old man who had been sleeping on his arms was disturbed by the clatter and moaned hoarsely.

"No more auditions tonight," I said in a vexed voice. "We don't need another singer."

After Daphne started to sing in the tavern, business became much better almost at once. Ali Pasha, merciless in his greed, set up additional tables that barely left room for the cursing waiters to squeeze by.

When Daphne sang an unhappy ballad or a lament, she had the old men weeping for the grand days of their lost youth. When she sang a dancing song from Macedonia and suggestively rendered the lyrics of a shy man and his bold wife, the old men went wild with delight. When the gray-beards finally rose to dance, they exhausted themselves to demonstrate their unflagging virility, and leaped off the floor like drunken and festive roosters.

Ali Pasha couldn't take his eyes off her. When she sang, he gripped the tips of his mustache in anguish. She held him off by a fury of blazing defiance in the same way she held off the countless other males who stampeded around her at the end of each evening. She provoked my grudging admiration in the ruthless way she cut them down.

But Apollo confused her. Against him she raised defenses that were not needed. He pursued her with a gentleness that was a source of wonder to her. Slowly, almost against her will, she must have felt herself drawn to him. Perhaps he stirred in her a memory long lost in the tide of dark days, a dream of fair love.

There was a day in the beginning of October when rain fell until evening and left a brief scent of freshened earth across the city. Late in the evening Apollo came looking for Daphne and seemed distressed. A while after that, one of the waiters relieved me at the bar, and I slipped out the kitchen door to smoke a cigar and get some fresh air.

Daphne called my name from the shadows.

"What are you doing out here?" I asked. "Apollo is looking for you."

"Let him look," she said defiantly. "He is as bad as all the rest."

"Is he?" I asked quietly. I sat down on a crate and with a sigh raised my burning feet to rest on another.

For a long moment she did not answer. I drew a cigar

from my pocket and struck a match, and in the brief flare of light I saw her pale and weary face.

"Perhaps he is," she said. "Perhaps he isn't. But there are times when I am sick and tired of all men."

"The fate of a handsome woman," I said.

She laughed mockingly in the darkness. "I only feel comfortable with you, Janco," she said. "Why is that?"

"My arteries and my bad feet," I said wryly. "You sense correctly they have immobilized me for any pursuit."

She fell silent again. Above us the rain clouds had disappeared and the stars glittered.

"Wasn't Apollo the name of a god?" she said.

"He was the god of life and light," I said. "And he loved Daphne above all other women."

"I knew the story as a child," she said quietly, "I don't remember now except that it was sad."

"Daphne was the daughter of Peneus, the river god," I said. "Apollo was seized with love for her, but she yearned to keep her freedom. Many lovers sought her, but she spurned them all.

"Apollo loved her and longed to have her as his own. She sensed he was different from all the others, but she was afraid. She belonged to the unspoiled woods and to the untamed rivers. He followed her relentlessly and told her not to flee from him as a lamb flies before the wolf or a dove before the hawk. He was the god of song and the lyre and played a mighty melody of love."

"A guitar player," she said softly. "Playing a sweet and sad guitar."

"She tried not to listen to him," I said. "She was innocent of the meaning of love. But he would not let her alone. Her strength began to fail, and she called upon her father to aid her, to change her form, which had brought her into danger. Scarcely had she finished pleading when a stiffness seized all her limbs. Her hair became leaves, her arms became branches, her feet stuck fast in the ground as roots. Apollo touched the stem of the tree and felt her flesh tremble under the new bark. And he wept for his lost love. 'Since you cannot be mine,' he sang, 'I will wear you for my crown. I will decorate with you my harp and my lyre. My songs will make you immortal.'"

When I finished, she moved restlessly from the shadows and for an instant stood in the strip of light before the door. "The legend does not tell the truth," she said, and there was a black and bitter edge to her words. "Do not believe she fled because she was innocent and cared nothing for him. She fled because she had known many men and did not deserve the kind of love he offered. She knew if they loved each other they might both be destroyed."

"It is only a story that belongs to the past," I said wearily. "A bit of foolishness for children and old men."

She went in the door, and after a moment I followed.

It was not long after that night that Apollo and Daphne became lovers. I do not know why she changed her mind. Perhaps even the daughters of gods have moments of mortal yearning. And the legend does not tell us whether in that unhappy chase the two of them did not pause for a moment together, perhaps in an hour of twilight when the darkening of the woods made them feel keenly the burden of being alone.

No one told me they became lovers, but I knew by the radiance that came from them when they were together. Sometimes when they had finished their last song after midnight they came to the bar, and I served them little glasses of wine.

"Is she not beautiful, Janco?" he said, and there was the intimacy of possession in the way his fingers touched her hair. She accepted his touch, and I saw their faces stir with the soft wind of each other's desire.

"Is he not mad?" she said and laughed her husky laugh, animated and deepened by affection.

"He is a guitar player," I smiled. "You are a singer of sad love songs. This gives you both a head start on madness."

"When I was a boy," Apollo said softly, looking at Daphne, "I had dreams of conquering cities and of ruling men. Dreams of loving countless fair and dark women." He paused, and the words came shaken from his throat. "I have found them all," he said. "In my love I have conquered cities and rule all other men. In my love I have spanned the oceans and circled the earth. In my love I possess countless fair and dark women."

"He is mad," Daphne said, and in her eyes there was a longing to believe him. "He is trying to make me as mad as he is."

"The mad are sane," I said, "and the sane are mad. Only love can harness both."

She raised her glass of wine and watched me as she spoke. "Legends are stories that belong to the past," she said, and a shadow swept her cheeks. "Is that not true, Janco?"

"That is true," I said quickly. "A bit of foolishness for children and old men."

She accepted my assurance recklessly and held tightly to Apollo's hand. "Then I drink to the future," she said. "A future that will make stories of its own."

"I drink to that," I said and spoke from my heart.

I am sure the ugly trouble began with Ali Pasha. When he could not have Daphne, his soul festered in rancor and wished to destroy that which he had been denied. He whispered in low malevolent tones to the waiters, falling silent when I came near. They followed his dark spoor and, like coyotes that feed on what the wolf brings down, added their own venom to the pot. Rumors and suspicions and whispers about Daphne and her past spread furiously through the tavern. There were sidelong smirks and muted laughter when Apollo passed the tables.

When he understood something of what was going on, he twisted in frustration and rage, but could find no adversary visible. I think he wished mainly to protect and defend her, and yet the baleful laughter nourished disorder. He knew that the shadows of her past concealed much he did not relish, and he began to brood over what could not be forgotten.

I fought to help him where I could and yet protected Ali Pasha as well. I knew that if Apollo suspected the origin of the vile whispering there would be violence. Ali Pasha kept a loaded gun in the top drawer of his desk and was coward enough to use it if he were attacked.

Under the taunt of these aggravations Apollo one night flung a patron violently from the platform when he sought to slip a folded bill into a pocket of Daphne's dress. There was a roar of catcalls and jeers. The man who had been shoved shrieked for the police. Ali Pasha hurried him into his office to conciliate him. A moment later Apollo came raging to the bar, followed by Daphne.

"He meant nothing," Daphne pleaded to calm him. "That was a good tip, and he meant no harm."

"Let him choke on his good tip!" Apollo said. "I should have smashed him. I saw him paw you. I should have smashed the pig!" He twisted on the stool, all the weeks of provocation and helplessness fused into explosive direction. "I have to sit there and watch them hour after hour," he said. "Drunken pigs who think their grimy dollar entitles them any liberty."

"Listen, please," Daphne said in a low, soothing voice. "I can tell when one is a bad apple. I would slap that kind down myself. Mostly they are old roosters with cut claws showing off for applause from their friends. They mean no harm."

"They harm me!" Apollo said. "I do not want the woman I love pawed by pigs!"

Her eyes began to flash fire of their own. "You forget one thing," she said. "I am a singer of bawdy songs in a tavern. In Cleveland and Detroit I earned my tips this way. This is the way I earn my bread."

"To hell with that," Apollo said, and his cheeks shook off heat. "To hell with earning your bread that way."

"Don't tell me how to earn my bread," she said, and the words came bitten from between her teeth. "From the time I was ten no one cared whether I had bread at all. I have made my own way and asked no favors and earned my bread. Don't tell me now what is right. Don't sit in judgment like a god over my life."

"What kind of woman are you?" he asked savagely. "Not to mind being pawed by a hundred men!"

She stepped back as if he had struck her. Then, without another word, she turned quickly and almost ran to the door. He made a sudden frantic motion with his hand to call her back and then changed his mind.

"Go after her," I said quietly. "You were not fair, Apollo. She cares a great deal for you. Don't let her grieve alone!" I looked uneasily at the closed door to the office. "Ali Pasha will be out in a minute."

"To hell with him," Apollo said. But the circles of anger around his mouth loosened slightly, and then he slipped off the stool and started after Daphne.

A moment later Ali Pasha came out of the office embracing the patron whose outrage seemed to have softened. "Give this gentleman two bottles of mastiha." Ali Pasha's voice dripped unctuous tones. "Drink them, sir, with my compliments."

After the mollified rooster walked away clutching his bottles, Ali Pasha quickly dropped the mask of civility. "Mark that down," he snarled. "Those two bottles come out of the guitar player's tips. Charge him the retail price." He glared around the room. "Where are he and the girl?"

"Out for the air," I said.

"You tell them when they get back," he said, spitting the words from beneath his flaring mustache. "You tell lover boy that one more outburst like that and he and his prize paramour can both clear out." The sweat glistened on his swarthy face. "Who the devil does he think he is to protect that tart?"

"He is only a man in love," I said slowly. "A poor man

goaded and tormented by dirty rumors and vicious lies spread by animals who only feel at home in the dark."

The blood left his face as if I had struck him.

November came, and the hours of daylight grew shorter. Dusk and dark advanced as the winter nights closed down. For the first time that I could remember I dreaded the coming of winter. The bleakness of the earth mirrored a desolation gathering in myself. I tried to validate this as the ominous premonition of an old man who did not have long to live, but I knew it was really because of my grief and despair for Apollo and Daphne.

The ugly whispering and mocking laughter had slowly faded away. Even Ali Pasha tired of the brutal game. But the baleful harm had been done.

Apollo could not forgive or forget the measure of mockery Daphne and he had endured. He tasted a bitter cup of brooding that would not let him rest. Each night that Daphne sang he devised in fury that the room secreted her former lovers, and he held himself tense and ready for violence. She sought to soothe and reassure him, but he was beyond reason. When they could bear no more, they raged loudly at each other and did not care who heard. At other times they fought in a dreadful silence.

In those dissembled moments when they sought to tear from the fabric of the nightmare a pattern for survival, they drew me with frenzied gaiety into their plans.

"Can you see me tending house?" she asked, and laughed a quick, shrill laugh. "Janco, can you honestly see me in an apron?"

"I see you clearly," Apollo said. "I will come home weary in the evening—"

"And Daphne will greet you with a song and a dance," I said, smiling.

"She will greet me with a tableful of food," he cried. "Roast chicken and white pilaf and salad garnished with Calamata olives and ripe mezithra cheese."

"Where will this splendid meal come from?" Daphne asked.

"You will cook it," Apollo said. "As my mother cooked for my father."

"Fine," Daphne said mirthfully. "I will cook for you as your mother cooked for your father. Fine."

"You will cook it," Apollo spoke with confidence. "And we will invite Janco to dinner several nights a week."

"I will work hard to learn," Daphne said. "You might both be surprised at how good a cook I become."

"I think you will become a fine cook," I cried. "And when you achieve this mastery, Apollo will create a ballad about your prowess in the kitchen."

There were those other bleak and furious moments when he stormed past the bar into the office, and she followed as if she were tied to his flesh. I could hear their voices through the thin panels of wood.

"You are a madman," she told him. "You are blind and mad."

"I see enough," his voice trembled. "The way that sailor looked at you. The things you promised when you sang to him."

"It is only you I care about," she cried. "Don't you understand that?"

"You knew him from before," he said.

"I have never seen him before tonight."

"You lie!" he said savagely.

"I'm not lying!" she said. "I'm not lying!"

"There were other men," he said. "You cannot deny there were many other men."

"What can I say about that now?" she said, and a terrible pain rang in her words. "What can I do about that now?"

There was a day in the beginning of December when I got to the tavern very early in the afternoon and found it deserted except for Daphne on a stool at the bar.

"You are hours early," I said smiling. "Are you that attached to this place?"

"I am leaving, Janco," she said quietly. "I came to say goodby."

I could not answer. A sadness settled upon me. After a while I said, "Where will you go?"

"I don't know," she said. "I don't care."

"He will follow you," I said. "He will not let you go."

She did not answer or move for a long moment. Then she slipped off the stool and turned and stared gravely across the shadowed room with the chairs piled upon the empty wooden tables. "These places are all alike," she said bitterly. "When you have sung in one you have sung in all. They are graveyards one moment and circuses the next moment. They all have the smell of damp cellars that never see the sun."

"If you went away for a little while," I said. "For just a little while and then came back."

"That would do no good," she said. "You know that."

She walked a few steps, and her shadow rose and swept along the wall behind her as if seeking a place to rest.

"In the world outside," she said, "there are countless people who love and marry and bear children. They live one day like the next. I have never envied them before." A stricken wonder came into her voice. "I try to remember the moment for me when there was no turning back. I try to remember the moment such a dream was lost to me forever. I cannot." She shook her head wearily. "All my life seems a long, bawdy song."

She came slowly to where I stood and kissed me. Her lips were cold against my cheek. "I could not say goodby to him," she said. "I say goodby to you instead."

"Will you leave him a letter?" I asked. "A message?"

"Everything has been done." She shook her head. "Everything has been said." She walked toward the door of the office. "I will fix my face and go," she said. "The first waiters may come soon."

She stood for a moment in the doorway. Her face, suddenly stained with tears, had imperfections, but no face is faultless, and still she glittered in that moment with some strange beauty. "So the legend is right in the end," she said. "Daphne and Apollo are lost to each other."

"Not really lost," I said. "They have loved each other. He will never forget her. He will wear her love for his crown and will decorate with her memory his harp and his lyre."

"You are a foolish old man," she said softly. "Life to you is a song and a harp and stories that belong to the past."

She closed the door behind her. I turned wearily to prepare for the evening, trying to ease my distress in the movements of habit, the opening of bottles and the wiping of glasses. A few moments later I heard the sound of a shot.

A cold wind from the grave swept my body, and I went quickly through the door to the office. She was sitting in an armchair with her head limply to one side and the tumbled waves of her lovely hair almost hiding her face. There was a small stain of blood on her breast above her heart and at her feet the gun of Ali Pasha from his drawer.

I made my cross and closed my eyes for a moment and cried out then, a terrible cry from the marrow of my bone, for Daphne and Apollo and for the earth which had lost their love.

The winter seems to last forever. March is still a cold and dreary month. Sometimes the snow falls softly during the night, and in the morning the earth is frozen and buried. I walk shivering to work, and when I breathe, a quivering mist rises like smoke from my mouth.

The tavern is not the same. Ali Pasha carries a dark burden of guilt and drinks savagely and alone. The wild old men still dance, but without the vigor they had before, as if they are only sad and futile ghosts. Apollo still plays the guitar, but he is changed as well.

Many come to hear him play in the evening. I swear there are tears off his strings, and his songs are great white stars that set dreams to weeping. And as I stand behind the bar late at night and listen, it seems to me that I am back in the mountains of the old country under Homer's glittering moon. Parnassus stands behind dark mountains. The olive groves and the ruins of columns lie among the age-old trees. The sea and Piraeus are white with light. Under the stars the shepherds sleep beside their flocks.

When I have to sit down because my ankles are swollen and my feet hurt, I return unwillingly to reality and know I am only an old man. A foolish old man to whom life is a song and a harp and a legend that will never die.

¶ This is a grim story, and rereading it still chills me.

The Judgment

Elias Karnezos entered the United States as an immigrant from Greece in 1919. He was twenty-six years old, the son of a farmer from a village near Tripolis, in the Peloponnese. He was short, stocky, with robust arms and shoulders, strong hands, and thick black hair. His good health and ebullient spirits made him confident he would achieve success and make a fortune in the new land.

A friend who had emigrated from the same village a few years earlier, working as a bellboy in a Chicago hotel, obtained a job for Elias as a shine boy in a neighborhood shoe-repair shop. Elias shined shoes zestfully while singing songs of his village. The old shoemaker liked him and began teaching him the rudiments of his craft.

When conventions were quartered in the hotel where his friend worked, Elias joined him as a bellboy. From his paycheck and tips, he sent money home to his parents and to repay the debt he had incurred for his passage to America. Whatever remained after deducting for rent and food, he spent in roistering with a group of young sports. They gambled, danced, drank, and visited whores with jocular enthusiasm. Some of the first words Elias learned in English remained his favorite ones: "Sonofabitch!" "Goddam!" "Jesus Christ!" He never used these words in anger but simply as explosive and fervent expressions of his excitement and delight.

When the old shoemaker died, the owner of the store gave Elias the job with a substantial raise. Elias bought several new suits and a wide-brimmed Borsalino like those worn by gangsters of that period. He gained a reputation as a dandy and a generous man with friendship and money.

Among the cronies with whom he gambled were two brothers named Varvari from a village not far from his own in Greece. Playing poker in their apartment, he saw Katina, a younger sister the brothers had brought a few months earlier from Greece.

The girl was sixteen, tiny and slim-boned, with a somber face. She had never attended school and could not read or write. At the pleading of their parents the brothers had reluctantly brought her to America to have her educated and married. But they found it simpler to utilize her as a menial. She scrubbed, cleaned, washed, and cooked for them and their friends without complaint. She was shuttered by shyness and paralyzed by ignorance and terror. Her brothers ridiculed her constantly, mocking her ignorance by tossing newspapers and magazines at her and demanding she read them aloud. When they grew surly because they were losing in the games, they pinched her and threatened her with beatings.

"Why don't you leave the poor girl alone?" Elias cried indignantly.

"Sticking up for her is a waste of time," one of her brothers sneered. "She's dumb as a sheep and hasn't as much meat on her skinny frame as a starving chicken."

Katina knew Elias was defending her and fled with flushed cheeks back to the sanctuary of the kitchen.

In the following weeks, on visits to the apartment, Elias found excuses to enter the kitchen. It took him a while to overcome Katina's shyness and fear. One night he brought her a small box of sweet chocolates and saw her laugh with pleasure for the first time. He noticed then with surprise that she was a pretty girl, her hair black and lustrous, her features delicate, her eyes bright and alert. And she was so tiny that, despite his own short stature, he felt huge and tall beside her.

Her brothers thought him crazy and wavered between encouraging his interest to get Katina off their hands and avoiding the dire prospect of losing their indentured servant. The fact that Elias did not seem concerned about the traditional old-country dowry decided the brothers to accept his proposal of marriage to their sister.

Elias and Katina were married in a small church ceremony. He wore a rented tuxedo too small for his brawny shoulders and she wore a cheap white gown grudgingly paid for by her brothers. On the first night of their weekend honeymoon in the hotel where he worked as a bellboy, Elias took his bride's virginity with gentleness and patience. Despite her fear and shock at the sight of her blood, he was surprised at the fierce passion in her small, slim body.

They lived in a shabby, two-room apartment overlooking an alley a block from the shoe-repair shop. For the first few months after their marriage he came home after work every night to the dinner Katina prepared. But he found her meekness and silence oppressive, and in the monotonous hours of the evening he ached with nostalgia for the revelries of the nights before his marriage. He began meeting his cronies again, explaining to Katina there were shoes to be repaired after hours in the shop. When she did not question his excuses, he discarded even that flimsy pretense, slipping easily back into his routine of drinking, gambling, and visiting the jovial, bountiful whores who laughed and shrieked in his arms.

When he arrived home late at night, stinking of wine and the colognes and powders of other women, he climbed heavily into bed beside Katina. He heard her fitful breathing.

"Katina?"

She did not answer.

"Katina, I know you're awake."

She did not move. He reached under the covers and groped clumsily with his fingers for her naked body under the cotton nightgown, a maudlin gesture of remorse and affection. She twisted violently away from him, and untroubled within his drunken euphoria, he fell soddenly asleep, unaware of the tears of shame and fury Katina cried into her pillow as he snored.

Katina's life resumed the pattern of her labor in the service of her brothers. She scrubbed, washed, and cooked for Elias and the friends he brought home. In addition, she received him into her body for the occasional spurtings of passion he salvaged from his whores.

Elias could not understand that Katina's inability to read and write locked her into a dark obsession with her own grievances. Although she had feared the cruelty of her brothers, their brutalities seemed trivial to those she now endured. She felt betrayed, her rage at Elias compounded of her own unsatisfied passion and the way he selfishly surfeited his needs. She began resisting his caresses, subduing her desire in a corset of tightly laced hate.

"What the hell's the matter with you?" he would say in aggravation. "You're stiff as a carrot! What's wrong with you?"

"Leave me alone!"

"What the hell is wrong?" he cried.

"Ask your whores!" she said hoarsely.

Stung by the justice of her condemnation, he would turn away from her in the bed.

"Goddam women!" he would mumble under his breath. "None of them understand a man needs a little fun. . . ."

At other times, however, when drinking dulled his guilt, he forced himself upon her. They warred with their bodies, his strength pitted against her spirit. Though she was determined to deny herself any pleasure, there were moments Katina's body betrayed her will and she cried out with a wild, unwilling joy. Afterward she bathed and scrubbed her breasts and thighs as if they had been defiled.

In the second year of their marriage Katina became pregnant. She accepted the doctor's diagnosis with resentment and distress. But as the baby grew within her body, she felt herself softening, curling warm and alive, the world less grim and forbidding.

Elias was jubilant. He sang loudly as he pounded on the

last, cut down his drinking, reduced his gambling, and subdued his whoring except for a few infrequent lapses when
desire drove him wild. On those occasions he did not linger
after he was relieved but would hurry to dress.

"Where you going so fast, honey?" a whore named An-
neta, who was fond of him, asked.

"I'm going to have a son," Elias said, as if that anticipated
event explained everything.

In the evenings after work he went home to Katina eagerly. He treated her with an awkward, uncommon gentleness as he watched her tiny belly rise and swell. At night
in bed when he felt her stirring restlessly to find a comfortable position, he spoke to her softly.

"Are you all right?"

"I am all right," she answered quietly.

"Do you have any pain?"

"I have no pain," she said.

"Can I get you anything? A glass of water or some tea?"

"I am all right!" she said impatiently. "Go to sleep!"

In the silence that followed he slid his body carefully
closer to her, gently touching her bare foot with his own
toes. He was overwhelmed with gratefulness when she did
not pull away.

The baby was born in the spring of that year, a dark-
haired, brown-eyed boy they named Peter. When he beheld
the infant in Katina's arms for the first time, Elias cried with
pride and joy. In that sacred moment he swore he would
never touch a whore again.

Their lives mended in the delight of their son. After each
day's work Elias rushed home to play with the baby. Katina
scolded him for his ardor but enjoyed the baby herself, her
days filled with the wonder of his beauty and his growth.

The following year, Katina gave birth to a baby girl. Almost a year to the day after that birth, in the same month
that Elias purchased the shoe-repair shop for his own business, Katina gave birth to a second daughter, their third

child. For all three children she was a devoted and capable mother, unhindered by her inability to read and write.

Contented in his home and family, Elias worked vigorously, and his business prospered. He bought a second shoe-repair shop and then a large dry-cleaning business. He had more than thirty employees working for him, joined a fraternal lodge and a businessmen's association, bought a new car, the first he had ever owned, and learned, not without some minor mishaps, to drive it.

For a while Katina firmly refused to allow the children or herself to ride with Elias, but when her apprehension lessened, she looked forward to their drives into the country on Sunday afternoons. Another favorite pastime was when they invited a score of friends to the park on summer weekends. Elias would buy a whole lamb and roast it over a charcoal fire and a spit, drinking and dancing and singing until it was time to eat.

And every Sunday morning they dressed the children and themselves in their best clothing and went to the Greek church. Standing stiffly beside Katina as they held the children in their arms, Elias felt his family blessed and sanctioned by God.

When Peter was three years old, the girls about one and two, an epidemic of influenza struck the city. All three children became ill, but only their son suffered complications. In the space of two nights, despite the frantic ministrations of a doctor and a nurse, the boy died.

In the anguish that followed their son's death Elias sought to comfort Katina, feeling a mother's loss even a greater calamity than his own. Yet he could not console himself. During the day he would suddenly burst into tears. Every small boy he passed on the street cut like a knife into his heart.

Katina, tearing at her hair in grief, came to feel the boy's death was a punishment for her acquittal and acceptance of the corruptions and debaucheries of Elias. By forgiving her husband's lechery, she had had delivered upon her a terrible retribution. She swore she would live the remainder of her life seeking to protect her daughters and herself, convinced that, in the end, God would exact damnation on Elias. Katina made her decision to mourn and remember, and to suppress every small pleasure and joy.

"What can I do?" Elias cried. "Sit in a dark room, day and night, remembering the boy?"

"Say your prayers and go to church!" Katina cried. "Light candles! Ask God's forgiveness!"

"Candles won't bring me back my son," Elias said bitterly.

"He is with God now."

"He doesn't belong to God!" Elias said. "He belongs to me!"

"Wait!" Katina cried. "Wait! God will answer your blasphemy!"

"I'm not saying nothing against God," Elias said. A resignation and despair swept his spirit. "I'm only saying that goddam candles won't bring me back my son."

In a frantic effort to anesthetize his sorrow, he invited friends to dinner several evenings a week. He spent money lavishly on wine, lamb, olives, and cheese. He sat at the head of the table, shouting for his guests to eat and drink. His arduous efforts at gaiety faltered before the somber presence of Katina. Sometimes she spoke a few words to one of the guests, but mostly she remained silent and unsmiling, casting her mournful shadow over the gathering. The uncomfortable guests would leave soon after dinner.

Sometimes at night, their daughters asleep, Elias and Katina in bed in their darkened room, he'd make an effort to embrace his wife. She pulled away as if the touch of his body had burned her.

"Let me love you a little," he pleaded. "It will be good for both of us."

"Never again," Katina said, her voice cold and relentless. "Never again for as long as we live. That is what God has decreed."

"How do you know that?" he cried in a low, hoarse whisper. "Why should he want that from us?" When she did not answer he turned away from her, trying to separate and calm the waves of fear and desire that swept his body. He remembered the oath he had taken, after the birth of his son, never to touch a whore again. He saw the balance of his life, cold and unloved.

"Sonofabitch," he murmured softly. "Sonofabitch."

Upon his small daughters Elias lavished all the generosity and affection his wife rejected. Despite her disapproval, he bought them frilly expensive dresses and small ermine coats. He spoiled them rampantly, loved to have them come running into his arms when he entered the door in the evening, their fingers eagerly searching his pockets for the gifts he always carried.

In contrast to his indulgences, Katina taught the girls the crafts of cooking and sewing, sternly pushing them to their books and studies, although she had no comprehension of the things they were studying.

When Elias sought to help the girls with some facet of their schoolwork, she turned on him resentfully.

"You think that's the way it really is?" she said scornfully. "You think because you can read, you know what's going on? You know nothing about life and the way people really are! You are a fool!"

To reinforce her argument she drew upon all the flotsam that floated unmoored in her head. Ignorant of the barest fundamentals of the knowledge in books, she lived in a teeming cupboard of superstition, myth, village theology, memories, fears, rumors, and the gossip of neighbors.

If Elias tried to argue with her, she'd burst into a rage. The girls would flee to their room and Elias would shield himself behind a newspaper, trying vainly to understand the reason for her vehemence and fury.

The years passed. The girls grew into dark-haired, dark-eyed young beauties. Katina was a vigilant tyrant, refusing to allow them to attend dances at school or parties in the homes of friends. The only organization she permitted them to join was the choir of the Greek church. On the holidays, she allowed them to invite a few friends into their home, but she subjected every boy who entered to so baleful a scrutiny, he fled, vowing never to return. When her daughters complained, Katina silenced them with angry, ominous warnings.

"All men are animals!" she cried. "Seeking to destroy girls, turn them into sluts! That won't happen to you while I'm alive!"

In the year their elder daughter graduated from high school, Elias suffered a disastrous fire that totally destroyed his dry-cleaning shop full of the clothing of his customers. His insurance covered only a fraction of their losses, yet he felt his honor required he pay the full amounts. When he had fulfilled this obligation, he was almost penniless, left with a single small shoe-repair shop, a shoemaker, a shine boy, and himself.

These reversals reinforced Katina's conviction that Elias was a shallow and indulgent man who accidentally managed some success that, in the end, his stupidity caused him to destroy. He, in turn, began to believe she was right in calling him a blockhead and a fool.

Within a year after their graduations, both daughters left home to be married. For the first time in twenty-five years, Elias and Katina were alone.

Elias aged quickly. Although he was only in his middle fifties, his thick black hair was mottled with strands of white. Futility cut deeper creases into the flesh of his cheeks and darkened the hollow circles about his eyes. He sought desperately to salvage his shattered business under a persistent burden of failure and defeat. He let the shoemaker go and returned to the last himself. But the years had dulled his fingers, and his poor workmanship was the final blow that caused him to close his business. They moved to a smaller apartment, grimly reminiscent of the dark rooms they had lived in during the first years of their marriage. Elias managed to pay the rent and buy food on a small insurance annuity he had taken out years before.

He looked for work but there was nothing for a man of his years without any special skill. He retreated to spending his hours before the television set, waiting for the visits of his daughters and the small grandchildren that had been born in the past few years. When they came to see him, he hugged them playfully, tickling and kissing them with delight. Katina shrieked that he would hurt them, confuse them with his insensate shouts. He'd make an effort to ignore her but, finally, pained and subdued, he'd let the children alone.

When they sat at the table, he slipped into the bountiful role he had always loved, urging food upon the children, wine upon his sons-in-law. Everything he did incurred Katina's displeasure.

"Shut up, old man!" she cried. "You think everybody guzzles and eats like you do! Not a dollar in your pocket and you still eat and drink like a pig!"

"Goddam, leave me alone," he'd say weakly and shake his head in resignation.

When he began to recite a story, some episode out of his past, his eyes would glitter and he'd laugh gaily. At some point in his excited recounting, Katina entered like a chorus.

"He was your good friend, that one, wasn't he? As long as you had money in your pocket and wine and food on your table. Where is he now?" She mocked him. "Where are all your other friends? Now that you have nothing but the pants you wear each day and the pants you wear on Sunday, where are all your friends? Answer me that, old fool!"

In order to evade Katina's nagging, he began leaving the house each morning, gathering with a few other old men in a coffee shop a couple of blocks away. They passed the hours telling stories of their youth.

Through the owner of the coffee shop, Elias heard of an old Italian shoemaker in the neighborhood who wanted to sell his small shop and return to Italy to die. Elias visited the shabby, narrow store, the fixtures decrepit, the machinery ancient. But the old shoemaker was willing to sell out for five hundred dollars, and the rent was only fifty dollars a month.

Elias borrowed two hundred and fifty dollars from his elder daughter's husband as a down payment on the purchase price and promised to pay the shoemaker the balance within six months.

When Katina learned of what he had done, she shrieked at him in fury and denounced her daughters for aiding him in his folly.

"Just wait a few months and I'll show you!" he cried. "I'll be on my feet again in no time! Jesus Christ, watch if I don't show you!"

Once more he rose with renewed hope at dawn and walked briskly to his shop, feeling a delight in turning on the lights, putting on his apron, starting the machinery. Yet, despite working from dawn until seven or eight o'clock in the evening, he barely made enough money to pay his rent. Rather than confront Katina's scorn, he borrowed a few dollars from one of his daughters and gave it to his wife at the end of the week as if it were a profit.

In the winter of that year, the wind and snow sweeping through the desolate streets, he sat huddled for warmth beside the small coal-burning stove, wearing his coat to conserve on fuel, staring through the window, vainly waiting for a customer to appear. Sometimes a whole day passed without a single person entering the store. The few pairs of shoes he repaired stood forlorn on the counter. At the end of the day he locked and shuttered his shop and despondently walked the few blocks home to the dinner Katina had prepared for him.

A new distress rose to plague him. His vision began to blur and the few customers who brought him work complained about the poor quality of the repair. Apprehensive of complaining to Katina, he kept the knowledge of his failing sight to himself for months. Only when he finally slashed his fingers on the shoe machines did he ask one of his daughters to take him to the doctor. An examination disclosed he had ripened cataracts in both eyes.

He entered the hospital for surgery, a dreadful period of darkness, sustained only by the faith that he would be able to see again. When the bandages were finally removed, his vision remained clouded by the failure of his eyes to heal properly. He sat for hours before the television set, watching the screen for that instant when the blurred faces and figures would once more come into focus. Instead of improving, his sight grew slowly worse. Each time one of his daughters took him back to the doctor for re-examination, he pleaded for help.

"Goddam, Doctor!" he cried. "Maybe something, some new medicine can make me see better. I can't work or read a paper! A man can't live like this!"

He could not accept the doctor's explanation that there had been incurable damage to the retina of his eyes, that although he might not become totally blind, his sight would slowly diminish and he would have to exist in a world of shadows.

With that irrevocable diagnosis, Katina ceased to nag him, fed him patiently, tended his needs without complaint. He was so grateful for her kindness, he was often moved to tears.

"I'll get better, Ma," he promised her fervently, holding tightly to her hand. "They'll find some medicine, some new treatment. You'll see, I'll find another store, get a new start, look after us both once more."

He marveled how calmly and stoically she accepted his plight. He praised her constancy and devotion to his daughters.

"Jesus Christ, that woman has become an angel," he said.

"The way she takes care of me every minute. That's what she is, an angel."

But as the weeks passed and his hope faltered, his anguish grew and the bonds holding him to life weakened. There was a night he woke with a strange heat burning through his body. He started to call to Katina, who slept in the bedroom across the hall, then slipped again into a fitful sleep. In his fevered dreams he saw the faces of his father and mother, the fields and groves about his village, the ship on which he journeyed to America. He saw the cronies of his early revels, the glittering bodies of whores, the laughing, carefree black men who worked for him, the mountain of shoes he had mended. He saw the countless wine casks he had emptied, the lambs roasting on the spit, the dancing friends who had shared his joy. He saw the cherub's cheeks of his son, the flowered mound of his grave, the eyes of his grandchildren glowing in the light of candles on the holiday tables. Above them he saw the figure of Katina.

He could not be certain whether she was part of his dream or whether he had wakened to find her standing over him, grown to a vast and stunning height, huge and broad as he had once felt when she was small and slim. But he suddenly recognized her as a vengeful, merciless, and satisfied witness to his fate.

In the great flood of water rising to engulf his body, a torrent rushing to clear his eyes, he uttered a single perplexed and bewildered cry, the last sound he made before he died.

¶ I don't know quite what to say about this story. I enjoyed writing it and am particularly fond of the last line:

"In a world of fools, the lout is king. . . ."

The Shearing of Samson

In a world where uncertainties abound, a man must depend on common sense. Reason is the only weapon with which to combat the hoary superstition and unbridled hysteria of fools. I tried often to explain this to my friend, Louie Anastis, but the man's incapacity to be reasonable merely confirms my observation that he is a lout.

In order that you might better understand the situation, I should first tell you something of Louie and myself. Before his retirement Louie had been a meatman specializing in animals that died natural deaths. He offered these beasts at substantial discounts to any restaurant owner foolish or greedy enough to purchase them. (I do not mention this fact to slander him but because it is the truth.)

As for myself, Alexis Krokas, until my own retirement two years ago I had been the owner of a restaurant. Nothing fancy, you understand, just a small lunchroom with sixteen stools in a factory district that kept me alive for thirty years until it was time to collect my social security.

Then there was Samson. Samson Leventis. He was our very close friend, a patron of the Parthenon coffeehouse where Louie and I drank mastiha every evening and danced to the bouzouki on Saturday nights. (We managed this feat in spite of Louie's weight and my wretched sciatica.)

Samson was a big man of about forty years, as strong a man as I had ever known. He owned the Zorah Wholesale Produce Company on Halsted Street and could open a crate of produce by shattering the wood with his fist. He had a voice as resonant as a clap of thunder. His clothing consisted mostly of mismatched trousers and coats and he never wore a tie. The most striking thing about him, however, was his thick black hair that he wore so long it concealed most of his ears and curled like a horse's nape over the collar of his shirt.

We were always pleased when Samson joined us and on that night in the spring when he came to our table in the Parthenon, we greeted him warmly.

"Your bottle is empty," Samson said as he sat down. "Waiting too long between bottles causes gas." He called out in his resonant voice and almost instantly old Barba Niko shot out of the shadows with a full bottle of mastiha. Samson filled our glasses.

For a long strange moment afterwards he was silent. Louie and I felt a curious suspense and waited for him to speak.

"My old friends," Samson said finally, "I think for the first time in my barren forty years of life, I am truly in love."

Frankly, I was startled and Louie was stunned. Respecting good sense and reason as I did, I had, of course, remained a bachelor. Louie had been married once for three years and his experience had been a calamity. His wife, a harpy who outweighed him by sixty pounds blacked both his eyes at least once a month and on one frightful occasion even kicked him down a flight of stairs. When he had despaired of ever attaining freedom he received a joyous parole. She deserted him to run away with a Turkish coffee salesman who had the brazen nerve to return to Louie three weeks later and plead with him to take back his wife. Louie hastily put his case in the competent hands of another mutual friend, counselor Pericles Piniotis (the poor devil suffered an untimely death when struck by an ambulance backing up) and achieved a separation. His tragic experience had completely unbalanced him on the subject of women and marriage.

"Well, is nobody going to speak?" Samson cried. "Are you both going to sit there dumb after such news?"

Louis was still so badly shaken he could not answer. I felt

it was up to me to observe the amenities. "Congratulations, Samson," I said. "Who is the lucky woman?"

"Not a woman," Samson said fervently. "A goddess."

Louie rose from the table with one hand across his stomach. Samson reached up and pulled him back down. "Sit, old friend, and drink!" he cried. "I know how delighted you must be for me." He caught me watching him and with one of his massive fingers gave me a playful poke in the chest that almost caved in my ribs. "How about it, Alexis?" he laughed. "Does an old bachelor like you know anything about great love?"

"Certainly," I said slightly huffed. "Love is a strong affection for a member of the opposite sex. Like Dante for Beatrice and Abelard for Heloise." I spoke these references modestly.

"Those are Turkish names to me," Samson shook his head. "I'm talking about real love and not fairy tales."

"Those people were real," I said.

"Is that right?" he asked and his interest was quickened. "That Dinty something or other must be an Irishman, eh?"

"An Italian," I said. "He was a man who loved a woman from the time she was a very young girl. He wrote poetry to her all his life and never said a word to her, never spoke to her."

"The only way," Louie said somberly.

Samson stared at me in disbelief. "Never spoke to her? What kind of nonsense is that? Of course he spoke to her."

"No," I said firmly. "He died without ever speaking a single word to her."

"God bless that man," Louie said.

Samson's cheeks quivered. "Where did you hear that?" he asked.

"That is something I learned back in school."

Samson slammed the table with his fist and made bottles and glasses jump. "That makes me glad I never went beyond the fourth grade!" he cried. "That's sheer nonsense."

"Let me tell you about my wife," Louie said. "My first mistake was talking to her."

"What about the other fellow?" Samson asked me. "That Abe something or other?"

"Abelard," I said. "He was a priest who fell in love with a beautiful girl and ran off with her."

Louie made his cross in dismay.

"That's more like it," Samson gave a long low whistle. "A priest too. That took guts. What happened?"

"Her kinsmen became angry," I said, "and sent some men to take revenge on Abelard. They severed certain parts of his body."

"I knew something terrible would happen," Louie said.

"What parts?" Samson asked. "His legs? Arms? Hands?" I shrugged grimly. A look of horror swept Samson's face.

"The butchers!" he cried in outrage. "The bloody butchers!"

"Violence and women," Louie said bitterly.

"In the end," I said, "Heloise became a nun and Abelard went into a monastery."

"Of course," Samson said with compassion. "What else could the poor devils do?" He sat in somber silence for a moment. "My own beloved is a widow whose husband has been dead five years now," he said gravely. "She moved here from Cleveland six months ago to buy the Sorek Bakery on Harrison Street. She bakes the bread and cakes in the kitchen. That's how I first saw her, her face flushed from the heat of the ovens, and flour smudged across her dark lovely hair. I tell you, old friends, I haven't been the same since." He made a gesture of resignation. "It took a week of going into the store before I mustered up the courage to talk to her. You know I am a pretty rough sort, not much for fancy ways, and enough to scare a real lady when I meet one."

"You are highly regarded," I reassured him and Louie nodded quickly in agreement. "You can outdance and out-drink any man on the street. All of us respect you."

"Old warriors like yourselves," he said, "but a woman

measures things differently. I've been seeing her for two
months now. I go and sit with her in the kitchen while she
works. Sometimes she lets me take her to dinner. She seems
to like me but she also says I lack appreciation of the finer
things, that I dress like a bum, and that I look like a shaggy
bear with my hair down my neck." He sighed and rose to his
feet to leave. "Maybe I could change," he said somberly.
"For a woman such as the Widow Delilah, I think I would
do anything." He nodded in farewell and walked slowly to
the door.

Louie moaned softly. "Delilah!" he said and struck his fist
on the table in a puerile imitation of Samson.

"Do you know her?"

"No," he shook his head in distress, "but in the Bible the
mighty Samson was destroyed by the wicked Delilah."

"Don't be a fool," I said impatiently. "The names are
mere coincidence."

"Any woman is a calamity," Louie said, "but one named
Delilah for a man named Samson!" He slapped his cheeks
with his palms in despair.

"Louie, listen to me," I said sternly. "Get a grip on your
head."

"We must save him," Louie said. "He is too noble a man
to be destroyed by an unscrupulous woman." He paused,
breathing heavily. "I must go to see the Widow."

"Just like that," I laughed wryly. "You will go and see the
Widow and ask her not to marry Samson because her name
is Delilah. She will throw you on your crooked head."

Louie rose and drew himself to his full, plump and quivering five feet and two inches. "I consider Samson almost a
son," he said with emotion. "I must make an effort to save
him."

I sighed. I knew the density of that man's head and how
impervious he could be to reason. "You will make a mess of
this affair," I said. "Since you insist on meddling, I will have
to go along and prevent you making a greater fool of yourself than you already are."

Early the next morning Louie and I met at the Sorek Bakery. We stood for a moment outside the window laden with frosted cakes and sugared rolls.

"Now let me do the talking," I warned him. "If you have a comment, make it sensible and brief, if that isn't asking too much."

Louie agreed uneasily. We entered the warm little store scented with the aroma of freshly baked bread. A young slim girl worked behind the counter.

"We have come to call on the Widow Delilah," I said. "We do not wish to interrupt her work but we would be grateful for just a few moments of her time."

The girl retired to the kitchen and returned to motion us around the counter. We walked into the kitchen and met the Widow Delilah.

She was a tall and stately woman in her early thirties. Her face was a flawless ivory oval within a frame of thick black hair gathered into a great bun at the back of her head. Her dark eyes had a startling brightness. There were stains of flour upon the apron which rose and swelled across her majestic breasts.

For a moment I thoroughly appreciated Samson's admiration for her. I gave her a warm smile. When I caught Louie watching me with suspicion, I sobered quickly.

"Widow Delilah," I said politely, "this gentleman is Louie Anastis and I am Alexis Krokas. We are very close friends of Samson Leventis. He has spoken of you with great respect. Since we happened to be passing we thought we would just drop in and introduce ourselves."

"We regard Samson as if he was our son," Louie said ominously.

At the mention of Samson, a deeper pinch of red appeared in the Widow Delilah's already flushed cheeks. "I am pleased to meet you," she said in a husky voice and her lips parted as if they were glistening halves of a ripe plum. She raised the tray of bread and pushed it into the oven with a supple grace. She turned back to us wiping her fingers on a cloth. "I am very fond of Samson," she said.

"Are you going to marry him?" Louie asked in a shrill voice.

A startled confusion swept her cheeks. I gave Louie a hard censuring look and spoke quickly. "Forgive Mr. Anastis," I said. "He cares greatly for Samson and sometimes this causes him to speak bluntly."

She made a gentle gesture of forgiveness. "No apology is necessary," she said. "Your concern for your dear friend speaks well for both of you. You will permit me to speak just as frankly. I am very fond of Samson but I am afraid that I could never marry him."

"Never?" Louie asked eagerly.

"Why?" I asked puzzled. "I don't understand."

"My husband, God bless his departed soul, was a good man," she said quietly. "With his insurance I moved here from Cleveland and bought this store. I am lonely, very lonely sometimes and I would not object to marrying again except that it must be to a man interested in music and art, the things that I am interested in. I am afraid I could not endure a rough and disorderly existence."

"Samson is rough and disorderly, all right," Louie agreed with satisfaction.

"He is a strong man, true," I said. "But he has a purity of spirit as well. He appears unruly and fierce but I have never known him to commit an unkind act against any man or woman."

"He never went beyond the fourth grade," Louie said looking at me indignantly.

"The neighborhood children adore him," I said. "After school they stop by his business for a banana or a peach. You may think, my dear Widow, that you know Samson but until you have seen him teasing and cavorting with a group of delighted children, you cannot know the real man."

"He drinks a great deal," Louie said shrilly. "Two, often three bottles of mastiha a night."

"He is a champion of the weak," I went on swept by growing enthusiasm. "When hoodlums threatened Gavaras, the tailor, and poured acid on his racks of clothing, it was Samson who drove them off Halsted Street. Three men he thrashed that day in a fight that will be remembered for years. They have never dared return."

"He fights a great deal," Louie said loudly and wrung his hands fretfully. "Every weekend, sometimes."

"Let us not forget the baskets he distributes to the needy on Christmas and Thanksgiving," I said. "Many families would go hungry if it were not for Samson."

The Widow Delilah listened in silence. When I paused finally out of breath, she raised her hand in a soft gesture of concession. "I did not know all these things about him," she said, and it was evident she was moved. "He is such a loud and boisterous man, one would never conceive of such goodness and gentleness being a part of him as well."

"Most of the time he is pretty wild," Louie said desperately. "Ask the priest what he thinks of Samson and he will make his cross."

"It speaks well of Samson that he has such loyal friends," she said slowly and nodded gratefully at Louie, "such honest friends willing to admit his faults as well as his virtues. I am sincerely impressed." She offered us her hand in a gracious farewell.

We emerged into the street and Louie trembled in agitation.

"She told us she could never consider Samson," I said to reassure him. "How could I malign him after that rejection? Louie, believe me, I am quite sure this woman was speaking the truth when she told us she would never consider Samson."

It was less than a week after our visit to the bakery when we were sitting one evening at our table in the Parthenon. Louie and I had maintained an uneasy truce since speaking to the Widow Delilah. I was sipping my mastiha slowly and scratching my ear when a wild triumphant bellow shattered the darkness of the coffeehouse. Louis was nearly blown off his chair.

The wild bellow rang out again and a big man came stamping between the tables waving his arms like windmills. It was Samson and he came almost at a run to our table. "There you are!" he cried.

The old men from the nearby tables gathered around our own. "Hey, Samson," a graybeard called. "Did you find a pearl in one of your bananas?"

Samson laughed loudest of all. "I don't need a pearl," he cried, "when I have friends such as these two."

"What have we done?" Louie asked fearfully, sensing disaster.

"What have you done?" Samson shouted. "I will tell everyone what you have done! By your loyalty and devotion to me you greatly impressed the Widow Delilah. She regarded me in a new and kinder light. Tonight she consented to be my wife!"

Louie's terrible moan was lost in the roar of approval from the old men around our table but I heard it clearly. Samson started to pull Louie and me from our chairs. "Come with me, old friends," he said. "Tonight I buy drinks for everybody and you will drink the best brandy old Barba Niko has in his cellar."

"You go ahead, Samson," I smiled faintly. "Louie and I will be right along."

He started toward the bar dragging a half dozen of the old men with him. Louie and I were left alone. He stared at me as if I had committed some infamous crime. "You convinced her," he said in a choked voice. "You sealed his doom."

"You are an idiot," I whispered angrily. "A woman isn't convinced by a few words of praise to marry a man unless she intended to marry him all along. She concealed her true feelings. And what if they do marry? The trouble with you, Louie, is that you let one deplorable female sour you on all

women. You should have made your wife understand from
the beginning that you were the boss."

"Are you mad!" Louie said in a shocked voice. "That
monster outweighed me by sixty pounds!"

"Louie," I said more gently, "it depends upon the man.
Can you imagine any woman getting the better of a man as
courageous and strong as Samson? Can you imagine such an
absurdity?" I laughed at how ridiculous the possibility
seemed but Louie did not crack even a glimmer of a smile.

"Hey, Alexis! Louie!" Samson shouted from the bar.

I rose from my chair. "Now cheer up," I said to Louie.
"Let us go and drink to Samson's nuptials."

"I would rather stop breathing!" Louie said. He rose and
fled to the door, waddling slightly under his burden of fat. I
went to the bar alone and told Samson that Louie had been
overcome by the joy of the announcement and had to leave.

We did not see Samson again for almost six weeks following that night. Two weeks after he came to thank us so
jubilantly, the Widow Delilah and he were married in Cleveland. Their honeymoon included a week at Niagara Falls.
The first awareness we had of their return was when Delilah
phoned us at the Parthenon one Friday evening and invited
Louie and myself for dinner the following evening. Louie
had still not subdued his resentment and apprehension and
was reluctant to go until I convinced him it would be a
gross affront to Samson.

The next night we dressed in our Sunday suits and walked
to the apartment on Blue Island which had been Delilah's
before she married. Ignoring Louie's disapproval I carried a
small bouquet of flowers for the new bride.

We rang the bell of their apartment. A moment later Samson's voice answered faintly from the mouthpiece beside the
mailbox.

"It is Alexis and Louie," I said loudly. "Welcome back,
Samson."

The buzzer sounded and I opened the door and started
briskly up the stairs. Louie came slowly and heavily behind

me. On the third floor Samson stood waiting in the doorway of the apartment.

"Hello, old friend," he said and his voice sounded low and subdued but there was another apartment on the landing and I thought perhaps a neighbor was ill.

"Hello, Samson," I whispered.

There was a single dim light in the hall, a small bulb on the wall near the stairs and I could not see Samson clearly. I noticed with surprise that he wore a white shirt with a tie looped around his throat as if it were a noose. He seemed to be swaying slightly and when I looked down at his feet I did not see the old cracked wide black brogues he had always worn but a glittering pair of two-tone shoes that tapered to an incredibly sharp tip. Samson swung open the door of the apartment and stepped back to allow me to enter. In the bright ceiling light I saw his head for the first time and I almost cried out in shock and consternation.

The great black tangled forest of hair that had curled over his ears and matted around his collar was gone, shorn from his scalp as if he were a sheep, leaving a short bristling stubble over an expanse of pale flesh. For the first time in twenty years I saw his ears and they were crooked and pointed like the ears of a sad dog and skewered at an incredible angle from his head.

Louie, breathing hard from his ascent, stepped in the door and when he saw Samson, he staggered as if he had been dealt a stunning blow.

"Some slight changes," Samson laughed nervously, and his big hand fumbled uneasily at his head as if in futile search for the mop that was no longer there. "Looks neater, eh?" He spoke with the pathetic eagerness of a child wishing to be consoled.

"Certainly, Samson," I said quickly.

Louie could only stare at him in horror. Fortunately, at that moment, Delilah swept down the hall to greet us. She was dressed in a long white gown, her hair coiled in great thick braids about her head. Somehow the sheared scalp of

Samson served to accentuate the vitality of her own abundant locks. From her ears hung silver earrings in the shape of slim glistening knives.

"So good to see you, dear friends," she said warmly. "And what lovely flowers? Aren't the flowers lovely, Samson?"

Samson nodded somberly.

"Shall we go in and sit down?" Delilah said. "Dinner will be served in a moment. Samson, put the flowers in water. There is a vase in the kitchen. This way, gentlemen."

Samson started down the hall taking short mincing steps as if he were practicing a dance for the wretched ballet. Louie watched Samson in agony and I had to pull at his arm to follow Delilah.

In a few moments we sat down to dinner at a table covered by a fine lace cloth and set with delicate china and crystal. But in spite of the splendid roast lamb with browned potatoes, the whole meal was a calamitous series of fumblings and admonitions.

"Not that fork, love," Delilah said to Samson, "the other one. Stir with the spoon, love," she said. "Don't hold it as if it is a stein of beer." She spoke gently but with a vein of iron in her voice.

Even Louie and I became apprehensive. Although she did not correct us, she watched us. A number of times I hesitated and let my food grow cold because I could not be sure what bloody piece of silverware to use. Louie seemed to lose control completely once and, missing his mouth with his fork, jabbed a piece of lamb into his cheek.

But I forgot my own discomfort in watching Samson. He sat huddled in misery in his chair, the bright lights burning down upon his bereaved head, not daring to pick up a glass or a fork without receiving an approving nod from Delilah. Every swallow of food seemed to stick somewhere in his throat.

At the end of that cursed meal we were allowed to relax slightly over small cups of sweet coffee. Samson mustered the courage to ask a few questions on his own.

"How are things at the Parthenon, Alexis?"

"Everybody misses you, Samson," I said eagerly. "The dancing is not the same without you. Next Saturday night they are bringing in a new bouzouki player from New York. There will be some wild dancing. Come and join us."

Samson started to nod with enthusiasm and then looked at his wife. Delilah smiled with a slight shrug of regret. "Our Saturday nights are taken for the next six weeks," she said. "Samson and I have reserved tickets on those evenings for the opera."

"The opera!" Louie gasped. "Samson?"

I coughed to cover his confusion. "The opera is very cultural," I said stiffly. "The very best people go to the opera."

Delilah nodded in firm agreement. She shook a gently reproving finger at Louie and myself and with a peremptory movement of her wrist included Samson. "You have all spent far too many nights in the coffeehouse," she said. "There are pleasures far above the bouzouki and bottles of mastiha. There are symphony concerts and the art galleries downtown. I want Samson to learn to appreciate these delights he has been denied up to now. Perhaps the four of us can visit some of these galleries and attend some of the concerts together."

"Certainly," I said, and then I pushed back my chair and rose quickly. "At the moment, however, I have just remembered there is a meeting of our lodge chapter this evening. Please forgive me if I run right off because I am late already."

"I am so sorry you must leave," Delilah said. "I planned for us to listen to some classical records for a while."

Louie rose with a bounce from his chair. "I must go to the meeting too," he said. "Forgive me."

We said goodnight and walked to the door. Samson came behind us. We stood waiting while he hobbled and swayed to join us. We stared at his feet and he smiled uneasily. "They're the latest style," he said. "They're my size too." He looked warily in the direction of the diningroom. "Those damn tips," he whispered. "They're built for men with two toes instead of five." He made a gesture of resignation. "I'll get used to them, someday, I guess."

"If you don't go lame first," Louie said in a choked voice. With a tight forlorn wave of his hand he started heavily down the stairs.

I gave Samson's hand a reassuring squeeze.

"She's a grand girl, Alexis," he said fervently. "She wants what is best for me. I try to go along with her. It's for my own good, you know."

I started down the stairs. Samson hung over the railing. "Say hello to all the boys," he called after me in a plaintive voice. "I'll stop by . . ." there was a wretched pause, ". . . one of these days."

"I'll tell them, Samson," I said, and there was a tightness in my throat. "I'll tell them, old friend."

When I reached the street, Louie waited for me. I expected tearful recriminations but the whole evening had been such a shock, he was apparently having difficulty collecting his senses.

"Just like in the Bible," he said, struggling for breath. "Samson was shorn of his hair by Delilah and lost all his strength. It happened just like in the Bible."

"You are an idiot!" I cried furiously. "Stop talking nonsense! The whole business is sheer coincidence!"

I turned away and Louie reached out and grabbed my arm.

"It will be all right, Alexis, don't worry," he said hoarsely. "Remember what happened when Samson's hair grew back? He pulled down the pillars of the temple and destroyed Delilah and the Philistines." He nodded in a spasm of delight. "It will be all right! Samson will triumph in the end!"

I looked at him in shock. He stood there with his plump cheeks quivering and revelation rising like mist from his pores.

"Louie," I said, and my voice trembled, "Louie . . ." I

closed my eyes and had a sudden and bitter vision of those crooked ears and that naked and wretched head. I felt my senses rattled and my reason succumb with a groan.

"Enough, Louie," I spoke in a shaken whisper. "Go to the church and light a candle for Samson. Light one for me too. Ask the priest for a prayer."

"Right!" Louie cried fervently. "At once!"

I turned and started hurriedly away. "Where are you going?" he hollered shrilly.

I did not answer. I assembled my quivering legs and set a furious pace for the Parthenon, staying well beneath the bright beam of the street-lamps.

When reason is staggered by dread and superstition, when sanity is routed by necromancy and spirits from the vasty deep, no recourse remains for a reasonable man but to drown the whole catastrophic dilemma in a bottle of mastiha.

In a world of fools, the lout is king. . . .

℧ I have written few stories with young college students as principal characters. This story was published by a campus literary magazine, but I seem to remember one or more of my sons observing I had not really understood the young people in the story.

Perhaps they are right. Any man and woman who have raised children are eminently qualified by that experience only to disqualify themselves as far as understanding them goes. I think this truth applies equally to the ignoramus and to the sage. Parenthood may well be the last true democracy, all of us leveled by our bewilderment into one great, classless society.

The Sweet Life

Mark and Jerry had gone to see the film "La Dolce Vita" a few days before they were to return to Michigan State for the fall semester. They first noticed the two girls in the lobby of the theatre during the intermission. Both girls were dark-haired, one tall and large-breasted with long strong legs and the other girl slender and smaller. She had a fragile high-cheeked face and great dark eyes and her black hair was brushed back into a simple coiled bun that gave her a smoldering Castilian beauty.

They were both smoking up a fog and talking loudly about the picture in a way that demanded to be noticed. Jerry worked his way over to them and Mark followed him. Jerry asked them with his swinging charm if they weren't a couple of Italian starlets touring with the picture for publicity purposes. They started laughing and the big girl, Norma, had a hoarse and throaty laugh and Senta laughed with a soft quivering of her lips around her small even white teeth. By the time the intermission was over they had made arrangements to meet after the movie. On the way back to their seats Mark and Jerry counted their money and agreed that Jerry had Norma while Mark would take Senta.

When the lights went on at the end of the film, the boys

hurried through the press of people up the aisle. The girls were waiting for them in the lobby and they walked over to Rush Street and entered a tavern and sat down in a shadowed booth. Norma ordered a Bloody Mary and Senta ordered a Daiquiri. The waiter asked to see her I.D. card. Jerry and Norma teased her as she dug irritably into her purse and showed the card to the waiter. Mark learned she was nineteen and a junior at Ohio State. Mark and Jerry ordered beer.

"I liked the ending of the picture," Senta said. "The marvelous expression on the little girl's face as she called to Marcello."

"She resented missing the party," Jerry said. "She wanted Marcello so they could have a party of their own."

Norma laughed loudly in appreciation and Jerry joined her, pleased with his wit. Senta made an effort to laugh politely but it didn't quite come off and Mark felt drawn to her because of her reaction.

"That perfectly horrible fish," Norma shuddered in disgust. "That round dead eye staring up at them. It made my skin crawl. What kind of fish was that?"

"A schooner fish," Jerry said.

"The fish was a symbol," Mark said. "A bloated monster reflecting the uselessness of their own lives."

Jerry grinned and motioned at Mark. "When he graduates next June he wants to become a writer like Marcello," he said. "I think his real reason is that he wants to go to parties like that blast in the film."

"I think he looks a little like Marcello," Senta said.

"The hell he does," Jerry snickered.

"More like the fish," Mark said.

"I mean it," Senta said seriously. "You have the same sensitive eyes."

"Don't let that sensitive look fool you," Jerry said. "He uses that look to draw a girl into his web and then . . ."

"Cut it out," Mark said.

The waiter brought their drinks. They cheerfully toasted

each other. Jerry took a long swill of beer and shifted closer
to Norma who made no effort to slide away.

"The best scene in the picture was that party," Jerry said.
"That crazy doll who did the strip and those fairies pranc-
ing around and Marcello trying to paste the chicken feathers
all over the blonde."

"Remember the way she flapped her arms," Norma said.
She flapped her own firm bare arms and crowed, "Oo-oo-
ahroo!"

"Take it easy," Mark said. "They'll throw us out of here."

"It was sure a great party," Jerry said. "Maybe I can get
the guys in the frat house to throw one like it."

"Be sure to invite me," Norma said.

"I'll invite you right now," Jerry slipped his arm around
her shoulders, "and let you know the date later on." They
both exploded into laughter and Mark looked wryly at
Senta.

"I've been to some pretty good parties myself," Norma
said with a smirk.

"The hell you say," Jerry said. "Tell us about them."

"You college rah-rahs ever hear of musical chairs?"
Norma laughed. "Well, I have played the same game with
beds."

Jerry chortled with delight. He let his hand slip over
Norma's shoulder, his fingers hanging very near her breast.

"She's just showing off," Senta said sharply to Jerry. "She
has a good job in an advertising office and helps support her
mom and dad."

"Mama doesn't think a girl needs any fun after a day's
work in a lousy office," Norma gave Senta a quick bitter
look. "After we graduated from high school, Senta was able
to go on to college but I had to go to work. That doesn't
mean I have to sit home and feel my arteries hardening."

"Not if I can help it, doll," Jerry said soothingly. He signaled the waiter to bring another round of drinks.

"Let's talk about the movie," Senta said with a silent plea

to Mark. The dim lights of the tavern threw restless shadows across her pale cheeks and dark eyes. "I thought Fellini did a marvelous job, a kind of parable of the emptiness of our materialistic culture."

"It was all right," Norma said, "but I still think it was a pretty dirty picture."

"It wasn't dirty at all," Mark said. "It was a very moral portrayal of immorality."

"Don't tell me he had to go into that much loving detail to make a moral point," Norma snickered. "All those nymphomaniacs and homosexuals and fairies."

"Fairies and homosexuals are the same thing," Jerry said.

"I know that," Norma gave him a slight playful shove. "Don't you think I know that?"

"Mark is right," Senta said. "There were many haunting and beautiful scenes that I will never forget."

"I liked the scenes with Steiner," Mark said.

"Why did Steiner kill himself?" Norma asked.

"I'm not sure why," Senta said.

"I'm not sure either," Mark said. "He seems to have had everything a man could want. A beautiful family, literary success and artistic friends. But he was terrified of something no one else could see."

"I liked the part where Marcello's old man visits him," Jerry said. "He lectures Marcello about sin and then wants to go to a nightclub where the old rip begins to fondle one of the dolls in the chorus. He sure reminded me of my old man. I know for a fact he's had at least a half-dozen girlfriends in the last ten years. I wouldn't be surprised if my old lady knew it too even though all she cares about is playing cards five nights a week."

"There's been a change in the structure of society," Senta said. "Marital loyalty for fifty years to the same person is sheer hypocrisy."

"Now who is showing off?" Norma asked loudly.

"I mean it!" Senta said and her eyes flashed. "In Hollywood movies, sex is a daydream for people who are scared they will never find the real thing. In French and Italian movies the people don't moon around wondering what sex is really like. If they want sex, they have it, and when they are done they forget about it until next time. It's more honest that way."

"I think you gals are both a little too fast for us," Jerry said and winked at Mark. He tried to catch the waiter's attention.

"I don't think we'd better have any more to drink," Mark said. He figured their combined funds would about cover the drinks they already had.

"If you're short I know how it is," Senta said. "Norma and I will be glad to share the bill."

"Speak for yourself, honey," Norma said. "That might be the way you little college girls do it, but I work hard for my money."

"We wouldn't consider it anyway," Jerry said and grinned. "I've got a better idea. My folks are in Washington. My old lady goes along on the old man's business trips to keep an eye on him. Our house is empty and the bar is loaded."

Senta gave Norma a long warning look. "I'm staying with Norma at her house," she said. "Her mom and dad asked us not to be late."

"By this time mama and papa will be sound asleep," Norma said, "their fannies snuggled and both snoring like bears." She smiled coyly at Jerry. "My papa is faithful to my mama," she said, "but he does have a cabinet full of nude girlie photos in the basement."

"What does your mama do for kicks?" Jerry asked with a snicker.

"She adores Cary Grant," Norma said. "She sees all his pictures at least a half-dozen times and dreams about him almost every night."

"They'll never miss you then," Jerry said. "C'mon let's go."

Norma looked hesitantly for a moment at Senta and then

shrugged and rose. "I don't feel sleepy yet anyway," she said. "Tomorrow's Saturday and we don't have to get up till late."

They paid the check and left the tavern. Jerry walked with his arm around Norma's waist, his fingers spread slightly on her thigh. Senta and Mark walked slowly behind them.

"They sure hit it off well together," Mark said. They walked in silence for a few moments. The summer night was marked with a trace of early burning leaves.

"Norma is a fine girl," Senta said. "She was my best friend in high school. We used to talk all night. She was terribly disappointed when she couldn't go to college."

"You are both very different," Mark said.

Senta was silent and when she finally spoke, her voice was pensive. "Two years can be a long time," she said. "I can even see the change at home. My mother and father think I have grown callous and hard. My father is a pharmacist and thinks all life can be reduced to the exact measure for a prescription."

"I know what you mean," Mark said. "After my second year in college I couldn't stand the whole summer at home. I took jobs in other cities. It seemed I couldn't say or do anything anymore without hurting my parents in some way."

They turned off Rush Street and left the bright noisy cafes. A wind came off the lake and blew the scent of burning leaves more strongly about their heads. Mark studied Senta's face in the light of a passing streetlamp.

"You're lovely," he said suddenly. "You're a very lovely girl." He couldn't tell whether she was pleased. "I bet you've heard that from many fellows before me."

"I don't object when someone tells me that I'm pretty," Senta said quietly, "but looks can be a handicap too. Men can be distracted by surface allure and forget a girl is also a human being."

"I understand that," Mark said quickly. "In addition to beauty you have a sharp and sensitive mind."

He could tell that pleased her and after a moment he took her hand. They walked a short way in silence.

"I enjoy reading a great deal," Senta said.

"What writers do you like?"

"Tolstoy and Dostoevski in the novel and Sartre in the drama," Senta said. "A lot of poetry but mostly the work of Pablo Neruda."

"I don't know him," Mark said. "I guess I should, but I don't."

"He's a great Chilean poet," Senta said. "And I love foreign films and my favorite actress is Sophia Loren . . . she's a woman in every sense of the word."

They reached the lot where Jerry had parked the car and could not see him or Norma. They walked to the car and saw the figures in the shadowed front seat curled in a tight embrace. Mark looked at Senta with a faint embarrassed smile and knocked on the windshield. Jerry and Norma disengaged themselves slowly and Jerry motioned for them to get in the back. Mark held the door open for Senta and climbed in after her.

"I'm sorry we disturbed you," Mark said with sarcasm.

"Never mind," Jerry laughed. "We can always pick up where we left off."

They pulled into the driveway of Jerry's house, a large spacious ranch building on a lot landscaped with evergreens and myriad trees. Norma gave a low whistle of appreciation.

"It's all right," Jerry shrugged. "The old man takes the suckers for plenty in his law practice."

He drove straight for the garage and the door opened. He parked the sport coupe beside a long gleaming Cadillac. On the dark steps before entering the kitchen Jerry walked behind Norma and suddenly she squealed. "You naughty boy!" she cried.

They passed through a long kitchen with a massive twin-doored refrigerator and a stainless steel stove into a livingroom paneled in walnut with an imposing array of lamps and sculpture.

"Lovely," Norma said with awe. "Just lovely."

"Wait till you see this," Jerry said. He walked to a corner and pushed a button. The wall panel slid back to reveal a compact bar with a glittering assortment of glasses and bottles.

"Better than any Rush Street tavern," Norma marveled. "If it's for real, make me another Bloody Mary."

Jerry moved briskly behind the bar and began mixing the drink. Senta sat down stiffly on the couch.

"What will you have?" Mark asked her.

"I don't think I want another drink," she said.

"Come on, honey," Jerry said. "Give me a chance to show how good a bartender I am."

"I just don't want another drink," Senta said.

"I'll take scotch on the rocks," Mark said.

When Jerry had finished mixing their drinks he picked up a glass and a nearly full bottle of Bourbon and came out from behind the bar. He stood looking at Norma with his broad shoulders hunched slightly and a reckless glint in his eyes. "I'm taking my bottle upstairs," he said slowly. "Anybody want to see the bedrooms?"

Mark looked uneasily at Senta. "For cri' sakes slow down," he said to Jerry.

Jerry loosed a short brusque snicker. "What the hell for? We sat in the bar an hour and a half. We all know why we came here. Let's not waste the whole damn night sparring around." He motioned with the bottle to Norma. "Coming, doll?"

Norma glanced hesitantly at Senta.

"Or was all that talk about musical beds just showing off," Jerry said. "The little working girl trying to impress the college crowd."

Norma turned back to Jerry with a defiant glitter in her eyes.

"You could at least put on some damn music," Mark said to Jerry.

"You play all the mood music you want," Jerry said in a flat hard voice. "Read some poetry too. Spend the whole damn night talking. I'm going upstairs now."

Senta gave him a scathing contemptuous look but he ignored her. Norma rose slowly from her chair and stood a moment staring at Senta. "Enjoy yourself, honey," Norma said in a tight and brittle voice. "La Dolce Vita."

She turned then and started up the stairs, carrying her drink, her firm thighs pressing against the skirt of her dress. Conscious of them watching her she affected a certain casual disdain. Jerry started after her with a cool smile of triumph. "The first floor is all yours," he said to Mark. He followed Norma upstairs.

Mark watched him out of sight and glanced uneasily at Senta. She sat a little stiffly in silence and after a moment laughed shortly.

"He must be the prize bull of sorority row," she said.

"He does pretty well."

"And how about you?" Senta said. "Do you do pretty well too?"

"Not nearly as well as Jerry," Mark said. He took a long swallow of scotch.

"You're the sensitive kind," Senta said.

"Sure," Mark said sharply. "That's why I brought you here."

"You didn't bring me," Senta said. "Your fast friend brought me. You just came along."

"All right," Mark said. "Don't bite my head off. I'm not going to attack you. You can just relax and read a good book until your friend comes down."

Senta rose and walked to the fireplace. She stood for an instant with her back to him and then whirled around. Her dark eyes glistened angrily.

"I'll do what I want to do!" she said. "The whole business

isn't that important. If only people would stop hacking at it like woodchoppers and show a little grace."

"Okay, okay," Mark said. "Your friend is over twenty-one but I'm sorry we came here. I didn't mean to hurt your feelings."

The tight angry circles loosened slightly in her face. She returned to the couch and sat down.

"Do you believe in fate?" Senta asked quietly.

"In what way?"

"Do you believe that whatever happens to us is predestined to happen long before we are born?"

"I don't think I buy that," Mark said.

"I feel that way about love," Senta said. "That I will find it someday as it was planned long before my life began." She looked so lovely, the shadows sweeping her face and her lips gleaming. Mark leaned over suddenly and kissed her, feeling her lips surprisingly soft under his mouth.

He pulled back sharply expecting her to protest. She sat looking at him quietly without a trace of warmth in the firm carved lines around her mouth.

He kissed her again pressing his lips harder over her mouth. She twisted in his arms and he thought he felt her kissing him back. A wild urgency caught at his body and he pulled her against him in a hard embrace that robbed them both of breath. He felt the agitation of her heart. His hand rose to touch the trembling swell of her small firm breast and she began to struggle. For an instant he thought it was because she was excited until he realized she was fighting him. He paused in surprise still holding her arms.

"What's the matter?" he asked.

She looked at him with her dark eyes open so wide they resembled cups. "I won't!" she said.

"What?"

"I won't!" she cried. "I won't!"

He had heard those words as a prelude before and he ignored them and bent to kiss her again. She began to struggle violently and he was startled at the strength in her slim body. He fought to hold her and suddenly she went limp in his arms. After a moment he relaxed his grip. Almost at once she cried out and with a hard vengeful sweep of her arm raked his cheek with her nails, tearing his flesh. He cried out in shock and pain and slipped to his knees beside the couch holding his torn cheek.

"Oh my God, I'm sorry," she said. "I'm so sorry." She sat there pale and scared, her blouse pulled askew showing the flesh of her shoulder.

Mark rose slowly to his feet. "That's all right," he said and his voice sounded strange in his ears. He turned and started from the room.

"Where are you going?" she asked quickly.

"To get some iodine," he said. "Do you mind?" He walked to the bathroom. He snapped on the lights and the faces that stared back at him from the multiple mirrors did not seem his own. The scratch ran an ugly red scar down his cheek. He washed it, grimacing with pain, and then found a bottle of iodine in the cabinet.

"Let me do that, please." She had come to stand quietly in the doorway. She didn't wait for him to answer but took the bottle from his hand. She began to apply the dauber to the long scratch.

"Take it easy," he said wincing.

"I'm sorry," she said.

"That's about the tenth time you've said you're sorry," he said with sarcasm. "Change the broken record."

When she finished applying the iodine, he looked at himself in the mirror.

"I look like a goddam Indian," he said dejectedly. "I don't know how I'm going to explain this to Jerry."

"Can't you tell him you cut yourself shaving?"

"Cut myself like this?" he asked. "Are you nuts? What do you think I shave with, a saber?"

They stared at each other and her lips quivered in a faint smile.

"Go ahead and laugh," he said angrily. "If you had

scratched Jerry like this, he would probably have beaten hell out of you."

"You're not Jerry," she said. "That's why I like you."

"God, I'm lucky," he said and loosed a short harsh laugh. "You like me so Jerry gets laid and I get a torn face to carry around like a badge of honor for days."

She stood watching him and he noticed the sadness of her eyes. She raised her hand and touched his cheek, her fingers fluttering softly as a bird's wing beneath the raw red line of the scratch. He had a strange feeling that she was touching the bone beneath the flesh of his face.

Something in her fingertips made him reach uncertainly for her again. She raised her small somber face to him, and he kissed her again, warily at first, and then with a growing jubilation as he felt her responding. He started to tug her into the livingroom and their feet tangled and she nearly fell. He held her in the circle of his arm while he snapped off the main light switch to darken the livingroom except for a small lamp in the corner.

"Tell me you love me," she whispered, and there was a dark anguish in her voice.

"I love you, Senta," he said, and the words tumbled from his lips. "I love you very much."

They were on the couch and he felt the frantic trembling of her body. For a moment a sharp remorse and shame possessed him. Then it was lost in a furious fumbling and twisting of their bodies.

A little before dawn it began to rain. A thin drizzle fell across the evergreens and walks and cast a shimmering mist around the post light near the gate. The first faint trace of daylight cut the rim of the dark night sky. Mark snapped off the post light and walked into the kitchen where Senta had made coffee.

Her cheeks were scrubbed clean of any remaining powder and without a stain of lipstick her lips appeared to be drained of blood. She had brushed back her hair and tied it with a strip of ribbon. He sat down across from her and poured himself a cup of coffee.

"Do you want sugar and cream?" she asked.

"Just a little sugar," he said.

They lapsed into silence and drank their coffee slowly. He gave a short and rueful laugh.

"Do you ever see those corny commercials on television?" he asked. "The ones that show the adoring newlyweds saying, 'Good morning, Mr. Jones,' and 'good morning, Mrs. Jones,' and a lot of jazz like that."

"I may have seen them," she said quietly.

"They should have a commercial for us," he said. "Some aspirin company should show us sitting like this, not talking, drinking our coffee with a kind of quiet desperation."

He fell silent again staring into his cup.

"Are you sorry?" he asked.

"I don't know," she said. "I don't really know what I feel."

He twisted restlessly in his chair.

"It's my fault," he said. "I'll assume the full blame if you feel like blaming somebody." He shook his head. "It was kind of a mess anyway," he said. "I guess the excitement and the booze didn't help much. I mean . . ."

"I don't blame you," she said.

"You're not mad?" he asked.

She shook her head slowly. "I'm just confused," she said. "I talked about people in the foreign films doing it when they wanted to do it and afterwards not worrying. But we can't be like that. I don't know why. We go at it like Jerry trying to prove something, or like me, mooning and brooding about whether to or not. We grow up into women like Norma's mother, dreaming of Cary Grant, and men like Jerry's father searching for something we cannot find." She paused and looked at him with a shaken sadness. "And in the end," she said, "a day may even come when we'll no longer remember that it once belonged to love."

Norma entered the kitchen, her face gray and weary in

the neon light. Her legs were bare and she pulled at her dress which was wrinkled and showed the lace hem of her slip.

"God, I could use some coffee," she said. "Pour me a cup of black and then let's go. My old lady will kill me."

Senta poured her a cup of steaming coffee from the pot. Norma took the cup and did not sit down but stood blowing across the coffee to cool it. She looked over the rim of the cup at Senta and then at Mark. For the first time she noticed the stained scratch on his cheek. "Some night," she said grimly. "Some night we all had."

She handed the car keys to Mark. "I took them from his pants pocket," she said. "He's out like a dead man. I tried to wake him thinking he might want to drive his little sweetie home," she laughed without mirth. "He opened one eye and looked at me like I was nuts." She took a sip of the coffee and grimaced as the steam curled from the corners of her mouth. "You know he resembled the fish in the picture," she said. "That goddam fish with the ugly dead eye."

They drove home to Norma's place silently except for Norma's directions to Mark. The three of them sat in the front seat watching the cold day sweep aside the final shadows of night.

Mark parked the car before Norma's small frame bungalow. Norma slipped out of the car, nervously watching the house, and motioned for Senta to hurry. Mark started to get out of the car to take Senta to the door but she caught his arm and shook her head. They stared at each other for a moment and then he looked away. "If I don't get a chance to see you before you leave for school," he said awkwardly, "Good luck to you."

"The same to you," she said. She twisted then to slide her legs from the car. She turned back to him and with a sudden impulsive gesture raised her hands to his cheeks. She held his face for an instant and then kissed him softly on the lips, a sad and fleeting kiss of farewell. Afterwards she left the car and walked quickly toward the house. Norma waited for her on the porch with the door open and they walked inside and the door closed. The gray still silence swept back across the house.

Mark sat there in the car for a long time. A curious weariness possessed him. His head felt heavy and his arms were burdens.

He turned the key, pressed down on the gas, and the car began to move slowly and then more quickly as he gathered speed. He opened the window and let the rush of cool damp morning air strike his face.

℄ I knew two old men just like the ones in this story and worked for both. I pressed clothes for the tailor who told me I had a heavy foot and suggested a cathartic of castor oil and barley water. I delivered groceries for the grocer who paid me off in dimes, slightly spoiled fruit, and a recital of his laments.

Some years after leaving their neighborhood, driving by again one day, I noticed the stores were still there. I made a vow to stop by to confirm if either one was still alive.

That was one of those vows we never get around to keeping until it is too late.

A Hand for Tomorrow

In the fifteen years since the end of the Second World War many changes had come to Bleecker Street. The Quality Delicatessen, which had once specialized in a fragrant potato salad, had been joined with a lunchroom and a small hand laundry to form a glistening supermarket dominating the street. Banners with great red letters and numbers were splashed across the windows, and shiny shopping carts rolled in and out of the parking lot all day. Farther down the street, the little dusty tailor shop of Max Feldman, who claimed at one time or another to have pressed the pants of every male within a mile radius of Bleecker Street, had been demolished along with a radio-repair shop and a candy store to make a bright and gaudy drive-in cleaners operated by his sons.

Of all the stores that had existed on the street before the war, only the small grocery of Kostas Stavrakas remained unchanged except for concessions to the miracles of modern packaging.

Kostas, ignoring the trend to health breads and protein breads and enriched breads, still baked his own loaves as he had baked them for thirty years in the oven in the back room of his store. He carried an assortment of Balkan spices and Greek and Bulgarian cheeses white as the foam on

fresh-whipped milk. Although he had accepted the utility of
neon lighting and had purchased a small sign to hang in his
window, his store stood out at night by appearing almost an
island of darkness beside the flaming, garish splendor of the
rest of the street.

What little business he did came mostly from the older
people who had traded with him for years. As they died or
moved away, there was nobody to replace them. In the
meantime he did some business in the morning before the
supermarket opened and in the evening after it closed.

He did not mind the leisurely pace of his trade. For some
years now his legs had been bothering him, and he wore
shoes slit along the sides to ease the swelling of his feet. But
he could not conceive of existence away from the store in
which he had spent thirty years. When his wife was alive,
they had planned together for his retirement, but after her
death of a stroke, a few years before, this dream had lost rel-
evance. He lived with his married son and wife, who had a
two-year-old daughter whom Kostas adored. This family
and the store with the warm, familiar scents of spices and
cheese and yeasty bread hot from the oven were the boundaries of his life.

The afternoons were long and quiet, and shortly after
lunch he would be joined each day by his old friend, Max
Feldman, the tailor whose shop had been surrendered to the
ambitions of his sons and the cornucopia of progress. They
would gravely set up the checkerboard within arm's reach of
the briny pickles in the barrel.

"Where does the count stand?" Max asked, and puckered
his thin, dry lips and wriggled his crooked ears. "I must be
leading by a dozen games this month."

"No more than three," Kostas said. "You have no conception of the difference between addition and multiplication."

Max shrugged that off. "This will be a short, sad game,"
he said. "Five, maybe six of Feldman's murderous moves
and, pfft! you will be gone."

A Hand for Tomorrow

"Your best game is with your mouth," Kostas said. "If hot air counted, you would be champion checker player of the world."

"Play!" Max cried. "Today I have no mercy!"

They made their first moves and settled down to the game, staring intently at the board. They played in a tight silence until the door of the store opened and a little bell jingled. A gray-haired heavy woman entered. Kostas rose to serve her.

"Don't cheat," he said in a soft warning whisper to the tailor. Max looked outraged.

"Good day, Mrs. Lanaras," Kostas said warmly. "How is your fine son, Thanasi?"

"Still growing," Mrs. Lanaras said, "and eating enough for three grown men. How is your family?"

"Excellent, thank you." Kostas smiled. "At two years of age my granddaughter is as beautiful as Aphrodite. Can I help you?"

"A little cheese, I think," Mrs. Lanaras said. "A half-pound of feta and a loaf of bread. Thanasi takes four sandwiches for lunch."

Kostas packed the items, rang up the sale, and Mrs. Lanaras walked briskly out the door.

"Yesterday as I was coming," Max said, "I saw her and that lummox Thanasi carry two bags out from the supermarket. Bags loaded like that only giants should carry. Here she comes to buy a little cheese and a loaf of bread. Such customers should do you a favor and pass by without stopping."

"She was good to come in for that," Kostas said. "The supermarket has a counter with cheeses from all over the world and varieties of bread. I am grateful she comes in for anything at all."

Max looked for a long, searching moment at Kostas. "Tell me something," he said slowly. "Are you making expenses?"

"Certainly!" Kostas said in a shocked voice. "What kind of businessman do you think I am? Every month a small profit is made here, although I admit not what it used to be."

"What about your son, Nick?" Max asked. "Does he still come sneaking in with a carpenter and an electrician under his jacket?"

"They were in here again last week," Kostas said and smiled. "They took measurements for hours and scribbled a padful of figures. Nicolas is so excited. He wants to do so much. I tell him to wait. When I am dead he can do what he wishes with the store."

Max shook his head somberly. "Believe me, they can't wait," he said. "Don't I know? Twenty-seven years in one location they should let a man walk out, but from my store they shot me like a shell out of a cannon. They came to me one afternoon and said, 'Papa, tomorrow the wreckers will be here.'" His lips curled with contempt. "A drive-in cleaners they wanted. So lazy louts never lift their rumps from the car. A girl they got in a short skirt and naked legs to take the clothing right from the car. Believe me, they can't wait."

"You admit yourself they are making a lot of money," Kostas said.

"Money, money!" Max cried. "Do me a favor and stop talking about money. A little money a man should make to live, but with dignity." He flung his arm up and cut the air violently. "Imagine! A drive-in cleaners with a girl in a short skirt and naked legs to take the clothing from your car!"

The door of the store opened, and the bell jingled again. Nick Stavrakas came in. He was a tall, thin young man with a serious twist to his lips and black curly hair and intense eyes.

"Hi, papa," he said. "Hello, Max."

He stood for a moment balancing on the balls of his feet. He looked up to the ceiling, and a shadow of annoyance crossed his cheeks. "Papa, that light is still burned out. I thought you were going to get Leon to fix it?"

"I forgot to tell him yesterday," Kostas said. "I will tell him for sure today."

"You can hardly see the canned-goods labels on the center shelf with the light on," Nick said. "With the light out, the shelf is in total darkness."

"I'll be sure he fixes it today," Kostas said quickly.

Max smiled slyly at the young man. "Tell me, how are all your friends?" he said. "The carpenters and electricians."

Nick frowned at the old tailor. "If you don't mind, Max," he said. "I wanted to talk to papa alone for a minute."

Max sighed and rose slowly from his chair. "I'll take a walk to the park and watch the pretty nursemaids for a while," he said. "There is one Bathsheba who is like a juicy strudel."

"Sit down, Max," Kostas said. "We have no secrets from you." He looked gently at his son. "You have some more estimates?"

With a final despairing glance at Max, Nick pulled a sheaf of papers from his pocket. When he spoke, his voice was vibrant with excitement. "Papa, these estimates are the best yet!" He motioned eagerly with his hand. "This plan would almost triple the area usable and let us stock three times the items we carry."

"How?" Kostas asked.

"By knocking down that wall," Nick said, "opening those partitions in the rear and utilizing all that lost space."

"What about my oven in the back room?" Kostas asked.

Nick shook his head fretfully. "That would have to go," he said. "That takes up space and yields nothing."

Max gave a sharp, pointed laugh and looked intently at the checkerboard. Kostas looked quickly at his friend and tried not to smile.

"Papa," Nick said, and his voice rose a little, "you know that oven is outdated. It costs you forty cents to bake a loaf of bread that you can't sell for more than thirty. In the supermarket, people get their choice of forty kinds of bread."

"Fifty kinds," Max said sagely. "Once I counted them."

"I have been baking bread for families here for thirty years," Kostas said.

"Papa," Nick said excitedly. "That kind of business you can afford to lose. We've got to streamline this store. Do you know that Tony Manteno, the real-estate broker, was telling me this block is a gold mine for business? This block draws a fantastic number of people. We've got to get our share."

"We do a fair business," Kostas said. "We make a fair profit on the items we sell."

"Not one-tenth the business we could if we remodeled," Nick said. "Papa, I've racked my head to plan every step. I tell you we can't lose. We would have our additional investment back in a couple of years."

Kostas did not answer for a moment. "I know there is truth in what you say," he said slowly. "Let me think about it a little more."

"Papa," Nick said in exasperation. "You've been saying that for three years, and you haven't made a move."

Kostas walked from the counter to the window. He stood silently for a moment, looking at the people walking past.

"Thirty years is a long time," he said finally. "Children who stood with their eyes open like big saucers before the jars of three-for-a-penny candy are grown into adults and married, with children of their own. Friends who once came in and sat and smoked and sipped a glass of wine have grown old, and some have died. This store has many memories."

"Papa," Nick said, and a softness entered his voice, "memories are fine, but you can't live today in a dream of the past. You've got to keep up."

"They can't wait," Max said somberly, as if he were speaking to himself. "They can't wait."

Kostas turned back to his son. "All this new business," he said, "will mean additional help. I have always managed this store alone. People who come in expect me to look after them."

"We would need some help," Nick said. "You could begin to take it easy and supervise everything. Sort of keep your eye on the whole operation."

"Tell me," Max asked sharply. "Do you think you might use a girl in a short skirt with naked legs?"

Nick looked at him in irritation. "What does that mean?"

"Nothing," Max said innocently. "I just happen to know where there is one such girl available."

"Nicolas," Kostas said. "We will talk further this evening. We will examine the figures together." He nodded at Max. "This boy has a marvelous head for figures," he said proudly.

"Papa," Nick said, "I know talking about this makes you unhappy, but something has to be done. I've become the laughingstock of the street. Always estimates and figures and plans and nothing more. Think of me."

Kostas looked for a long, silent moment at his son. "I am always thinking of you," he said softly. "Of you and Lucy and Katerina. The three people I care most about in this world."

Nick lowered his head to conceal the flush risen suddenly to his cheeks. "I'm sorry, papa," he said. "I know how much you think of us." He paused for a moment and tasted his defeat and could not resist one final assault. "Look now," he said, and his voice shook under an effort to speak quietly. "I've been in here almost twenty minutes now, and not one customer has entered in that time. Do you call this a business? It's more like a cemetery."

"I am a small grave on the hill," Max said wryly. "Before you leave, water my plot."

Kostas could not help smiling. Nick glared in sudden anger from one to the other. "Laugh!" he said shrilly. "Laugh and sit in this cemetery and play checkers all day. At least admit you aren't really in business. You don't want this place to become a business because it would interrupt your game. You sit in here, and outside the world has changed, and you go on playing checkers and ignoring burned-out lights."

"Nicolas," Kostas said with concern.

"I'm sorry, papa," Nick said. "I'm fed up! I'm your only son and I love you more than anything else in the world, and I swear to God I want what is best for you and Lucy and the baby. I'm full of energy and ambition, and I want to repay you for all the good years and take care of you, and all you can do is sit and worry about playing checkers."

He turned and stumbled once in his haste and then went quickly out the door.

"They can't wait," Max said grimly. "They can't wait."

Kostas returned to his chair and sat down and shook his head in despair. "Maybe we are the selfish ones," he said. "We have forgotten what it is like to be young." He paused and looked around the dimly lighted store, breathing the warm, familiar scents that came from the darkened shelves and the hidden corners. "Maybe the boy is right," he said. "Maybe this place is a cemetery."

Max shook his head violently. "Better a cemetery than a circus!" he cried. "A circus with a girl in a short skirt and naked legs so the lummoxes won't raise their rumps from the car. Big, flashing neon signs and tinsel waving like every day is the Fourth of July."

"They are young," Kostas said sadly. "The world seems to move by quickly if they fall out of step. They cannot bear to be left behind." He shook his head in some stricken wonder. "Where has the time gone?" he said. "It seems like yesterday that we pushed their buggies in the park on Sunday afternoons and wiped their running noses and dreamed of their growing up to be President of the United States." He stared at the board without seeming to see the checkers. "Now my Ethel is gone, and your Sarah is gone. The babies are grown into men who live in a world different from the one we remember. And the time goes by so swiftly."

Max pulled out his handkerchief and blew his nose in a harsh trumpeting of sound. "Move!" he said. "It's your move for a half-hour now. You are maybe planning to move sometime before closing? Do me a favor and move, why don't you?"

They finished their third game late in the afternoon. Max dozed a little in his chair, his bald and bony head nodding slightly. Kostas quietly swept out the store. When Leon, the maintenance man, came in, Kostas had him replace the burned-out bulb. A few customers came in for several small purchases.

As twilight fell across the street and Kostas turned on the window light, Nick returned. He brought his wife, Lucy, and their daughter, Katerina, sitting upright in her stroller.

Kostas saw them coming and held the door so Nick could push the stroller in. He looked quickly at his son's face to see what vestige of the morning's disturbance remained. Then he forgot everything in his pleasure at seeing his grandchild.

He lifted her squealing from the stroller. He kissed her warm, soft cheeks and raised her high above his head. She shrieked with delight, and he held her close and poked her gently with his nose.

Lucy, a pretty, slender, dark-haired girl, kissed him on the cheek. "We have lamb and green beans for supper tonight, papa," she said gently. "I fixed them especially for you. Nick and I came to watch the store so you can go home and eat while the food is still warm."

Kostas looked at Nick, and for a moment the young man did not meet his father's eyes. Then Nick managed a slight, repentant smile, and Kostas smiled in warm and grateful response.

"Lamb and green beans?" Max said, coming out of the shadows. "Is there perhaps enough for an old tailor who eats no more than a sick baby?"

"All sick babies should eat as well as you," Kostas said. "They would become well in a hurry."

"Always enough for you, Mr. Feldman," Lucy said. "You go along and keep papa company."

"There is plenty of food," Nick said. "Lucy cooks enough for six men."

"She knows lamb and green beans are my favorite," Kostas said proudly to Max. He patted his daughter-in-law's cheek with tenderness and affection. "I am a lucky man. I have a fine son, and he married a grand girl, and together they produced this incomparable child." He made a face at the baby.

"My sons married monsters," Max said somberly. "Wailing harpies who cook like poisoners. Believe me, every meal at their table freezes my blood."

Nick took the child from his father and returned her to the stroller. He gave her some cellophane-wrapped candy canes to play with. A customer entered, and Kostas started behind the counter. Lucy waved him away. "I'll take care of the store, papa," she said. "You and Mr. Feldman get started now. The lamb will become cold."

Nick went into the back room and returned with his father's jacket. He held it for Kostas to put on.

"Papa," Nick said, and he spoke softly so that only his father could hear. "I'm sorry about this morning."

"It was not your fault you became angry," Kostas said quickly. "Max and I should not have laughed."

"No, papa," Nick said, and shook his head in muted despair. "I've been thinking about it all afternoon. I talked to Lucy for two hours. I been fooling myself for a long time, but I got no right to change you or change the store. Anybody who has worked as many years as you have worked this store has got a right to keep it just the way he wants."

"Nicolas," Kostas said. "I am not saying my way is right."

"Let me finish, papa, please," Nick said. "I guess I'm not as smart as I think sometimes, but when I stop and figure it out, a light begins to dawn. I've been bothering you for three years, but you don't have to worry or become upset any more. Starting now, I'm through with estimates and figures. I'm going to leave you alone about the store. That's the way Lucy and I decided."

Kostas looked silently at his son for a long time and then impulsively embraced him. He held him tightly for a moment and then, suddenly self-conscious, stepped away quickly, looking to see if Max or Lucy had noticed. He turned his face slightly and spoke slowly and carefully. "This is my store," he said quietly. "And I have made up my mind what must be done. This place is a disgrace. It was fine for thirty years ago, but it has become a rusty bicycle on a street of fast new cars. Changes must be made."

"Papa," Nick said, and he shook his head in wonder. "What are you saying?"

Kostas did not trust himself to touch the boy again. "I've made up my mind I want to see what you can do for me," he said briskly. "I am not that bad a businessman. I am satisfied you have looked into the matter thoroughly, and I put my faith and trust in you. Don't let me down."

"Papa," Nick said angrily. "You're doing this because of what I said this morning. You're doing this because of me. I won't have it."

"Will you shut up about this morning?" Kostas cried. "Am I a child that a few words spoken in excitement cause me to change my mind? I am not married to this old store. It has provided me a living and memories, but it has also given me swollen feet and aching legs. Now go and help your wife and let me go home and eat my lamb and green beans, and in the morning call the carpenters and electricians and make plans for the work to get started."

As he finished speaking, Max came silently to stand at his side. Nick turned on the tailor with enthusiasm. "Did you hear, Max?" he cried. "Papa and I are ready to go! We are going to make this the finest little store on the street! We'll show them all!" He turned fervently to his father. "Just wait! You won't be sorry! I'll make you proud!" He turned and walked quickly toward his wife.

"They can't wait," Max said softly. "And because they are flesh of our flesh, we give in."

Kostas watched Nick talking earnestly to Lucy. He turned on Max. "The trouble with you, Feldman," he said loudly, "you live in the past. You lack vision. Your sons were right to throw you off the premises. You have a brooding face that invites disaster and despair."

He started for the door, and after a moment of outraged silence Max followed. Lucy and Nick called to Kostas and started toward him, but he waved them away. "Later," he said. "The lamb and beans grow cold. Later."

He fled to the street. Max followed him out, and when he caught up, the old tailor laughed dryly.

"Moses Stavrakas," he sneered. "So I lack vision. I live in the past. You rushed out of that store because maybe in another minute you would have been crying. Ha!"

Kostas glared at him and did not speak. He walked with as quick a stride as his swollen feet would allow, and the tailor had to half run to keep up.

"You know what this means?" Max paused for a moment to catch his breath. "The song is familiar. When all the painting and renovating has been finished, the only old antique left sticking out of place is you."

"I know," Kostas said. "I know."

"But do not despair," Max said, and he laughed a dry, ironic laugh. "I will be here to help you. I will teach you to sit in the park and watch the pretty nursemaids and argue politics with the Irishmen who sit like black roosters in the sun. I know the best benches for checkers, the ones shaded beneath the trees. And when the weather turns cold, there is always the public library with newspapers from all the big cities."

"Feldman!" Kostas said wrathfully. "Feldman, go to the devil!"

They walked on together without speaking. They passed

under the bright, flashing glitter of the signs and the neon night streaked with multicolored lights. As they approached the great, gleaming festival of the supermarket, Max fell a step behind and fiercely brandished his fist at the long window with flaunting banners. With a violent gathering of his body, he spat on the ground before the store.

℄ This story came out of a gray, desolate period during the last year of my father's life. My wife and I had been married only a few years and had moved into a house with my mother and father. He was ill then and not sleeping well, suffering the slights and arrows of trustees of his church who wanted to eject him for a younger, more vigorous priest. I would come home at dawn from the night shift at the steel mill to find him alone at the table, his briefcase of papers and letters and petitions open before him.

The steel mill and my father near the end of his life were the beginning. From that point, the story wove its own strange and marvelous design. In the end, I was surprised and awed at what had been revealed.

The Witness

That winter seemed to last forever. At the end of March the ground was still frozen. Walking home from a night shift at the mill, I huddled my head into the collar of my jacket to shelter my cheeks and ears from the biting cold.

By the time I reached home the first traces of daylight had broken the rim of the dark sky. I went in the back door and found Pa in his bathrobe in the kitchen with a pot of fresh coffee brewing on the stove.

In the past weeks he had been having trouble sleeping. Even after taking the pills the doctor had given him, he lay awake through most of the night. Just before dawn he would come quietly downstairs. He would light the oven to warm the kitchen and put on a pot of coffee and wait for me.

I came in cold and tired with the dust of the mill on my cheeks. I wanted only to wash, peek in on my sleeping son and then climb into bed beside my wife, between the sheets that would be warm with her body. But Pa waited for me with a pot of coffee and I had to sit with him for a while.

"Didn't you get any sleep again, Pa?"

He pulled the cord of his robe tighter and turned his face slightly away, because he was no good at deception.

"Better than I have slept in weeks," he said. "Maybe those damn pills are beginning to work."

He poured me a cup of steaming coffee and the sharp aroma pulled at my weariness. "Pa, you made it too strong again," I said, sitting down. "I can tell by the look of it." I was sorry the moment the words were out of my mouth.

"I only put in six scoops," he said. "You told me six scoops was just right."

"Sure, Pa," I said. "Six scoops is right. I just remembered Ethel saying she was going to switch to another brand. Maybe she got one that is stronger."

He walked to the pantry and brought down the canister of coffee. He raised the lid and stared intently at the beans.

"Don't worry about it, Pa," I said. "Sit down and have a cup yourself."

He came to sit down at the table. He dropped two slices of bread into the toaster. Then he raised the pot and poured himself a cup of coffee. His hand trembled slightly because he was old and not well. But his hand still looked big and strong, with the large powerful fingers I remembered as a child. I would get out of school in the afternoon and run to wait for him at the north gate. He would come across the bridge with his crew from the plate mill at the end of the turn. He would see me waiting outside the fence and holler and wave.

He would swing me to his shoulder and the men would laugh and slap my legs. I would ride home high on his back, his hands holding me securely, proud of his strength and his love.

"How did it go last night?" Pa asked as I sipped slowly at the coffee.

"We beat the other two turns by eleven ton," I said.

"No fooling!" His face flushed with pleasure for me. "Who was rolling?"

"The Dutchman," I said. "On all three furnaces."

"He must have been going like hell!" Pa laughed and his pale and tight-fleshed face seemed to flood suddenly with color. Whenever we spoke of the mills he seemed to feel the heat of the furnaces, the glowing slabs bobbing on the rolls.

"You boys still can't touch our record," he said. "I'll never forget that night. Bungo on the furnaces shooting the slabs out like shells from a cannon. Montana on the crane over the hookers. Fuller thinking we were nuts when we gave him the tonnage at four."

He sat up straight in his chair with excitement flashing in his eyes. The doctor did not want him excited, because of his heart and, besides, I had heard the story of that night a hundred times. The stocker with a smashed hand who cried when they took him to the hospital because he didn't want to leave the crew. The way old steel men who had been there swore the crane was a bird snatching up the slabs like a crust of bread. And Pa up and down the length of the mill hustling his crew in a voice that could be heard above the thunder of the roughers and the shrill whistles and bells of the cranes.

". . . And that fool, Barney," Pa was saying, "getting his hand pulped and refusing to go to the hospital. Even taking a poke with the other hand at one of the plant cops who tried to force him off the line."

"Pa, listen," I said. "We both enjoy talking about the mills, but this morning I'm really beat. I run myself crazy trying to keep up with the records set by my old man." I laughed as I stood up and gave his shoulder a slight punch. "Every few days a damn foreman asks me when you're coming back, so they can start breaking tonnage records again."

He smiled up at me then and I saw the thin clean line of scalp under his thick gray hair. "You're a damn good mill-man," he said. "Better than I ever was, bigger, and a hell of a lot smarter."

"Sure, Pa," I said. "Go tell that to some of the old-timers and they'll lock you up." I arched my shoulders and stretched. "Let's go up," I said. "Maybe you can get a couple of hours' sleep before the kid gets up."

"You go ahead," he said, "and I'll be along in a minute. I'll just rinse the cups and make the kitchen look nice for Ethel when she comes down."

He stopped me when I reached the stairs. "Don't forget the kid's birthday party," he said, and all the love and devotion he felt for Alex was in his warm wink of anticipation. "Tonight is the night."

I stopped for a moment in Alex's room. He was asleep in his crib, looking like some kind of dark-haired angel. He was quick and bright and a joy to be near. I spoiled him a little, but Pa was worse than me. When Ethel cracked Alex across the behind for something he had done wrong, Pa left the room because he could not bear to hear the kid cry.

In the bathroom I stripped and shivered as I washed. I went quickly into the bedroom and slid carefully between the sheets. Ethel stirred beside me and I kissed her soft warm cheek. She moved gently against me, warming my body with her own, until I stopped shivering and fell asleep.

Alex woke me a little before one. His habit was to creep softly into the room and climb up on the bed. If this wasn't enough to wake me, he would bring his mouth to my ear and, like a puppy, begin nibbling at my lobe.

There was a joy in waking to the boy's great brown eyes and clean-child smell. I would hug and tickle him till he shrieked in delight.

Afterward I showered and dressed and went downstairs hungry. I kissed Ethel, standing before the stove, and gently stroked her swollen little belly that pressed up against her apron.

"Potato pancakes again?" I said.

"Don't eat them," she said cheerfully.

"Anything else?"

"Eggs."

"I married a cook," I said.

"We get what we deserve," she said. "My mother used to say, Ethel, marry a rich man and keep off your feet."

"You didn't get that little belly standing up," I said. She took a swipe at me with her dish towel and we both laughed.

Alex came into the kitchen with cookie crumbs around his mouth and wanted another one. Ethel told him no and I winked at him and slipped him a chocolate chip from the jar. He ran out of the kitchen with his prize.

"It's his birthday," I said.

"You spoil him worse than Pa," she shook her head.

"Where is the old man?"

She motioned toward the back yard and the garage. "With Orchowski," she said quietly.

I sat down at the table and she brought me the potato pancakes and several slices of sharp salami.

"They should play in the house," I said. "Find a place somewhere in the house. That small stove doesn't keep the garage nearly warm enough."

She stared at me silently. I ate slowly, without looking up from my plate. We had covered this same ground often before. I kept bringing it up, even when I knew what she would say.

"Mike," she said wearily, "Mike, what's the use of talking?"

"I know, honey," I said. "But he's not well."

She made a helpless gesture with her hands. In that moment I realized how much of her day was spent in the kitchen cooking for us, washing the dishes, ironing the clothes. The potato pancakes stuck in my throat.

"I know, too," she said, and she spoke softly. "I want to do right, but I want to be fair to Alex, too. Why don't they play in Orchowski's house?"

"You know why," I said. "His son-in-law doesn't like his cigars or his beer."

"They don't have a child like we do," she said. "When they play inside here I can't keep Alex out of their room. Pa hasn't got the heart to lock him out. I don't mind Orchowski's cigars, how bad they smell in the house, but I mind the hollering and the cursing. Honest to God, Mike, you've heard them."

"They're roosters with cut claws now," I said, feeling my cheeks hot. "All they can do is swear and holler."

"I know that," she said patiently. "But curses and hollering are no way to bring up a child." She twisted the dish towel uselessly in her fingers. "This neighborhood is bad enough," she said. "They call it the bush and laugh at the number of bars. When Alex grows older he will need all the strength we can provide him now, all the decency we can give him now."

"All right," I said. "All right, for God's sake, Ethel, let it alone." There was a senseless anger in my throat, because I felt she was right.

She came over and stood for a silent moment beside my chair. I leaned my head against her breast and smelled the flour on her apron.

"Eat," she said gently, and her small soft fingers rubbed my neck in a soothing caress. "Eat your food before it gets cold."

I ate a little more and left the table. I called Alex and got him ready for a walk. He rolled on the floor while I tried to pull on his leggings. I crouched above him and he pressed his tiny hands against my chest, begging me to crush him. My chest dipped against his body and he squealed with fear and delight. I got up and slipped on my jacket and tied a muffler around his throat.

In the yard the ground felt cold and hard beneath my feet. The dark gabled roofs of the mill loomed at the end of the block, throwing a shadow across the houses built closely side by side. The shrill whistle of a crane rang through the clear cold air.

We walked into the garage and Pa and Orchowski were bent over their checkerboard on a small table. Even though the small oil stove in the corner glowed with a steady flame, Pa wore his coat and had a wool scarf wrapped around his throat. Orchowski was dressed in a sweater and jacket and a pilot's cap with the flaps pulled down over his big shapeless ears.

Alex broke from my hand and made a dash for Pa, tumbling into his lap. Orchowski grabbed the board and held it aloft while Pa wrestled with the kid.

"If it ain't the steel man." Orchowski smirked between his pitted cheeks. He was a bull of an old man, a roller and turn foreman in the old days, and a terror on Saturday nights. "Tell me, steel man," he said. "You still picking up hot slabs with bare hands and swinging on the crane like Tarzan?"

"Leave the boy alone, you bastard," Pa said. "Today they make steel with their heads, not their backs like we used to do."

"I know," Orchowski sneered. "Sure, sure." He scratched his nose. "Play checkers. You're losing and you're trying to turn over the goddam board."

The kid listened to them intently and I remembered what Ethel had said. I stood there a moment and shivered in the chill of the garage.

"Why don't you guys play inside?" I burst out. "This place is an icebox."

Orchowski and Pa looked at me. Even Alex stopped wiggling between Pa's legs and stared up at me as if he understood I had said something foolish. Orchowski looked at me with that smirk cracking his lips. Then he turned back to the board and waved impatiently for Pa to move.

Pa kept watching me with concern. "This is fine, Mike." He shook his head at me, slowly at first, then faster and beginning to grin. "Teddy and me like it fine out here."

For a moment Orchowski did not look up. Then he seemed to feel the waiting in the silence and raised his head. Something in Pa's cheeks must have stung him.

"To hell with playing inside," he growled. "Out here we can breathe." Then he slapped his leg with his fist. "You gonna play checkers!" he yelled at Pa. "If you don't make a move I'm gonna go get a goddam beer!"

"Shut up, you bastard!" Pa cried. "You're a poor loser and a scab!"

I took Alex by the hand and we left the garage. We stood outside in the yard and the shifts had changed and the mill-men walked past our fence. Some called greetings to us and some walked tired and silent with their heads bent against the cold. After a while Alex told me he was getting cold and I took him into the house.

After supper that night, while Ethel decorated the cake, I took Alex upstairs and put him into the tub. While I soaped and rinsed him with the spray, Pa sat on the laundry hamper and laughed as he watched him splash. When I lifted him dripping out of the tub, Pa caught him in a big towel and began to rub him gently dry. Then he carried him into the bedroom and they tussled on the bed while Alex screamed.

"I got to dress him, Pa," I said.

"OK," Pa said, and he gave Alex a soft final swat across the fanny. "I'll go down and give Ethel a hand."

I finished dressing Alex and combed his hair. He was a handsome boy with Ethel's fine features. I looked at him with pride and love, thinking of him as a part of my flesh.

Ethel came upstairs and she smelled from the warm and fragrant kitchen. She gave Alex a kiss and waited until he left the room. When she turned to me there were bright spots in her cheeks and a weariness around her mouth.

"Mike," she said, "Pa wants to decorate the dining room and he's making a mess of it. I told him Blanche was bringing a few Japanese lanterns to put over the lights, but he's found some old faded crepe paper in the basement." She paused a moment, with her cheeks pale, and moved her fingers to tug helplessly at her apron. "I hate myself," she said, and she spoke softly, almost in a whisper. "I hate myself every time I complain. He's got no one but us and I want him to know this is his house, too. But I can't help myself." Her eyes became red and I could see her trying hard not to cry.

"I'll tell him," I said. "I'll tell him I want to fix it a certain way."

She shook her head, sorry suddenly that she had come upstairs, sorry that she had spoken. "Let him alone," she said. "Don't tell him anything. Don't make me feel more ashamed than I am already."

"If he would take a walk," I said, "up to the corner or over to Orchowski's for a half hour, we could finish decorating the way you want." I paused. "Orchowski is coming to the party, isn't he? You told Pa to ask him, didn't you?"

I could see the misery working behind her cheeks. Then it was my turn to feel ashamed, because I was glad she had not invited Orchowski, not for any other reason but that he made Pa seem worse than he was.

We did not speak again. There didn't seem to be anything either of us could say. I started down the stairs and Pa waited for me at the bottom. I muttered something about turning the thermostat higher to warm the house.

"Is Ethel all right?" he asked. I looked away, because he seemed to sense quick when something was wrong.

"She's got a little headache," I said.

He turned away and I looked down on his gray-haired and strong head and the slight slump that rounded his big shoulders.

"If you think Ethel won't be needing me for anything special," he said, "I might take a little walk. Maybe there's something she wants from the store." He had to pass me to reach into the closet for his coat. I looked at him closely, but he only smiled.

"That's OK, Pa," I said. "I'll see if she needs anything." I called up to Ethel and knew that she was standing silently on the landing at the top of the stairs. For a long moment she did not answer, as if she were trying to compose her voice.

"No," she said, "but tell Pa to hurry back. He's sitting next to Alex at the head of the table."

Pa tugged on his coat and walked to the door and closed it behind him.

In about an hour the dozen or so guests for the party had arrived. Ethel's sister, Blanche, had come from the North Side with her husband, who was an insurance executive. He kept walking around sniffing the house. There were a couple of women Ethel had once taught school with and a couple of the turn foremen with their wives. Pa had not come back.

We waited a while longer and Ethel passed around some more cheese and crackers and I opened some more beer. Everybody was getting restless. Alex, becoming impatient, began to whine. I went next door finally, to Max's place, and asked to use their phone. I called the Burley Club, but the bartender hadn't seen Pa. I called Orchowski's brother-in-law's house, but no one answered. On the way back I peered into the garage, but it was dark.

In the house I told Ethel to cut the cake. Alex was crabby and didn't want to blow out the candles. The insurance executive and Blanche had bought him a $22 dump truck and he didn't want to even open the other presents. I was angry and suddenly sick with worry about Pa, thinking something might have happened to him. I went into the kitchen to get another pint of ice cream and when I got back to the dining room everything was strangely quiet.

Pa stood in the front hallway. His hair was mussed, his collar unbuttoned, and his eyes were bright and glistening. Orchowski, an idiot's grin on his pitted cheeks, stood behind him. The stink of whiskey covered them both like a cloud and fell across them into the room.

I looked once at Ethel and her cheeks were the color of chalk. Pa took a step forward and stumbled and then braced himself against the doorway of the room.

He swept his arm up recklessly in a swing that included everybody in the room. He kept staring at all of us and then he fumbled behind him, catching Orchowski by the coat and tugging him forward.

"I brought my goddam friend home for the party," Pa said, and the words came slurred and thick from his tongue. "My goddam friend who worked with me at the plate mill for thirty-six years."

"Thirty-seven years," Orchowski said, swaying and grinning beside him.

Alex yelped then for his grandpa and one of the foremen laughed and walked forward to greet them. Ethel moved and smiled across the pale band of her cheeks. I helped Pa off with his coat and Ethel took Orchowski's jacket, and for a moment in the closet I felt her hand, cold and trembling against my own.

A short while later I got Pa upstairs and helped him undress. He was sobering, his eyes suddenly blurred and melting, and he kept mumbling under his breath. When he was under the covers, I sat down on the edge of the bed near his head. I heard the last of the guests saying good night and the door closed for the last time. Ethel brought the kid upstairs and put him to bed. All the while, the old man lay there with his eyes wide open, staring up at the ceiling.

Ethel came into the room. She stood for just a moment inside the door and then she walked to the bed and leaned down and put her cheek against Pa's cheek.

"It's all right, Pa," she said, and she was crying, the tears running silently down her cheeks. "It's all right and I'm glad you brought Mr. Orchowski."

Pa touched her cheek with his fingers and moved his lips without making any sound. He touched her cheek that was wet with tears, in a kind of caress, and tried to smile to reassure her, and then turned his head helplessly to the wall. I motioned to Ethel to leave the room.

I sat for a while longer beside him. He twisted and thrashed beneath the blankets.

"I was drunk," he said. "Honest to God, boy, if I hadn't

been loaded I wouldn't have come in like a goddam fool. I wouldn't have hurt Ethel like that."

"Let it alone, Pa," I said. "What are you making such a big thing of it for? Ethel said it was all right. We were wrong."

But he would not be comforted. He would lie still for a few moments with his eyes closed and I thought he had fallen asleep. Then he seemed to startle awake and his fingers moved in restless tremblings along the spread.

I got scared and left the room and called the doctor. He came and gave Pa a shot. After a while Pa fell asleep, his rough breathing eased and quieted.

It was not very long after that night, only a couple of months later at the beginning of summer, that the old man died. In May we sowed a bed of columbines and Pa talked of seeing them flower and just a few days after that he was dead.

When he died he had been in the hospital two days with a hard and heavy pain in his chest. The second night a blood clot formed and he died in his sleep. We had seen him early in the afternoon of that day, and when they called us back to the hospital, all I remember noticing was how really thin his wrists had become, how slim and pale his strong fingers were.

We buried him three days later. The old rollers and turn foremen who were still alive came, and a bunch of the men from my turn. It rained a little on our way to the cemetery, the drops glistened on the bankings of flowers around the grave. Ethel cried a lot and she was near enough her time for giving birth that I was scared for her and for the baby.

On the way out of the cemetery I saw Orchowski. He was dressed in a baggy gray suit, a stiff collar around his broad throat. I wanted to talk to him a few moments, there beside the old man's grave, but someone took my arm and I lost him.

We stopped on the way home to pick up Alex from Mrs.

Feldman, who had looked after him. The rest of the way,
Alex between us in the car, Ethel and I didn't speak. I
parked the car and carried the kid into the house because of
the puddles that still gleamed in the gutters and made small
pools along the side of the walks.

The house was damp and quiet. I turned on some lights
and put up the heat. Ethel came in behind me and we stood
like that for moments, listening as if there were sounds and
noises we expected to hear.

"I'm tired," Ethel said. "I've got a headache. I'll get Alex
ready for bed and go to bed myself."

"I'll bring him up in a minute," I said. "Let him play for a
while."

She stood in the hall and slipped off her coat and the
jacket of her suit. The light fell across her body and I could
see the great swell of her belly, the slow labored movement
of her arms. She saw me watching her and came over and
kissed me on the cheek. I held her close in the circle of my
arm.

"We tried," she said, and there was a thin tight edge to
her voice, and she looked at me out of her weary and swollen eyes. "We did what we could for him, didn't we, Mike?
Didn't we?"

I remembered the night of Alex's birthday and the way she
cried against the old man's cheek.

"Sure," I said. "Sure, baby, you did."

I sat for a while in the back room watching Alex play with
his toy cars on the floor. Outside, the cars passed in the twilight and from the mill I heard the whistling of the slab-mill
crane.

I listened to the kid humming a foolish song as he played.
I thought suddenly of Ethel dead, someday, like my ma, and
me having to live with the kid and his wife.

I got up and went into the kitchen. Through the window,
night had fallen over the back yard. A few fireflies flickered
over the garden. The outline of the garage loomed silent and

dark against the lighter sky. I moved to the sink, feeling a tightness breaking in my throat.

When I began to cry, the water running so the kid would not hear, I didn't know for a few crazy moments who I was really crying for—the lost old man or myself.

℃ I wrote this long story during the late 1960s, with the agony of Vietnam poisoning so much of our spirits, and bitter confrontations between students and police taking place in the streets. No other story I have written came from as vulnerable a part of me as this one did.

I make a confession now I have never made before. Earlier drafts of this story had the principal character a middle-aged writer going through the anguish of wondering what his role in the struggle should be, distraught because he could no longer conceal from himself how much of his early hopes and ideals he had forsaken for spurious comforts and liberal aphorisms.

In later drafts, that naked exposure became almost unbearable and I lost my courage and masked the principal character by making him a priest.

Looking back on that decision now, it doesn't seem too implausible. During the Middle Ages many writers became priests, and, in our own tumultuous times, priests, in turn, become writers.

The Waves of Night

That Sunday morning in late March, Father Manos rose, as usual, before daylight, not shivering quite as much as he had on previous Sunday risings for months. He walked to the window and pushed aside the curtain to peer out. Darkness still covered the sleeping city, misted stone and brick peaks of buildings, a single ring of light under a corner lamp. For the first time it seemed to him he could hear the heart of the earth beating faster, a thin promise of early spring, a forerunner of green feast and fruitfulness in the weeks ahead.

He washed and dressed briskly and left the house, walking the deserted streets to his church as the fragmented dawn glimmered across the roofs and parapets of the city.

The shops he passed were shadowed and silent, the taverns that had throbbed with revelry a few hours before, padlocked now, their muted neon signs creaking gently in the stillness. A tomcat emerged from an alley, fur ruffled and wary, idling its way home after a night of errant and promiscuous love. I will expect you at confession, Father Manos thought wryly, as the unrepentant rake glided by.

Even inside the church, sombrous and damp with the chilled shadows of the night, he seemed to feel the stirring of the earth beneath his feet. Then, with a laugh, he realized that it was the old sexton, Janco, raking up the coals in the basement furnace. Soon the old man would come up and begin lighting the candelabras before the icons of St. John the Baptist, and the Holy Mother with the Child-Christ. In another few hours the great chandelier would be lit and the light representing the stars in the sky would shine down upon the nave full (well, almost full) with the members of the congregation.

It was his custom in these quiet and serene moments to pray. He knelt before the Royal Gate of the Sanctuary, the portal decorated with the icon of Christ as Shepherd. He prayed for the end of the war in Viet Nam, for the starving children in Biafra, for the welfare of the poor, for the general condition of the country. He prayed for the wellbeing of his parishioners, for the perpetuation of the faith, and, finally, he spoke a prayer of gratefulness for the plenitude of his own life.

He was fifty-nine, in good health although somewhat overweight, and with (some exceptions, unfortunately) a good parish. It was true there were a few of the wealthier parishioners with an unholy penchant for distressing him. There was the peculiarly Greek conception of the priest having to spin like a dervish to fit the parishioner's vacillating moods and needs. He had, over the years, managed to balance these unreasonable demands in a way that produced a minimum of resentment. The blessed St. John himself could not have accomplished more.

Not all of the priests in the city were as fortunate. Father Peter of St. George's Church was caught between two rabid factions in his parish, one seeking to banish him and the other to retain him. Father Theodore of St. Dionysios was also in trouble although it was common knowledge that he gambled and drank. But many of the weaknesses which the priests developed were not really their fault. The young priests came from Pomfret and Brookline, eager to serve their flocks and God, but their years of prayer and study provided no inkling of what they would find in their new parishes. The malicious, envious individuals, the myriad groups in reckless rivalry, the constant bickering, the vanity of the wealthy and the resentment of the poor, all took their toll.

Our priests are forced to wear the masks of clowns and fools, the savage Father Grivas of Holy Trinity Church often cried. He responded by affixing a single fierce and unrelenting demeanor to his own face, ignoring the angry threats of his trustees to petition his removal. That he was able to remain in his pulpit and serve as priest was simply due to the fear in which they held him. They regarded him as a ruffian, capable of murder if he were crossed or betrayed.

Wasted effort and lost energy. Father Manos tried to counsel him. He met similar problems with a more subtle and political response. He did what he could and if this were inevitably less than was expected of him, he apologized earnestly for his infirmities.

Playing their dirty, hypocritical game, Father Grivas would storm at him, but Father Manos saw no reason to whirl in a tempest of anger and bitterness when some amicable diplomacy could smooth issues out.

The sexton, Janco, came up from the basement into the church. He was a crooked-limbed old man who moved in a disjointed scramble of elbows and knees, his speech all but limited to mumbles and grunts. He lived in a room in the basement of the church and did not require more than a few dollars a week for food. Father Manos supplemented the meager wages the trustees gave the old man with a little money from his own salary, but he found him an ordeal.

Now he directed him in the lighting of the Kandilia and patiently pointed out several pews that had not been swept. By that time the first of the black-garbed, stony-faced old women appeared bringing a Prosforon, the offering bread he would use in making communion. Another old woman brought in a small plate of Kolyva, the boiled wheat garnished with raisins and almonds, a reminder that the dead will rise again as the wheat which is buried in the earth sprouts out and bears fruit.

When it was time for him to dress for the service, Father Manos entered the Deacons' door into the anteroom adjoining the Sanctuary. He slipped on his Stiharion, the long tunic that covered his body from the shoulders to the feet. He put on the stole, belt, cuffs and the felonion, the scarlet vestment cape, kissing each holy article before adding it to his person. By the time he had finished tying the cords and ribbons, the first young acolytes appeared in the anteroom on the opposite side of the Sanctuary, slipping noisily into their white altar gowns. He caught the eye of one of them and waved sternly for silence.

"Good morning, Father Manos," Elias, the choirmaster said, as he entered the anteroom.

"Good morning, Elias," Father Manos said.

The choirmaster, a handsome man with pomaded hair that glistened in blue-black swirls, changed into his cassock.

"Looks like a good turnout this morning," he said. "They should fill the collection trays."

"Let's first fill their souls," Father Manos smiled.

The choirmaster left the anteroom and a few moments later his strong and resonant voice chanted across the church.

Father Manos entered the Sanctuary. "Blessed is our God, always now and ever . . ." he whispered. He adjusted the Evangelion and the candlesticks on the great marble Holy Table. He motioned the young leader of the acolytes to silence all movement and speech and then he took his place before the closed panel of the Royal Gate. He folded his hands gravely.

In another moment the old sexton, his brittle, awkward frame harried as usual, rushed past the acolytes into the Sanctuary, crossing himself clumsily, taking up his place at the Royal Gate. When given the signal he would slide open the panel and Father Manos would stand revealed in the total firmament of the church, all eyes drawn through the charismatic union of crosses, icons and candles to him. It was a moment that he had always, secretly, and he admitted honestly to himself, vainfully cherished, imagining the resurrective effect of the sanctified light across his colorful and brocaded vestments. Behind him the great Holy Table and large wooden crucifix on which the carved, life-sized body of Jesus Christ was nailed, heightened the effect.

The sexton crouched with his skinny arms against the panel, his scrawny old rooster's neck twisted toward the priest. Father Manos nodded somberly. The old man grimaced in a violent effort to match the high solemnity of the moment and slid the panel open slowly, making certain as Father Manos had often warned him, to keep his own figure hidden. The glitter of the church burst across the priest's head. He raised his hands slowly. The congregation filling the benches in uneven rows rose with a sound of woodwinds for the beginning of the Mass.

At the end of the service he divested himself of his vestments, the young acolyte leader helping him. He put on his black cassock and walked from the anteroom to stand on the Soleas, the elevated section of floor between the Sanctuary and the main part of the church. He felt the pangs of hunger rumbling in his stomach and quickly appraised the number of people waiting to see him. There were about five or six, no more than usual, but he had somehow hoped to be spared even that number today. Then he sternly admonished himself for his impatience. Lantzounis would wait, would indeed expect to wait. The luncheon his good wife prepared for them would be even more delicious when they finally sat down to eat.

He motioned toward the group. Hesitantly, the first man walked forward. He was a poor visitor, he said, from another section of the city, asking for a little money to buy food and clothing. He had the uncertain manner and nervous demeanor of the chronic alcoholic. Although there was a contingency fund that would have allowed Father Manos to give him a few dollars, he brusquely promised instead that one of the church organizations would send the man a basket of food and some articles of used clothing. The man left unappeased, mumbling a disappointed thanks. Father Manos was pleased to see a second man among those waiting leave with him.

The second parishioner to come up was a man in his late fifties, stocky and broad of build, with thick gray hair. Father Manos had seen him in church a number of times but could not recall his name.

"I am George Yalukis, Father," the man said in a harsh, anxious voice.

"I know you, Mr. Yalukis."

The man nodded gratefully.

"You know my son, Sam, Father," Yalukis said. "He played baseball in the GOYA tournament last year."

"I remember Sam," Father Manos said. "A fine boy and a splendid athlete."

"Father," Yalukis leaned forward slightly and lowered his voice. "I don't know what to do. Last week Sam got notice to go into the army. He's been 1 A and passed his physical. But he won't go. Says he'll go to jail first."

"Why won't he go, Mr. Yalukis?"

"I don't understand him, Father," Yalukis said. "He talks about the war in Viet Nam being wrong, things like that."

Father Manos shook his head somberly.

"These are difficult times for a young man, Mr. Yalukis," he said. "No youth wants to go to war but to serve one's country is a solemn obligation and responsibility. If he refused and went to jail it might ruin his life, place a stain upon him for as long as he lives."

"I know, Father," Yalukis grimaced as if he were in pain.

"Try to explain that to him," Father Manos said. "Explain how serious the whole matter is, the catastrophic results. Meanwhile I'll say a prayer for him as well as for you and your family."

The man stood staring mutely at the priest. What does he expect of me, Father Manos thought uneasily. What more can I tell him now?

"Father," Yalukis looked shakenly down at the tips of his shoes and then raised his head. "Can you come over with me to my house now, to talk to him? He came home today to see his mother, not me, but he won't stay long. If you could come and talk to him . . ."

Father Manos wavered. He found it more and more difficult to communicate with many of the young people in his parish, particularly the militant and unreasonable ones. He might go with Yalukis to talk to Sam but would probably accomplish nothing if the youth's mind were already made up. Yalukis, obviously a strong-willed and stubborn man, had probably totally alienated his son. How could the priest be expected to pacify him?

"I'm sorry, I can't come now," he said regretfully to Yalukis. "I have another appointment. But tell Sam I want to see him, ask him to come to church and see me tomorrow."

Yalukis shook his head silently and patiently as if he were resigned to his fate. He bent and gripped one of the priest's hands and kissed the back of the palm. He turned and started walking slowly and dejectedly down the center aisle.

For a moment watching his retreating figure, Father Manos felt pinches of remorse. There were so many problems he was helpless to resolve, one aging man trying to administer to a parish of more than four hundred families. Did they want his blood as well as his flesh and bone?

He sighed and looked up at the small windows in the

dome of the church. The sky gleamed a vibrant blue through the panes of glass. It seemed to him a bird winged past with a shimmering grace. The winter had been long and hard, he had felt it like a cold stone in his body, but the spring was coming. There would be sun to warm his bones and the scent of flowers in the gardens and the laughter of children on the walks.

"Father Manos?"

He turned back to the church and a young woman stood at the foot of the steps of the Soleas. He recognized Angela Fotakis, a plain, pale-cheeked girl over thirty. Her father, Kostas, was one of the wealthiest men in the parish, owner of four large resplendent restaurants, a substantial contributor to the Coal and Easter offerings.

"Yes, my dear?" Father Manos said.

"Father, my parents are waiting outside," she said. "I've only got a minute." She stared up at him with watery eyes. "They have found a man willing to marry me. He's old . . . more than fifty." She paused, stricken suddenly by what he might feel to be rudeness.

Father Manos smiled to console her. "Don't fret," he said. "My graying hair and arthritis have made me immune to the vanity of thinking over fifty is young."

"I'm sorry, Father," she said. "I know I'm just past thirty now. I know what they tell me is true, that no other man may be found who wants me if I wait. But I hoped . . . at least . . . for someone just a little younger."

"I know the man your parents are considering," Father Manos spoke earnestly, and with a measured degree of caution because of her father. "He is a good man who will be a good provider. If he is not as young as you wish, that is, after all, not his fault." He took her hand between his palms, felt her fingers tense and chilled. "There are worse things than marriage to an older man. You could marry a young wastrel, a drunk, someone who would beat you. Would youth compensate for cruelty? I know, my dear. We have several cases like that in our parish now." He felt the disquieting rumble of hunger widening in his stomach. "You think about it a little more. Measure the benefits against the disadvantages. I'm sure your good parents would not make you do anything against your will. Let me know what you decide. If you think the aspect of the man's age too distressing, come back and see me. I'll promise to talk to your father."

Angela nodded slowly, her face still pensive and sad. He reached out and patted her cheek gently. She smiled faintly and turned and started toward the narthex.

Father Manos hurried back into the anteroom and slipped off his cassock and put on his suitcoat and coat. He noticed a button hanging precariously on one sleeve. Iota would have to sew that on.

He emerged from the anteroom again. "Janco!" he called, and his voice echoed across the silent church. When there was no answer he called again more sharply, "Janco!" An instant later the old sexton came stumbling out of the shadows.

"I'll be at Mr. Lantzounis' for lunch," he said. "Remember we have a baptism for four o'clock. See that everything is prepared. I'll be back a little after three."

The old man nodded dolefully. His face seemed incapable of cracking a smile. Iota at home and this grim old devil here, Father Manos thought. They were enough to age a man before his time.

But sitting at the head of the bountiful Lantzounis table, Father Manos felt young and ebullient. The platters were heaped with grape leaves stuffed with rice and meat, broiled chicken in a lemon-butter sauce, tureens of creamy avgolemono, leafy green salads with black olives and chunks of white feta cheese and loaves of warm, crisp-crusted bread. There were, as well, several decanters of chilled retsina wine.

He bent his head and blessed the table and the family, his palate quivering with anticipation. When he raised his head the silence was broken by an eruption of amens and hands moving swiftly through the stations of the cross.

"Eat, Father!" Mrs. Lantzounis cried. "Eat and drink now and relax." She was a cheerful, incredibly obese woman with a roll of fat around her neck so thick it resembled a collar of fleshy fur.

Father Manos patted his midsection. "I have too much weight here now," he said. "Iota starts me dieting every week."

"You're just right, Father," Lantzounis said. "Let me refill your glass." He was a tall, handsome man with strong arms and dark, curly hair. It was common gossip throughout the parish that Lantzounis had a mistress, a young Spartan girl who worked in the office at his meat packing plant. But looking at his poor wife, Father Manos thought, how could one blame him? The rule against adultery must still be tempered by justice. That was the difference, he had always felt, between an enlightened priest and a clerical fanatic.

Sixteen-year-old Caliope Lantzounis whispered into the ear of her sister, Aspasia, and then broke away to giggle shrilly.

"What's so funny, young lady?" Lantzounis snapped.

"Leave the child be, Cleon," Father Manos smiled. "At her age all of life is a source of mirth. I laughed often when I was sixteen." He looked at Aspasia, slender and lovely and dark-eyed. "And at eighteen."

"Have some more wine, Father," Mrs. Lantzounis said. With his mouth full of grape leaves he could not answer but motioned eagerly to his glass.

The wine warmed him and he saw the great bulk of Mrs. Lantzounis flitting with the grace of a nymph around the table, filling plates over again, and pouring endless glasses of wine. The hunger of his stomach was fully appeased. He could feel the wrinkles filled out with the warm, savory food. He managed to stifle a belch and decided, regretfully, that he had eaten enough.

The girls rose in a few moments to help pick up the

dishes. They wore print dresses with frilly skirts, modestly miniskirted. As Aspasia bent beside him to pick up his plate, her skirt rose up her legs and he caught a glimpse of her bare white flesh above the hem of her silk stockings. He felt a sudden frivolous impulse to pat her slender bottom.

The urge was disquieting. It is the wine, he thought. The barriers that age and the habit of abstinence had erected crumbled like faulty dikes under the flow of the juice. It was true that what had once troubled him a great deal, now bothered him rarely. He was immensely grateful for the quietude of his body, something achieved after considerable hardship. Even now it was never completely dead. There were vagrant moments when it returned to trouble him and he found himself prickled by the most carnal thoughts.

There was the magazine he had confiscated from an eighth grader in the parish school some months before. In the privacy of his office he had leafed through the pages and was shocked at the photographs of totally nude women in incredibly suggestive poses. His first reaction was one of outrage against the publishers and then he considered sending for the boy to give him a thrashing. But he remained rooted in his chair, the magazine in his hands, his feelings suddenly changing. A curious lassitude settled over his limbs. He saw the breasts of one woman, not as young as some of the others, a certain maturity in the proportions of her flesh, in her dark prodigal nipples. To sleep at night, he thought, against such breasts. To feel the warmth of them against my back in frozen winter. He stared then at his hands, at the fingers and the palms. They seemed desiccated and bloodless like the hands of the saints in the icons. He imagined them caressing the breasts of the woman in the magazine and he groaned and snapped the magazine shut and tossed it into his bottom drawer. But the vision continued to burn him and he opened the drawer and took out the magazine and using all his strength he tore it into pieces too small to tear any more. He threw them into the wastebasket beside his desk. He looked down at the torn pieces and felt a curious and plaintive sense of loss.

"Father?" Lantzounis' voice startled Father Manos from his reverie. "What were you thinking of?"

Father Manos looked into the laughing face of Aspasia staring at him with a certain intuitive wisdom and he felt a rush of blood to his cheeks.

"The wine," he said loudly, in an effort to cover his disorder. "The wine has made me drowsy."

"A cup of coffee then," Mrs. Lantzounis said and she emerged from the kitchen carrying a silver coffeepot and Caliope followed her carrying a great silver tray laden with powder-sugared kourabiethes and honey-nut baklava.

"Mercy!" Father Manos cried with such vigor that they all laughed with him, their voices blending into a happy and harmonious warmth.

Father Manos returned to church some time later than he had planned and found the parents with the child to be baptized waiting. He donned his robes quickly and assembled the relatives and friends in the baptismal corner.

The baby was a girl of about eleven months, a fair and plump child with a fuzz of golden hair. The godfather was Spiro Marketos, President of the Board of Trustees of the church, a man who had made a fortune by speculating in real estate.

Father Manos found him a pompous and insufferable man always determined to have his own way. On a few occasions they had quarreled but for the most part they observed a certain wary truce. Because Marketos was the godfather, Father Manos would be obliged to attend the celebration dinner following the baptism, although he had no more desire for additional food and drink. He also knew, unhappily, that Marketos was fascinated with the sound of his own voice, punctuating his tedious speeches with countless "now in conclusion's" and never ending.

The moment came during the ceremony to immerse the

baby under the water in the baptismal font. It was a time for Father Manos that contained all the mystery and beauty of faith. That this naked, squirming pullet of flesh, only some months removed from her mother's womb should now be receiving the sacrament of baptism and anointed with oil in the sign of the cross, filled him with fervent satisfaction. He tried to remember, holding the baby in his arms, the number of infants he had baptized in the past thirty years. A few of them endured the ordeal silently but most screamed shrilly in outrage, thrashing their small limbs violently. He had learned to hold them firmly and gently, without fear, and dunked them for a second, completely under the water. He enjoyed the pleased murmurs that came from the watchers as the body of the infant emerged from the water, dripping and breathless, to be enfolded in the warm, fleecy towel.

When the baptism was over, Father Manos congratulated the parents and relatives. Marketos looked at him with a certain bovine haughtiness. "You are coming to the reception, of course?" His tone suggested no other action would be tolerated.

"I am coming," Father Manos said and within himself sighed.

He sat at the table of honor staring out upon the half-dozen tables grouped together in the private diningroom of the luxurious Regis Hotel. The pleasure of eating and drinking he had sustained earlier in the day had vanished and he found the presence of so much food suddenly repugnant. He reproached himself for not having eaten less earlier and left a margin of space. He sipped his champagne without savor. Simple good Greek wine would not do for any child that Marketos baptized.

". . . now in conclusion," Marketos said, for the fifth time, and it seemed to Father Manos that the buffoon had been talking for hours. "I want to relate to you how I came to baptize this lovely baby. Her dear mother, daughter of one of my closest friends, the distinguished owner of the Salonika Laundry, came to see me. She had already been to church to visit Father Manos . . ." Marketos paused and looked toward the priest, half perhaps for confirmation and half to ascertain whether he was paying attention. Father Manos sat up a little straighter and nodded although for the life of him he could not remember when the girl had come to him.

"I could discern at once the young lady was troubled," Marketos paused to allow the audience time to absorb the sensitive attunement of his perceptive powers. "She told me there was a young man she wanted to marry."

God have mercy, Father Manos thought, that was more than three years ago. No wonder I couldn't remember. Will the simple flit never stop?

". . . now in conclusion." But by then the voice of Marketos faded into an intermittent mumble and the stain of wine spilled on the tablecloth nearby made Father Manos remember the wine glass the girl's father had shattered when he learned the boy she wanted to marry wasn't Greek. For a year the father had not spoken to his daughter, remaining angered and embittered. Not a trace of Marketos all that time but Father Manos had argued and pleaded the cause of the young people. Now the father sat beaming on the other side of Marketos, all rancor and animosity forgotten, the son-in-law's managership of a lucrative Ford agency helping to obliterate the parental wrath. All the hours of anguish they caused me, Father Manos thought, and now they sit here like lovers, their souls entwined in each other's arms.

He was conscious of a sudden oppressive silence. He looked up startled to find Marketos glaring at him, the eyes of everyone else in the room on him as well. I listen to him faithfully for forty-five minutes, Father Manos thought unhappily, and the moment my attention lapses, the booby quits.

"Our esteemed Father Manos works too hard in his spiritual duties," Marketos said with an edge of malice in his voice. "He finds it hard to remain awake, or perhaps I speak too long, is that it, Father?"

The crowd laughed goodnaturedly and for a fleeting moment of bravado, Father Manos considered saying, yes, that is true, Marketos, you go on and on like a cracked old record and say nothing. But his courage subsided quickly into the rigid propriety of his position and he rose to his feet.

"Forgive me, Mr. Marketos," he said gravely. "I was carried away by your eloquence and moved by your recollections. When you spoke of the day Demetra came to the church to see me, I was reminded of that fateful hour myself, my own feelings as she informed me of her wish to marry this fine young man . . ."

The parents beamed. Demetra clapped her hands in delight and embraced her husband. The guests joined in applause. Marketos sat down to nurse his defeat. Father Manos could not refrain from a sly feeling of triumph. O I can play your game, he thought gleefully, when you cross lances with me, you nincompoop, you had best bolster yourself with a sturdy rod shoved up your starched backside.

Then, ashamed of his vengeful incontinence, he lowered his head and with sincerity invoked the benediction, wishing the guests, the parents, the grandparents, the baby, and yes, even Marketos, a long and fruitful life.

At eight o'clock that evening there was a meeting of the Daughters of Sparta where he spoke concerning the needs of the Boston orphanage. At nine, a half-dozen members of the picnic committee met in his office at church to discuss plans for the Hellenic Federation picnic in July. By the time they had finished a little after ten o'clock, Father Manos was exhausted and Rexinis, one of the members, drove him home.

He walked wearily up the steps of the house he had left near five that morning. He took off his coat in the hallway and went into his study. He sat down in his armchair and bent burdensomely to untie and remove his shoes. He wiggled his toes, unbuttoned his trousers and leaned back in his chair uttering a deep fervent sigh. He yearned suddenly for bed and for sleep.

There was a brusque knock on the door of his study and without waiting for his answer, Iota entered. She was the withered, almost bloodless old lady who tended house for him, an ancient crone with hard blue veins webbing her parchment flesh.

"A call for you, Father," she said and blinked in annoyance at the open buttons of his trousers. "They phoned the church just after you left."

He sighed again, a vexed, loud sigh, not caring that the old lady heard and pursed her thin lips in disapproval. He rose heavily and walked to the hallway for the phone. He had been pleading for a year for an assistant rector to replace young Deacon Botsis who had been transferred to a parish in Atlanta. The trustees were reluctant to pay another salary and the only concession they made was to allow him a priest to help him during the Christmas and Easter holidays. Meanwhile he felt his life being shortened by the excessive burdens and demands of the parish.

The call was from the floor nurse at the Mercy Hospital with a message from Peter Kramos. His nine-year-old son, suffering from leukemia, a boy that Father Manos had visited several times in the hospital and twice given communion, was dying and not expected to survive the night. His father requested the priest to come.

Father Manos slipped his swollen feet back into his shoes and buttoned his pants while Iota called for a cab. He felt a surge of pity for Kramos and his wife, the anguish of parents losing a young child. At the same time he could not help thinking there was nothing he could really do besides join them in their suffering. He had been witness to death many times over the years, felt it a blessing for the aged and incurably ill, a cessation to their suffering. But there was nothing more shattering than the death of a child and at such

times he whirled in a helpless desperation to find words to
console the bereaved parents.

Carrying his small bag containing Bible and chalice for
communion, he walked down the steps to the cab. They
drove through the darkened streets. By the time they
reached the hospital and he paid the driver, making sure to
get the receipt he would turn in to the parish treasurer at
the end of the month, his weariness had been submerged
under a determination to meet the ordeal ahead.

He was taken by a nurse to the eighth floor. As he came
out of the elevator he recognized the boy's uncle who had
come to the end of the corridor to grieve alone. His face was
stained with tears and when he saw Father Manos he bent
and pressed his lips fervently against the back of the priest's
hand. Father Manos embraced him silently and walked
down the corridor to the boy's room.

The child lay almost lost within the huge bed, only his
thin, frail face visible, a thatch of dark hair against the stark
whiteness of the pillow. A white-coated doctor stood at the
foot of the bed and on either side were the parents. Mrs.
Kramos with her hands pressed to her mouth to stifle her
moans. Peter Kramos staring down at his son with a mute
and terrible grief.

Father Manos looked at the doctor who slowly shook his
head. The priest moved closer to the bed, pausing a moment
to console the mother. He placed his bag on a chair and removed the chalice for communion. He read a brief prayer
and then raised the chalice and with the tiny golden spoon
forced a little sip of the bread and wine between the boy's
blue lips. The liquid bubbled for a moment from the child's
mouth, running a thin scarlet line down his chin. At that instant the child shuddered, his mouth opened, his small teeth
glittered in a frightful grimace. After one short shrill explo-
sion of breath, he died before their eyes.

Father Manos almost cried out in shock at the abruptness
of the end, only moments after he had entered the room. If
the taxi had been delayed even five minutes, he thought

frantically, the child might already have been dead when he arrived. Then he remembered the father and mother and looked at them with stark compassion. The doctor had moved from the foot of the bed and bent over the boy. The mother stared uncomprehending at her son. The father took a step closer to the bed and stared down in disbelief. He pushed the doctor aside and put his big hand against his son's frail throat, his fingers touching the boy's flesh in some taut and ghastly effort to revive him. A low hoarse moan broke from his lips and he put his mouth down over his son's mouth and screamed against the pale still lips.

The mother wailed and Father Manos embraced her, the tears burning in his own eyes. He led her from the room while the doctor tried to draw the father off the body of his son. The uncle hurried past Father Manos and the mother to enter the room.

Father Manos helped the sobbing, shuddering woman up the hall. She tried once to turn and go back but he urged her gently and firmly toward the small waiting room at the end of the corridor. He made her sit down and tried shakenly to console her.

When he looked up, the doctor and uncle were bringing Kramos into the room. His face was still shattered, his eyes anguished, the image of the boy's dead face torn across his cheeks. Father Manos left Mrs. Kramos and went to him.

"God bless you in this moment," he said fervently. "God sustain you, my dear friend . . . provide you the strength to endure your terrible loss . . . may God console you with his balm of compassion . . ."

For an instant Kramos stared at the priest as if he were not really seeing or hearing him. Then his face seemed to break apart. He opened his mouth and with a kind of horror Father Manos saw the scream trying to break free. Then Kramos lashed out his fist and struck the priest in the face.

It was a terrible blow. The priest felt his senses cracked apart and as he fell, he cried out in shock and fear. He landed sprawling on the floor, the room rocking wildly around him. His arms flew up in a weird broken flutter of his fingers. He saw the face of Kramos swooping down to attack him again.

The doctor and uncle grabbed Kramos. In his wild fury to get to the priest he dragged them along. His wife screamed and ran to fling her arms around her husband's throat, dragging the weight of her body against his lunge. For a few moments their arms and bodies held him, the three of them barely enough, while in terror and panic Father Manos scrambled to his knees looking vainly for a way to escape.

"Goddam you priest bastard!" Kramos screamed. "Goddam your God! Goddam animals who let my son die!"

They struggled to hold him while he screamed and raged and another intern and orderly came. They dragged him from the room into a vacant room across the hall and closed the door which could not shut out his screams.

A nurse and doctor came to Father Manos where he still huddled on his knees. They helped him to his feet and he heard the solacing voices dimly and to every question he could only shake his head. They washed his face and offered him a bed to rest in, but he begged for a cab to take him home. They took him down to the lobby and called a cab and a nurse offered to accompany him but he insisted on riding home alone. He did not remember getting out of the cab or paying the driver. He fumbled in his pocket for the key and could not find it. He rang the bell. The sound echoed back shrilly and he looked fearfully behind him at the shadowed street. When there was no answer from inside the house he knocked loudly and urgently against the wood.

Iota finally opened the door, drawing a robe about her gaunt body, mumbling complaints about being awakened. He hurried past her up the hall to his bedroom. He entered and closed and locked the door. He sat on the side of his bed and for a long time did not move. Iota knocked on the door and spoke to him. He did not answer. After a while, still grumbling, she left him alone.

When the rooms about him were silent, he rose and

undressed. In his underwear he slipped into bed. He pulled the blankets to his throat and shivered. He slid his hands down across his stomach and gripped his genitals. He held himself tightly in a trembling frenzy. Great waves of cold followed by surgings of heat swept his flesh.

"O God," he whispered. "O God, why . . . O my God, why?"

He could not have slept more than a few moments when something startled him, a strange bursting within him and he cried out in terror. He felt sleep abandon him as if it were a soul leaving the body of someone dead. He flung off his covers and rose and left the room. He had a sudden fear of being left alone and he made deliberate noise in the kitchen hoping Iota would wake and come to scold him. At that moment he would have been grateful for even her skinny shanks in their cotton stockings and the sour line of her bloodless lips.

He returned to his bedroom for his robe and then back in the kitchen heated some milk. He sat at the table sipping it, the silence whirling in circles that grew tighter around him. He looked at his hands and was suddenly conscious of them in a way he had never been before. The myriad lines of the palm that laced together in a weird and disturbing pattern, a dark vein pulsing beneath the pale skin of his wrist.

He walked to the bathroom, relieved himself, and felt a burning in his organ. He let water run into the basin and soaked his face with a cloth. He saw his reflection in the glass, the raw ugly bruise that discolored his cheek.

He stared at his face silently for a long time and then felt another sweep of terror rack his flesh. It started in the small of his back, a knife between the ridge of his buttocks, and traveled up as if a frozen blade were rending his body. His mouth opened, his tongue and teeth appeared, and then he screamed . . . not very loud, but thinly and shrilly striking the tile walls and falling back upon him. He put his hands to his ears and felt them as if they were wounds.

I am going mad, he thought. This is the way it must begin.

When the first light of dawn broke over the city he looked up from his Bible with an exhausted relief. He leaned back in his chair and for the first time in hours dared close his eyes. When he opened them the light had spread, glinting across the bedposts and the bureau. He rose wearily and left the room.

In the kitchen, Iota turned from the stove to confront him sullenly.

"What's the matter with you?" she asked sharply. "You rushed in last night like the devil was chasing you and I heard you moving around all night. I couldn't sleep a wink."

"I'm sorry," he said. He stared at her waiting for her to identify the bruise. But she looked at him without a sign that she noticed anything unusual. "You want eggs or oatmeal?" she asked shortly.

"Nothing," Father Manos said, and turned away uneasily, his fingers rising to touch his tender, swollen cheek.

He started toward the bathroom, his muscles sore and cramped from sitting up through the chilled night. He felt the ache with a grim relief, a physical pain that had its origin in something he could understand.

When he moved before the vanity mirror, he hesitated with apprehension. The bruise was clearly there, a raw, red-black blemish that marked his face like a leper's taint.

The remainder of the reflection that stared back at him was familiar, the soft and ordinary face he had known for many years, changing only as age changed it. Yet he saw it now with every vestige of dignity and grace stripped away. The thinning gray hair that he wore long and brushed to cover the area of scalp that was balding. The arched, wry line of his eyebrows above the sockets of his indecisive eyes. The small brush of ridiculous mustache under his nose. Every wrinkle and fold, dreary and common.

For a while he considered remaining at home. But as the

morning wore on and he could not sit or rest, he dressed and left the house for the church. He kept his head lowered and his collar up in an effort to conceal the bruise.

In the church he went at once to his office and closed the door. The parish secretary was visiting her mother in Denver, but Janco had heard him entering and brought him several messages from people who had called. As he handed them across the desk to him, Father Manos waited again anxiously for the old man to see the bruise. But the sexton merely stood waiting for some command, shifting from one crooked leg to the other. The phone rang again and with a peremptory motion of his head, the priest signaled the sexton to take another message. Then he fled into the church.

It was dark and sorrowful in the nave, only a few forlorn candles flickering before the icons. He walked through the Deacon's door to the anteroom and from there into the Sanctuary. He stood motionless for a moment in the dry, ascetic air, absorbing the Evangelion, the Blessing Cross, the candlesticks, the Ark for the Sacrament of Communion.

He went to the small basin and washed his hands. Before the Oblation table he began to prepare the communion. He cut out the middle square of the Prosforon and pierced the bread with the lance. He poured water and wine into the chalice and cut the square of bread into tiny pieces, for the Holy Virgin, for the Saints, for the Bishop, for people living or dead, for himself. He put the pieces of bread into the chalice and spread the coverlet over it. He kissed it and prayed to God to accept and sanctify it. He removed the coverlet and with trembling hands raised the chalice to his mouth. The wine tasted warm and sour on his tongue, trickles seeping into the pockets of his cheeks.

Through the configuration of his arm and the chalice he saw the wooden cross on which the Saviour, Jesus Christ, was crucified. He stared up at the pierced palms and at the anguished countenance and felt a burning in his soul.

"O my merciful God," he whispered to the figure on the

cross, "tell me thy name." He held the chalice numbly in his fingers, his voice faint and shaken in his ears, "I pray you, tell me thy name."

He waited in an entombed silence, feeling the pounding of his heart. From the rear of the church came the sexton's hoarse voice summoning him. He was reluctant to leave the Sanctuary, moving further back into the dense shadows for concealment. The sexton came to the anteroom door and called him again and he walked out to answer the call.

The hours of that day passed unlike any he had ever experienced before. He spoke to the visitors who came to his office, feeling his features altering stiffly from frown to wan smile, hearing the words he spoke echoing as if from far away. He was conscious of talking with his head lowered, one cheek turned aside, his fingers raised often to conceal the bruise. Yet no one seemed to notice it, or if they did, made no sign. And the mystification of that veiling fed his disorder.

When the last visitor left, he rose and in the doorway of his office saw the narthex empty. Through the single lone paned window in the corner he marked the fading light and his terror of the night came storming back.

Back in his office he noticed on his calendar that he was to meet Father Grivas for dinner at the Hellenic Cafe that evening. Earlier in the week he had planned to cancel the dinner with the savage priest but he was grateful now that he had not. He phoned the Holy Trinity Church, afraid Father Grivas might have forgotten about the dinner, and asked him if they could meet a little earlier, as well. The other priest's harsh voice agreeing filled him with a measure of consolation.

Father Manos instructed Janco to lock up and then hurried through the twilight streets. Entering the Hellenic Cafe, a shabby grocery and restaurant, he passed the counters filled with dark green and black olives, ripe white cheeses, and crisp crusted breads. He usually paused to enjoy the plethora of food, often buying some to take home with him. Now he walked directly into the shadowed back room. There were a dozen booths lit only by candles that masked the drab and faded cloths. He sat down wearily in one of them, grateful for the shadows and the dimness. When a lean-hipped waiter with a soiled apron tied around his waist came for his order, he asked for a bottle of retsina. As the waiter left the booth, Father Manos saw the other priest.

Father Grivas came striding through the shadows, pulling off his coat on the way. He was a big, stocky man in a shapeless, dark suit. His hair hung shaggy and unkempt over his clerical collar. He had a swarthy, pocked face and a full-lipped mouth that he twisted into a sardonic grimace of greeting.

"It's been a long time," Grivas spoke in a rumbling voice, "since I've heard anybody so eager to see me."

The waiter reappeared with the bottle of retsina, Grivas stared up at him in irritation. "Don't just stand there, boobhead," he said. "Bring another glass." As the waiter walked away, he added, "That one would make a great Deacon." He stared sharply at Father Manos.

"You don't look well," he said. "Did you have a meeting with your damn Board of Trustees?"

"I didn't sleep well last night," Father Manos said. He kept his face averted slightly in an effort to conceal the bruise even though he was not sure the other priest could see it. At the same time he felt a swift, compelling yearning to reveal his terror. He restrained himself with an effort. Like a child, he thought for a vexed moment, like a child I will blurt out all my absurd fears. "It's nothing," he said impatiently. "Insomnia that bothers me now and then."

The waiter returned with another glass. Grivas filled both glasses with the wine. He handed one to Father Manos. "Drink up," he said, "and then drink some more. You'll sleep soundly tonight." He dismissed the waiter with a sharp cutting motion of his hand. "Get lost until we want you," he said.

They sat together drinking for a long time. Some men they knew entered the restaurant, ate dinner, and then left. Instead of eating dinner themselves, they ordered another bottle of retsina. Father Manos was aware he was drinking too much, that other patrons were staring at them, but after a while he didn't care. The wine warmed him, relaxed his body, seeped into the dark, hidden hollows of his distress.

Across from him, Grivas drank steadily, pausing only to order still another bottle when the second one was empty. Although a wilder glint entered his eyes, he showed no other visible trace of the amount of wine he had consumed.

"They are plump and well-fed, shallow and mundane," Grivas said.

"Who?"

"Who else?" Grivas curled his heavy lip with contempt. "You know damn well who I mean. Our blessed brothers in white collars, wallowing in their sties."

"They haven't done you any harm," Father Manos said.

"Just seeing and hearing them harms me enough," Grivas said stridently. He refilled his glass. The wine spilled over the rim and sloshed across his fingers. He raised his big, hairy hand to his mouth and with his tongue recoiling swiftly between his teeth, licked his fingers. "But the fault isn't theirs alone," he said. "They reflect the nescient cretins who make up their congregations. Forced to pander to every idiot who throws a stinking dime into the tray, they become freaks themselves, lambs who live with snakes so long they learn to shed their skins."

He made a move to refill both their glasses. Father Manos tried to stop him with a half-hearted gesture that Grivas brushed aside.

"You are a relentless man," Father Manos said slowly. "Relentless and cruel. A shade of compassion would make all these frailties bearable."

"I have compassion for them," Grivas growled. "The compassion Herod had, and that is more than they deserve."

With a sudden resignation Father Manos remembered he had heard all these denunciations many times before. He raised the glass of wine to his mouth and took a long swallow. The liquid flowed down into his body, into caverns where his organs lay inert and still.

"I tell the bastards where to go!" Grivas struck the table with his heavy fist and the glasses jumped. "Gluttonous swine wallowing in food while millions starve! Pimping merchants obsessed with spoils while children burn in Viet Nam! Coming to me on Sundays to absolve them of their filthy, necrophilic sins! I'll send them to hell! Let them ask for absolution there!"

"Grivas," Father Manos said, and suddenly he did not care how he might sound to the other priest, "Grivas, something is happening to me."

Grivas fell silent, his chest still heaving in agitation. His harsh breathing grew calmer and he stared at Father Manos with a wary curiosity.

"I don't know what it is," Father Manos said. "I have the feeling it began with a nightmare but I can't be sure." He looked for a long moment helplessly at Grivas, then slowly turned his bruised cheek into the candlelight.

Grivas looked at him silently.

"You see nothing?" Father Manos said. He put his hand to his cheek and felt the tender swollen scale of the wound.

"What should I see?" Grivas asked.

"Nothing," Father Manos said, and shook his head, and felt a flare of panic rising in his gullet. "I'm afraid I'm losing my mind."

For a long moment Grivas did not answer. When he finally spoke, his voice was a shade less harsh.

"Why shouldn't you lose your mind?" Grivas asked. "You wouldn't be the first priest who did, especially in these times. I know one cleric who has twice slashed his wrists and another who tried to conduct his Sunday services stark naked."

Father Manos closed his eyes and held them tightly shut. He fumbled for his glass of wine and raised it to his chilled lips.

"I'm weary and alone," he said. He opened his eyes and stared across the table at Grivas. "The God who was with me as a child, who grew with me as a man, as a priest, He's suddenly hidden from me now."

"Some modern priests think God is dead," Grivas said with a shrug. "That's the new faith now."

Father Manos shook his head slowly. "I don't think He's dead," he said in a low, shaken whisper. "I think He's examined my spirit and my heart and found them wanting. He has turned his face from me because I'm not worthy. He is no longer my rock."

Grivas looked down with an uneasy shrug. "I don't know what's happening to you," he said. "It could be many things. Despair, loneliness, fear and trembling. A man can go on mouthing the clichés for just so long and then a part of him caves in."

"I'll go and see a doctor," Father Manos said, and he clutched at that thought as if it were a raft in the whirlpool of his soul.

"Go ahead," Grivas said. "He'll probably find something wrong to reassure you, but your trouble won't be over then." He finished the last of the wine in his glass, the end of the third bottle and wiped his mouth roughly with the back of his hand. "I think you're a moderately decent man who has suddenly awakened to the absurdity of the whole charade. The pious frauds and bleating hypocrites that you try to anesthetize with candles, incense and dull sermons."

Father Manos felt a sudden ripple of anger in his body, welcomed it for the assault upon his despair.

"Are you any less of a hypocrite?" he asked, feeling the words bitten through his teeth. "Are you any less a fraud than the worst of priests? Tell me that, Grivas!"

"I'm as bad as any of them," Grivas said quietly. "With one difference. I admit my worthlessness and accept my hell. I don't fool myself with false hopes and futile dreams of sacrifice or service. Like the poor priests trying to find meaning in their lives who march with the blacks in Mississippi and get their heads broken by rednecks, or the priests who march into draft boards and pour blood on the files in protest for Viet Nam and for that Christian exercise are sentenced to rot for ten years in some filthy prison with cutthroats and thieves. Leave your pulpit and raise your voice and they'll burn you or crucify you." He paused, a wry grin twisting his lips. "But that might be your salvation," he said. "Join the marchers and protesters. There's always room for a benign, grayhaired martyr."

Father Manos looked shakenly at Grivas. "Once I marched in such a group," he said slowly. "With Blacks into a white neighborhood. They screamed and cursed us and the Rabbi walking beside me was struck with a brick. I panicked and ran. I was sick for three days, told everyone it was the flu, but it was simply terror." He shook his head wearily. "I'm afraid," he said. "I've grown old, soft and afraid."

"Screw them all!" Grivas said, his face dark with a rush of blood. "Let them devour each other! In the end we may leave the earth as clean as it was before Adam and God's curse!"

Father Manos stared at him in shock and wonder.

"How do you live, Grivas?" he asked. "How do you endure your days and nights despising yourself and all other men?"

Grivas looked at him without answering. He rose soddenly to stand swaying for a moment beside the booth and then clutching his coat, turned and walked unsteadily toward the exit. At the door he paused. After a moment he started back to the booth, reached it and bent forward, putting his hands on the table for support. His face was close enough for Father Manos to smell the rank pungence of wine, close enough to see the marks of suffering like dark etchings around the priest's eyes.

"I live on my hate," he said, and the anger and bitterness were gone from his voice, a terrible anguish in their place. "Hate alone keeps me alive."

After Grivas had gone, Father Manos remained at the table for a little while. His knees trembled and he was afraid that if he tried to walk, he would fall. Finally, he rose and left the restaurant, surprised how quiet and desolate the streets were. He was anxious to reach home and the pavement tossed under his legs as if it were the deck of a ship on a stormy sea. He looked vainly for a cab, peering with apprehension at the occasional car that rumbled past as if it contained parishioners who would recognize him. A drunken priest, he thought helplessly, a drunken priest who will fall into a gutter where they will find me in the morning.

But he did not fall down. After a while the night air, cool and damp with the faint scents of spring, cleared his head. He raised the collar of his coat about his ears and walked with his head lowered, charting the path his steps would follow. At each corner he raised his head to take a renewed measure of direction.

Then he stood before the house. He walked up the steps with a silent, grateful prayer that nothing had happened to him on the way. He found his key and fumbled it into the lock and opened the door. In the dim hallway he was assailed at once by the staleness of the rooms around him. The thin mist of cologne the old lady sprayed under her fossiled arms and upon her withered breasts. His own odors, dry, thin scents of prayer and flat, rheumatic spoor of aging, useless flesh.

He went to his bedroom and pulled off his topcoat and suitcoat together. He unbuttoned and removed his collar and took off his shoes. He pulled up the blanket from the bed and lay down and covered himself with it. He lay curved on his side, his head bent forward, his knees drawn

up almost into his stomach. Dear God, he thought, merciful
God, let me sleep.

Whether because of the wine or his exhaustion from the
night before, he slept. He woke with his head buried in his
pillow and could not be sure the length of time which had
elapsed. For a moment he was stung by the fear it might
still be night. He kept his eyes tightly closed and raised his
head slightly to listen for some familiar sound. When he
heard nothing he tensely opened his eyes a slit and with a
spasm of gratitude opened them completely. The rim of
window around his shade was bright with sunlight. He rose
quickly from the bed, remorseful at his terror of the night
before, ashamed when he remembered drinking with
Grivas.

The shower spray struck his naked flesh with a piercing
satisfaction. The water ran in torrents down his legs and
into the drain, flushing the crust of despair from his body.
As he was dressing, Iota knocked brusquely on the door of
his room. He asked her cheerfully to prepare eggs and toast
for his breakfast.

His mood of ebullience carried him into the afternoon. A
steady stream of parishioners came to see him on various
problems and the hours passed quickly. Late in the afternoon a young man and girl came to see him about plans for
their marriage. Happiness radiated from their pores and for
a while he basked in their joy. After they had signed the
necessary papers he walked with them through the narthex
to the outer door of the church and outside on the stone
steps. They waved to him from their car and he raised his
hand in a final flutter of farewell. He saw his fingers out-
lined like the claw of a skeleton against the darkening sky
and the first streaming shadows of twilight. He could not
believe that the day was already gone and he felt his flesh
tighten in a sudden, haunted distress. He turned and fled
back into the church.

He spent the evening at home with the television playing

loudly, for the first time not minding the inane noise and chatter. Finally, Iota asked him to lower it. She was peeved at him anyway because he had not eaten any of the dinner she had prepared. He tried to engage her in conversation to postpone her going to bed. But she told him she was tired and went to her room.

He went to his own bedroom and brought his Bible back to the parlor. He sat down again and began to read. The words blurred before his eyes. He made an effort to concentrate, speaking the verses out loud. They echoed with a stark hollow ring back in his ears.

He closed the Bible and leaned forward in his chair. He listened for sound in the silence of the house. His tongue felt dry, his throat tight, and he rubbed his palms in quick nervous flutters across the cloth of his trousers. The table, chairs, curtains, all seemed washed in a strange, eerie light. Even a bowl of unripe plums on the table caught the cold sparkle, their yellow glow glaring into his eyes.

He closed his eyes, felt them seal his flesh like the lid closing on a coffin. A great scream burst somewhere deep in his body. He slipped from the chair to his knees and then, unable to help himself, pitched forward to the floor. Prostrate and exhausted, his body swept by waves of trembling, he began feverishly to pray.

On Saturday morning he sat in an anteroom of the Archdiocese waiting for his appointment with the Bishop. He huddled in his chair, his head down, faintly hearing the voices of people around him. He felt a tugging at his sleeve and looked up, startled, into the thin, pale face of the Deacon.

"You can go in now, Father," the Deacon said. "His Eminence is waiting."

Father Manos rose and followed the Deacon toward the large double doors. The Deacon opened them and he passed into a huge chamber and the doors closed behind him.

Bishop Okas rose from behind his dark-oak desk and

crossed the room, his robe sweeping about his ankles. "How are you, my dear Father?" he said. He extended his hand, almost in apology, as if knowing yet regretting that ritual required he do so. When Father Manos bent and kissed the back of his palm, he withdrew his hand quickly as if the gesture of obeisance somehow embarrassed him.

The Bishop was a young man, still in his early forties, with a face and body made lean and spare by prayers and fasts. He had a mustache and a small trim black beard. His face might have been that of any ordinary parish priest but for the way, Father Manos had noticed before, it radiated a capacity for love and devotion, suggesting a grace that came through fulfilling God's will.

"Thank you, Eminence, for consenting to see me this quickly," Father Manos said. "I know how busy your schedule is."

"Not at all, Father," the Bishop said. "I am always delighted to see one of my brothers in Christ." He motioned to a chair. "Please come and sit down."

Father Manos sat down on a stiff-backed armchair and the Bishop sat down across from him, spreading and smoothing his black cassock across his long, lean legs. His eyes, large, dark and intense, stared somberly at the priest.

"What is it, Father?" he asked softly.

Father Manos raised his hand to hesitantly touch the bruise on his cheek. He had ceased expecting that it was visible to anyone but him, yet now, in the Bishop's consecrated presence he had a quiver of hope that the wound might be seen and healed.

"Something has come to me in the night," he said, and even the words filled him with foreboding, and he made an effort to keep his voice from becoming shrill. "I'm filled with a terrible fear." He shook his head in bewilderment. "I have never known anything like it before."

Bishop Okas listened earnestly. It seemed to Father Manos that a flutter of compassion swept the younger man's face and he was ashamed of his confession. As if sensing his discomfort, the Bishop leaned forward and reached out to touch the priest on the arm in a gesture of consolation. How beautiful his fingers are, Father Manos thought, long and slender and so pale they were almost white. They might have been the fingers of one of El Greco's saints, stretched toward an unfathomable, unreachable height, toward a vision visible only to the spirit.

"I have been a priest so long," Father Manos said. "Spoken so many benedictions, performed so many sacraments. And now I shrink and tremble and fear. Is it because I have failed God? Nothing is clear to me anymore. The night brings phantoms and demons. I feel my soul cry out."

The Bishop stared at him silently. He looked once toward the ceiling and for an instant his finely curved lips were visible within his silky beard. Then he rose, unfolding his body to his lean, full height. He stood with his back to Father Manos.

"Life is a jungle," he said softly. "All around us is murder, avarice, brutality. The jungle is tangled and thick and the animals scream in the dark." He turned slowly to look down at the priest. "But a road runs through that jungle, a rough and stony road that seems to fall away in places, or is sometimes hidden, yet it is still there. The road of faith."

His eyes blazed with a lucent fervor. "You are older than I am, Father, you have been on this road longer, have more reason to grow weary, more reason to feel anguish. These are times more wicked than the time of Sodom and Gomorrah. A bitterness rises through our lives, a nausea, a mist of melancholy, things that sound a knell." His voice fell to a sibilant whisper. "He who loves his neighbor burns his heart, and the heart, like green wood, in burning groans and distils itself in tears. We must understand, Father, that the evil of our suffering can be cured only by greater suffering."

Father Manos looked down at his hands, the soft, trembling fingers, the backs scarred with spots like the back of a toad.

"We can no longer save Man from himself," the Bishop

said. "We can only keep the faith alive until He returns, for He must return. Meanwhile we must have a passion for God. It must possess us and fill us with such fire that we are conscious of nothing else. God can keep us in sight of the road. God! Only God! And if we remain on the road, the Church will survive, and our Saviour will return to redeem us!" His voice rose slightly and he clasped his hands together and extended them to Father Manos in mute and quivering entreaty. "Let us pray together, Father," he said, and he slipped to his knees before the priest.

The sight of the Bishop kneeling before him swept Father Manos with a fit of trembling. He reached out and clasped the Bishop's fingers and then slipped to his knees on the floor beside him.

"O my God," Bishop Okas whispered. "O my God, help your servant who is in sore need of your light and consolation. Help him, my God, do not forsake him now in his hour of need."

He lowered his head toward the floor. His cassock spread like a mantle about their ankles. His slender shoulders trembled. "Abandon despair," he said. "Abandon anguish. Give yourself freely to God's spirit."

"I will," Father Manos said.

"God is love!" Bishop Okas said.

"God is love," Father Manos said.

"God is light!"

"God is light."

"God is eternity!" Bishop Okas cried.

"God is eternity."

Tiny beads of sweat had formed on the Bishop's forehead, a vein pulsed in his temple, dark with a rushing through of blood. A small bubble of saliva ran from his mouth into his beard. He swayed slightly and let out a great long sigh that seemed to surge from deep in his body.

Father Manos reached to him and bent and kissed the lovely and slender hands again, feeling the flesh moist and warm, a scent of some fragile, delicate greenhouse flower rising from the palms, a flower able to thrive only in compounds of heat and filtered light.

Bishop Okas turned his head slightly and for a moment their eyes met.

He must see me now, Father Manos thought. He must recognize the wound I bear now, in this moment, this unmatched moment when our souls have been joined in a solemn and tender benediction.

But Bishop Okas made no sign that he had seen anything but his own visions. He turned aside and rose to his feet, smoothing down his cassock. Father Manos rose slowly and made his cross and left.

That night, again, he did not sleep. But the frenzy and terror of the preceding nights altered now for him into a strange resignation. In his darkened room he floated upon the waves of night, watching the moonlight curl around the shade of his window, hearing the floorboards creak. In the passage of that night he recalled the years he had lived, unrenowned and unmemorable years marked by futile words, wooden gestures, faltering faith. What had happened to his dreams of life with purpose and fulfillment? He felt his soul poured out like water, his bones out of joint, his heart like wax. He heard a bough blown against the house and raised up his head and quietly prayed for death.

Before daylight he dressed and walked through the darkness toward the church. He heard his short, stiff steps echo on the pavements as if he walked in a great hollow chamber. At the rim of the sky darkness and light raveled their threads.

He unlocked the heavy church door, swung it open, and entered the darkened narthex. He walked into the silent nave and sat down in one of the pews. He sat for a long time staring into the shadows until the shades of dawn lit the ceiling of the dome and seeped down into the hidden corners, unveiling angels and saints, winged and fluted seraphims. The Royal Gate of the Sanctuary emerged glittering from the darkness. From there, blinded in his vanity and pride, he had taken the name of the Lord vainly. If he did not murder, his silence condoned the murderers. If he did not starve the poor, he comforted those who ate while the poor hungered. If he did not burn the innocent, his complacence sanctified the burners.

After a while he rose and walked to the anteroom. He began dressing himself in his robes and vestments for the beginning of the service. He heard the first of the young acolytes entering the anteroom on the opposite side of the Sanctuary. Then the choirmaster entered.

"Good morning, Father Manos," he spoke cheerfully without looking at the priest.

"Good morning, Elias," Father Manos said.

"A lovely, early spring morning," Elias slipped into his cassock. "Winter will be over soon now."

"Yes, Elias," Father Manos said. He walked into the Sanctuary, crossed himself, and took up his place before the closed panel of the Royal Gate. He heard the choirmaster begin his chant, the rustling and murmuring of people moving into the pews, the whispering of the acolytes in the anteroom. And in those moments that he listened and waited he understood he would hold his bond to the earth and to his church until it was God's will to sever him from them. He would live joylessly watching the coming and going of the seasons. Yearning for death and peace he would be burdened with mortality, each year like ten he had passed before, the long thin drawing out of his soul to cover them.

But in those years remaining to him he would seek to build again the shattered temple of his faith, seek to renew that vision of something surpassingly fair which had haunted him in childhood, make the words of his mouth and the manifestation of his spirit acceptable in the sight of God.

And if he still failed because he had lived too long with hypocrisy and deceit, then he would bear the bruise on his face and soul for as long as he lived. When he died, he would have nothing to render the Lord but the thin, futile ashes of his suffering.

The old sexton entered the acolyte's anteroom and came in his broken-gaited jog into the Sanctuary. He crossed himself hastily and took up his crouched position before the panel, twisting his face fearfully and anxiously toward the priest.

For the first time in all the years the two of them had waited together before the panel, Father Manos recognized the sexton's terror. He suddenly understood how each Sunday morning the simple act of pushing aside the panel was a pillory and an anguish for the old man, an endlessly repeated ordeal wherein he might commit some terrible indiscretion before his priest and his God.

"Don't be afraid, Janco," Father Manos said softly, and he reached out to clasp the old man's bony shoulder in a gesture of consolation.

The old sexton gaped up at him numbly for a moment and then slowly, awesomely understood that the priest had recognized and forgiven him his fear, had touched him in absolution. He bent renewed to his task, his crooked, twisted shoulders shaking.

Watching the old man begin to cry, Father Manos felt tears breaking slowly from his own eyes.

He bent his head and as the panel slid open, he saw the tears glitter into specks of flame on the scarlet cloth of his gilded vestments.